FEMINISM and
the CINEMA of
EXPERIENCE

FEMINISM and the **CINEMA** of **EXPERIENCE**

Lori Jo Marso

DUKE UNIVERSITY PRESS
Durham and London
2024

Project Editor: Livia Tenzer
Designed by A. Mattson Gallagher
Typeset in Minion Pro and Retail by Copperline Book Services

Library of Congress Cataloging-in-Publication Data
Names: Marso, Lori Jo, author.
Title: Feminism and the cinema of experience / Lori Jo Marso.
Description: Durham : Duke University Press, 2024. | Includes
bibliographical references and index.
Identifiers: LCCN 2024013446 (print)
LCCN 2024013447 (ebook)
ISBN 9781478031222 (paperback)
ISBN 9781478026969 (hardcover)
ISBN 9781478060215 (ebook)
Subjects: LCSH: Feminism and motion pictures. | Feminism on
television. | Politics in motion pictures. | Politics on television. |
BISAC: SOCIAL SCIENCE / Women's Studies | POLITICAL SCIENCE /
General
Classification: LCC PN1995.9.W6 M377 2024 (print) |
LCC PN1995.9.W6 (ebook) | DDC 791.43/6522—dc23/eng/2024072
LC record available at https://lccn.loc.gov/2024013446
LC ebook record available at https://lccn.loc.gov/2024013447

Cover art: Chantal Akerman filming *Dis-moi* (*Tell Me*), 1980.
Illustration from a photo by Laszlo Ruszka/INA via Getty
Images (detail).

This book is for the students in my "Feminist Film" classes at Union College. Those spaces, and the films, feelings, and conversations we shared, remain with me and are reflected in these pages.

Contents

Acknowledgments

Before expressing my deep appreciation for colleagues, friends, and family, I want to thank several groups of people I've never met but who have shaped my thinking and writing, and to whom I feel connected. Some of these people exist only in fiction, as characters in film and television. My book is about how certain kinds of films and television, because of style and theme, invite the discomforting and disorienting feelings of their viewers by depicting the experiences of characters on screen. Ambivalence, disgust, cringe, tenderness, pity, horror, the sharing of trauma, existential angst, joy—these are some of the many feelings that get stirred up as viewers feel with and against characters in a cinema of experience. I feel connected to these characters! Experiencing these experiences, which I may or may not have had myself, and feeling these difficult feelings often makes me feel less alone in my existential dilemmas and strong emotions, as they envelop me in their collective energy.

The creation of film and television is always a collective endeavor, and I want to acknowledge the many people who write, film, produce, adapt, edit, and do all the other tasks involved in bringing to fruition the film and television that inspire, antagonize, or somehow move me. Likewise, I'm grateful to curators, podcasters, critics, and members and supporters of institutions that are involved in creating spaces and opportunities for film lovers like me to gather in public to encounter cinema. With others in these spaces, we can share space and feelings too—feelings that, like the ones I explore in this book, can be hard to name but are sometimes contagious. But sometimes not: you start talking to the stranger next to you in the theater, or you read a review, or you chat with your friends, to discover that we were *not* sharing the same feelings at all, and the space of sharing becomes one of agonism, encounter, politics, and imagination.

Several of the films I include in my cinema of experience, and the great majority of the films I teach in my "Feminist Film" course, were first encountered (or re-encountered) in collective viewings at Film at Lincoln Center's New York Film Festival (NYFF), Rendez-Vous with French Cinema, and New Directors/New Films; and by attending film series and retrospectives sponsored by the Museum of Modern Art (MoMA), the Brooklyn Academy of Music (BAM), Anthology Film Archives, Film Forum, the Metrograph, and the International Film Center.

I first saw Chantal Akerman's *No Home Movie* in early October 2015 at the NYFF, and I was especially looking forward to her introduction of the film, as I had long admired Akerman and had been regularly teaching *Jeanne Dielman*, *News from Home*, and *Je tu il elle* in my classes. But that was not to be, as Akerman died of suicide in Paris just two days before that screening. The film begins with a nearly four-minute shot of a barren tree buffeted by wind (for a screenshot, see figure 1.6). These first moments onscreen—in a film that charts the aging and deterioration of Akerman's mother—moved me in ways that I am still trying to figure out. Seeing the film for the first time, I was struck by how disturbing, inexplicable, intimate feelings can be invited and heightened by the least sentimental and most abstract objects and choices, and how films can touch your life in ways unexpected and transformative. That screening of *No Home Movie* was the beginning of this book. In the first year or two after Akerman's death, retrospectives of her work were sponsored by Film at Lincoln Center, BAM, and MoMA. These events gave me the opportunity to see many of her difficult-to-find films in the company of appreciative and grieving audiences, and on the big screen.

I am very lucky to be part of a family of political and feminist theorists whose writing, and individual and collective camaraderie, helped me bring this book to fruition. Bonnie Honig has talked with me for countless hours about films, feminism, and political theory. I have an entire desk drawer filled with scribbled notes containing eureka insights gleaned from conversations with Bonnie on the phone, over email, by text, on long walks, in subways, in taxis and Ubers, and during meals. Some of these notes are written on napkins and theater programs. When talking with Bonnie, a work breakthrough can strike anywhere and anytime, spurred by our mutual appreciation of a Broadway show or being antagonized by a bad movie. I have learned so much from her work in political and feminist theory, and I am grateful for our friendship.

Davide Panagia was the first person to talk to me about why I should pay close attention to formal choices in film. His work on why and how film matters to political theory has helped me clarify my own thinking on film and politics. Years ago, Davide also introduced me to new literatures in aesthetics that have been crucial for me as I've developed this project. I am in debt to his writing and very grateful for our friendship now reaching back many years.

Longtime friends Mort Schoolman, George Shulman, Joshua Dienstag, Jason Frank, and Mark Reinhardt have each written important works on aesthetics—film, fiction, art, and photography—and have each generously read my work-in-progress, written me long emails, conversed, laughed, and dined with me, always in these contexts helping me think in creative and generative ways about the intersections of art and politics.

When Lawrie Balfour asked Jill Frank and me to be consulting editors for *Political Theory*, I anticipated the often difficult, occasionally controversial, frequently boring but at times creative work of editing, but what I didn't anticipate was how meeting in person or over Zoom to have conversations about our writing projects and everything else would become, particularly during COVID, a vitally important intellectual lifeline. In lively exchanges with Lawrie and Jill, I was freed to think about my chapters in new ways (for example, creating stand-alone interpretations of the films), and they soothed my anxieties about making claims about my strong feelings. Lawrie also took the time and energy to provide incredibly insightful feedback on the entire manuscript in its first draft, which further buttressed my resolve to keep moving forward with the project.

Torrey Shanks, Laurie Naranch, and Patricia Moynagh are co-conspirators in all topics and situations related to feminist theory (and beyond). Torrey revealed herself to me as one of the anonymous readers for this manuscript, and I thank her and my other (still anonymous, also brilliant) reader for their generous, close readings and inspired suggestions, all oriented toward helping me draw out and emphasize the most important aspects of my own way of thinking about film and feminism. Çiğdem Çıdam and Guillermina Seri have taught me about Proust, Barthes, Benjamin, memory, political organizing and activism, how to persevere in the face of adversity and keep good cheer, and much more. I also thank Union colleagues Andrea

Foroughi, Joyce Madancy, Zoe Oxley, Erika Nelson Mukherjee, and Jenelle Troxell for their friendship, steady counsel, trust, and good times over the years.

Over drinks one late afternoon in Montreal, Jane Bennett gave me the courage to follow my instincts to see what I might find by acknowledging and exploring the differences in the ways Chantal Akerman and Simone de Beauvoir approach experience. Jane's writing, as well as her orientation to work, life, and basically all things, inspires and resonates with me, and I feel very lucky to have her in my life.

Courtney Berger, editor extraordinaire, has been my editor and friend for many years. Courtney has talked with me about *this* book in particular over several meals, in many cities, on Zoom and on the phone, and in exchanging countless emails. I am extremely fortunate to have Courtney in my corner and to benefit from her vision and advice. I am also indebted to the care and expertise of Livia Tenzer and Laura Jaramillo at Duke University Press, who shepherded this book into being in its final stages. Annie Berke, film editor for the *Los Angeles Review of Books*, deserves a special shout-out for her keen intelligence, line edits, brilliant title ideas, and good humor. My readings of *Titane*, *Happening*, and *Barbie* began in conversation with Annie.

Funding from the Faculty Research Fund at Union College enabled me to travel to West Texas in March 2023, to visit Marfa, the film site for Joey Soloway's *I Love Dick*, discussed in chapter 4. Tom Lobe and I dined in the restaurant that is the setting for the dinner between Chris, Sylvère, and Dick where Dick tells Chris, "Unfortunately, most films made by women aren't that good"; we wandered the town to see the walls and shopfronts where Chris posted her letters to Dick; and we hung out in the bar where Chris was ordered home by Sylvère after her wild dancing. Most memorable and transformative was encountering, in person, the work of Donald Judd, Soloway's inspiration for the character of Dick. I had seen Judd's work in MoMA's 2021 exhibit of his colorful "boxes" and "stacks," and this was a very moving experience for me. But walking around and feeling the presence of Judd's massive sculptures on the Chihuahuan desert border between Texas and Mexico, walking among his one hundred boxes of mill aluminum (41 × 71 × 52 inches) housed by the Chinati Foundation in a shuttered army base enveloped by desert views, and seeing his paintings, drawings, and furniture in the downtown Marfa studio stunned and amazed me in ways I have trouble putting into language. My encounters with Judd's work have made me feel more intensely the many ways that Chris might love Dick in Soloway's series, and to think more expansively about the way "Dick's" art can seem to take up all the space, but at the same time still *make* space for more.

I was delighted to be invited to present work-in-progress at Political Theory Workshops and other venues over the years I was developing the argument and trying to see the shape of this book. These opportunities, listed below, and the several interlocutors who attended, stopped me from making major mistakes, and offered me their good ideas are very appreciated:

Johns Hopkins University, Political Theory Workshop ("Cringe Comedy"): Jane Bennett, Perry Moskowitz, Jennifer Culbert, William Connolly, and Sam Chambers;

The Graduate Center, City University of New York, Political Theory Workshop ("Chantal Akerman's Domestic Politics"): Paisley Currah, Corey Robin, Jade Macri, and Robyn Marasco;

Northwestern University, film series and symposium *The Cinema of Chantal Akerman, Time, Borders, Politics* ("Camera Materna"): Domietta Torlasco, Brian Price, Jane Blocker, Meghan Sutherland, and Penelope Deutscher;

Columbia University, Political Theory Workshop ("Mothers and Motherwork"): Ayten Gündogdu and Çiğdem Çıdam;

Union College, Inaugural Lecture for Stillman Prize for Excellence in Research ("Find Our Mothers"): Leo Zaibert, Çiğdem Çıdam, Daniel Mosquera, Jenelle Troxelle, Jim de Seve, and Michelle Chilcoat;

University of Chicago, Political Theory Workshop and the Center for the Study of Gender and Sexuality ("Camerawork Motherwork" and "Cringe Comedy"): Linda Zerilli, Agatha Slupek, Rose Owen, and Annie Heffernan;

University of Edinburgh, Centre for Ethics and Critical Thought ("Camerawork Motherwork"): Mihaela Mihai, Marion Schmid, and Bracha L. Ettinger;

Brown University, Democracy Project ("*Happening* and Feminism as a Democracy Project"): Bonnie Honig, Veronica Fitzpatrick, and Amanda Anderson;

Brown University, Cogut Institute for the Humanities ("Cringe Comedy"): Bonnie Honig, Amanda Anderson, Juliet Hooker, and Noga Rotem;

University of Washington, Political Theory Workshop ("Feeling Like a Feminist"): Noga Rotem, Chip Turner, Jamie Mayerfeld, and Becca Peach.

Input and advice from discussants, fellow panel members, and members of audiences at meetings of the American Political Science Association and the Association for Political Theory and at the Conference for the Study of Political Thought also influenced my thinking at key points. In these and other contexts, in addition to people already named, I thank Kelli Fuery, Rosalind Galt, Anna Kornbluh, Jodi Dean, James Martel, Deva Woodly-Davis, Nancy Luxon, Michael Shapiro, Kathy Ferguson, Lilly Goren, Alissa Kessel, Michaele Ferguson, Lida Maxwell, Patchen Markell, Kathi Weeks, Judith Grant, Lorna Bracewell, Suzanne Dovi, and Mie Inouye. Mary Caputi, Jennifer McWeeney, Cristina Beltrán, and Libby Anker worked with me on earlier iterations of parts of this book in their roles as journal editors, and for a special issue of *Cités* on Simone de Beauvoir, Marie-Anne Lescourret graciously and beautifully translated into French a shorter and earlier iteration of the introduction that positions Beauvoir as a lover of cinema and a cinematic writer.

In addition to sewing my Barbie clothes and the many other ways she cared for me when I was young, my mother, Jo Marso, attended my University of Edinburgh Zoom lecture on Akerman's "camerawork motherwork," and prepared several on-point questions so she would be ready if she were called upon to ask them. My daughter Luci Lobe read this entire manuscript in one of its later drafts, was brutally honest about what did not quite come together, and talked with me for hours about how to say things better. Even after she completed this enormous task, I continue to force her into multiple conversations about everything from *Middlemarch* to the television series *Poldark*, and her sharp insights are all over this book. My son Lucas Lobe helped me with screen grabs and all things art-related and challenges almost everything I say about any film. Conversations about art and film with May Parsey make me smarter, and her ridiculous puns always make me laugh. Along with Luci and May, Danielle Powell and Rita Siebels shared my enthusiasm for Greta Gerwig's *Barbie* in the summer of 2023 and each of them brought my attention to details in the film that I did not see.

I come up short on words to thank Tom Lobe for his abiding love and steadfast cheerleading, not to mention his always insightful counsel and conversation about film, politics, theater, and everything else. Tom's support has been my anchor for too many years and in too many ways to count. As postscript, I would be remiss if I failed to mention that our adored dogs, Taki, Zucchini, and Guaka, are always ready with the most excellent cuddles, unwavering good cheer, and unbridled enthusiasm for treats, belly rubs, walks, and sniffing. The dogs and Tom share a love for me and love of life that is always needed and appreciated, but especially so on the most difficult days.

INTRODUCTION:
FEELING LIKE A FEMINIST

feeling: an emotional state or reaction; a sense that something is true

feminist: participant in feelings and activities committed to dismantling patriarchal, racist, capitalist, and extractive practices, and imagining new ways of living and ways of relating intimately in sex, love, family, and friendship

FEELING LIKE A FEMINIST most often doesn't feel good. Feeling like a feminist provokes anxiety, summons deep ambivalence to norms of femininity, and triggers worry and confusion about sex, love, marriage, children, and friendship.[1] It can be upsetting to notice that the roles, relationships, projects, and even futures that girls and women have been taught to strive for, to hold on to, to cherish, are the very ones that solidify women's status as what Simone de Beauvoir calls "the second sex."[2] It can also feel very disorienting to discover our (unchosen, structural) connections to other women, to recognize that our actions and failures to act harm others, and to slowly or suddenly understand that we may have unwittingly chosen our own harm. It seldom feels good or empowering to learn we are each assigned locations within racist, capitalist, imperialist, patriarchal, extractive (of people and nature) structures that have deep interests in concealing these connections and these interests.[3] But while feeling like a feminist is most often uncomfortable, getting glimpses of possible feminist futures buried within our own present tense, waiting to be summoned, can bring an unexpected surge of joy.

I have studied the complicated feelings of feminists in the autobiographies and biographies of key feminist thinkers (Marso 2006), I have felt them in my own life, and I have tried to work through them with students in classrooms. I have written about these feelings and the books, films, movements, and reflections they have inspired. Always, I insist that there is no *one* definition of feminism.[4] There are several "feminisms," reflecting ongoing debates and actions in historic and contemporary struggles for the liberation of woman-identified subjects.[5] These conversations vitalize and revitalize the movement across geographies and history, and in the here and now. But the feminism to which I subscribe is antiracist, anticapitalist, anti-extractive. The quest for women's freedom must be collective and relational, rather than focused on the individual. Feeling like a feminist is not the appropriative position of bourgeois white feminism, nor is it the feeling good of what is called "choice" feminism (i.e., as long as I choose it, it's feminist).[6] Keeping with the definition of "freedom in the encounter" that I developed studying the writings and actions of Beauvoir, I insist that no one is free until all are free, that we can only be free together, even as I recognize that there are conflicts among differently situated women that are not only agonistic, but likely irresolvable (Marso 2017). These are some of the difficulties and the ambivalences of feeling like a feminist.

Turning my attention explicitly to feminist aesthetic forms, the individual and collective experiences they depict, and the feelings they invite, I argue in this book that to feel like a feminist demands a willingness to encounter and acknowledge feelings we would rather push away.[7] These feelings might result from trauma we have denied, relationships we would rather ignore, or what cultural theorist Lauren Berlant (2011) has called "cruel optimism"—the mistaken belief that attachments to the things that diminish us can make us happy. Feeling like a feminist crushes cruel optimism. Feeling like a feminist offers fraught community, but not individual empowerment.[8] Feeling like a feminist destroys any certainty that the arc of history is bending in the right direction. Feminist waves never move without undertow (Marso 2010). But in spite of all this, feeling like a feminist can also incite laughter and make us feel a kind of collective giddiness![9] To feel good in *these* ways (collectively, in struggle), however, is not our usual way of feeling good.

At the undergraduate liberal arts college in upstate New York where I teach, I have offered a feminist film course for roughly ten years, mostly to women (sometimes there are a few men) that is cross-listed in the fields of Political Science, Gender, Sexuality, and Women's Studies, Africana Studies, and/or American Studies, depending on the films, directors, and texts assigned. I change the syllabus every time. It has focused solely on French avant-garde filmmakers and solely on films directed by American women of color; sometimes it is a mix of Hollywood, European, and foreign films from across the globe. In the years before I crafted this course, I curated an on-campus "Women in the Movies" film series screened weekly in the spring trimesters. The "Women in the Movies" series included all kinds of films, not all directed by women—foreign, American independent, classic Hollywood, and avant-garde. I often included some (derogatorily called) "chick flicks" or romantic comedies, and the screenings were always followed by discussions.

I estimate that over the years I have discussed more than two hundred films with my students. The classroom has become for me a kind of experiential site for watching and talking about films with others, registering how cinema matters to the ways I theorize "feeling like a feminist." In the course, the films some of my students like the most are ones where the characters overcome the odds, inspire, dazzle, outsmart, accomplish, and succeed. Think of Reese Witherspoon as Elle in *Legally Blonde* (2001), a stereotypical feel-*good* feminist film that proves women can do anything, not by mimicking men but *as women*. Dressed in pink from head to toe, Elle wins her legal case because she knows that you cannot shower with newly permed hair.[10] Woe to those who discount women! Do not underestimate women's embodied knowledge and our connections to our (sorority) sisters!

Others of my students tend to like films that make them feel bad. Eliza Hittman's *Never Rarely Sometimes Always* (2020) is one such film. Finding herself pregnant, working-class teenager Autumn (Sidney Flanigan) tries to abort on her own. When this fails, she and her cousin Skylar (Talia Ryder) travel from rural Pennsylvania to New York City to procure an abortion. The giant suitcase they drag around the city from the Port Authority to various Planned Parenthood clinics is a symbol of not only the situational baggage they carry but also their struggle to navigate while lugging it. Several students identify and sympathize with Autumn's predicament, are frustrated by the obstacles the two teens meet, and feel angry as they are confronted by various forms of toxic masculinity all around them. *Never Rarely Sometimes Always* brings the two young women to life so realistically that viewers are easily able to identify with them.

The films many of my students tend not to like are the ones that make them feel things they have a hard time describing or categorizing. These are films that they need to be persuaded to appreciate after working through the reading and participating in discussion. These films take viewers places that my students, like the rest of us, do not want to go and will visit only very reluctantly. These films disorient in several ways, sometimes thematically, sometimes stylistically, often both. They might feature women who inhabit the margins of the category "women," or women who too directly or too obviously betray the demands of femininity (unattractive, angry, sad, unlucky in love, or in some way embarrassing). They surprise and often frustrate viewer expectations by featuring a stationary or unfocused camera, discordant noise or silence, long takes or too many cuts, unexplained or confusing images, music that fails to give viewers emotional cues, editing that scrambles the narrative, or narratives that frustrate viewer desire to detect clear messages and morals. In other words, they use discomforting and disorienting style and narrative to invite viewers to feel like feminists.[11]

My examples from film and television summon discomforting feelings, feelings we would rather not confront or even acknowledge, as they depict uncomfortable but common experiences for woman-identified subjects—ambivalence, stasis, horror, cringe, and plasticity. My examples deliberately refuse to offer accomplished and inspiring role models, to comfort, and to partake in the forms of representation that increase what we have come to call diversity. This book asks what is going on when we can't take our eyes off, or we *must* look away from, horror movies, cringy television, durational scenes of female anxiety, and other varieties of uncomfortable, discomfiting scenes.[12] My examples offer a way to feel and think our way through and about these encounters, as I insist that they are worthy of our feminist political attention. They offer tastes, sounds, moods, fleeting images, durational focus, ambiance, atmosphere, or architecture that capture the "real" of marginalized experiences and help viewers sense what freedom (existential, relational, antiracist, nonhierarchical) might feel like. The films and television I explore within these pages (there could be many more examples!) belong to my cinema of experience because their formal and narrative styles invite viewers to cinematically experience women's experiences as an appeal to feeling.

When I call my archive a "cinema of experience," some readers may think of Miriam Bratu Hansen's book, *Cinema and Experience* (2012) on Siegfried Kracauer, Walter Benjamin, and Theodor Adorno. In the book's preface, Hansen says that the concept of experience emphasized by thinkers in the critical theory tradition on which she draws is one where individual lived experience is recognized in its collective and relational dimensions marked by the fragmentation, alienation, and blockage that characterize life in modern capitalism. Hansen says cinema can be a kind of "public sphere," where viewers can "mobilize their own experience," to understand it differently and imagine different futures (2012, xiv). Likewise, the emphasis on experience in the work of phenomenological film theorist Vivian Sobchack is also important for me as she highlights experience "in the flesh" as the concrete foundation for a distinctly materialist and "bottom-up emergence of aesthetic and ethical sense" (2004, 3). Exploring the "reality" of screen images in an image-saturated culture to ask about how these images "touch" us, Sobchack builds on the writings of Maurice Merleau-Ponty to discuss (generic) embodied, involuntary (affective) responses to film, theorizing cinema as an "expression of experience by experience" (1992, 3).

My turn to the writings of Simone de Beauvoir builds on the works of Hansen and Sobchack. With Beauvoir and with Chantal Akerman, I bring attention to how structures of racism, capitalism, and patriarchy are bolstered by aesthetic objects that reproduce, circulate, and make attractive certain feelings but can be challenged by aesthetic objects that offer new ways to feel and imagine. Beauvoir is especially good at attuning us to the impacts of the male sensorium (and male common sense) on the bodies of those who are perceived and identify as girls and women.[13] I add to Beauvoir's astute observations about the male sensorium an exploration of how we can identify and feel these impacts in the holding spaces made available in a feminist cinema of experience, as exemplified in the cinema of Chantal Akerman.

As I write this book, I imagine myself as saying "yes" to Hansen's 1986 invitation to feminist film scholars and critics to interpret cinema through a feminist lens. By that, she means a lens that seeks out moments and spaces for resistance, a practice Beauvoir expressly prepared us for in *The Second Sex*, and that Akerman's uses of camera, sound, editing, and play with genre and color attune us to in the most remarkable ways. Akerman is the filmmaker who, for me, best typifies the aesthetic, affective, and political work from which we can begin to learn to feel like feminists.

(with) Chantal Akerman

Chantal Akerman released her first feature-length film, *Jeanne Dielman, 23, quai du Commerce, 1080 Bruxelles*, in 1975 when she was only twenty-five years old. Toward the end of 2022, it was named as *Sight and Sound* magazine's "greatest film of all time." The poll that decided this, which has occurred once every decade for seventy years, was taken by 1,639 film critics, academics, curators, archivists, and programmers.[14] Akerman's film, the first winner directed by a woman, displaced Alfred Hitchcock's *Vertigo* (1958), which held the top spot for ten years, and Orson Welles's *Citizen Kane* (1941), which topped the list for fifty years. This is a significant achievement for feminist film and for women directors. Upon release of the news, film scholar Laura Mulvey (2022) remarked, "Things will never be the same."

Although never recognized so broadly as upon release of this 2022 list, Akerman was one of the first, and remains one of the most significant and critically acclaimed, filmmakers in what is now a more-than-fifty-year history of feminist alternatives to a male-dominated media scene. Feminist directors, film critics, and theorists have collectively contributed to efforts to disrupt the male gaze and its cultural sensorium, and to diversify characters and their experiences to reflect, represent, and inspire our own as viewers. Beginning in the late 1960s and early 1970s, groundbreaking feminist filmmakers fused radical aesthetics with radical politics, even when they, like Akerman, refused modifiers such as "feminist," "lesbian," or "queer."[15] From 1968 with her first short film *Saute ma ville* (*Blow Up My Town*), and until her death in 2015, Akerman's themes, style, and characters—and her specific use of camera, sound, editing, and expansion and play with genre—exemplify, for me, a cinema of experience. Akerman's cinematic style, and its reverberations in contemporary film and television, summons complex feelings intertwined with longing for feminist transformation by depicting the experiences of women and girls in startling and discomfiting ways. Akerman's attention to bodily gesture and inscrutable or unreadable faces, her framing of shots from midrange, often with a static camera, and her expectation that viewers will endure very long shots, disorienting editing, and innovative use of sound can place us in uncomfortable situations vis-à-vis our relationship to characters, plot, narrative, and our own expectations. Actors and characters defy our quest to know their inner thoughts, and we have no access to their interiorities as we watch them navigate the gaps that exist between themselves and others, and those within themselves.

Published the same year that *Jeanne Dielman* was released, Laura Mulvey's article "Visual Pleasure and Narrative Cinema" (1975) named the male gaze and drew feminist attention to the nexus of Hollywood cinema, commodity culture, spectacle, and the white female star, raising consciousness about the passivity of female spectators in our "to be looked at" status as objects of the gaze. Mulvey's article named as culprit not only the cinematic apparatus, or the objectifying look of the camera, but also the structure of a certain kind of narrative itself—the familiar (and familial) arc of beginning, middle, and end whose signposts are determined by a gendered structure of reproductive patriarchy. She insisted that the only way for feminist filmmakers to counter the male gaze and break these pernicious myths was to take up avant-garde filmmaking, eschewing narrative to create radical new film forms to alter our way of seeing. Akerman did just that with *Jeanne Dielman*. As Mulvey (2022) puts it,

> The film that collected the most votes in 2022 is made with a cinematic style and strategy closer to avant-garde than mainstream traditions and, furthermore, at just under three and a half hours, demands dedicated viewing. Although confrontational, idiosyncratic and extraordinary films have consistently appeared lower in the lists, the experimental tradition, to which *Jeanne Dielman* belongs, is—apart perhaps from the recent appearance of Dziga Vertov's *Man with a Movie Camera* (1929)—absent. While it has brought this tradition to the top of the list, *Jeanne Dielman* is inescapably a woman's film, consciously feminist in its turn to the avant garde.... In a film that, agonisingly, depicts women's oppression, Akerman transforms cinema, itself so often an instrument of women's oppression, into a liberating force.

Focusing static cameras on the ordinary housework, mothering, and prostituting that one opaque woman performs over the course of three days, *Jeanne Dielman* completely upends viewer expectations. First, film length: as Mulvey notes, it clocks in at three hours and twenty minutes. The length of the film might be received by some as a violation of regular time and timing.

Film theorist Daniella Shreir (2019) calls it an act of "feminist arrogance": an insistence to take up space in the heteropatriarchal cinematic sphere. Taking up our time as viewers and inviting us to feel time with Jeanne (in 1975) still today remains a kind of "feminist arrogance," even and especially as the willingness of contemporary male filmmakers to boldly take up our time in this way proliferates—think of Kenneth Branagh's *Hamlet* (1996), Martin Scorsese's *The Irishman* (2019), and Christopher Nolan's *Oppenheimer* (2023). Scene duration also scrambles our sense of how time passes in films.[16] Viewers watch Jeanne (played by the amazing Delphine Seyrig) perform household duties such as cleaning the bathtub, making coffee, tidying the bed, and boiling potatoes, and we stay with her, task by task, for each action, all of which extend well over one minute, many two minutes or more, and some as long as four minutes.[17] In the BFI Film Classics text on *Jeanne Dielman*, film scholar Catherine Fowler calls this Akerman's "phenomenological obsession . . . with how the lived body occupies and moves through space" (2021, 32). The subject matter is also new—the life of a widow caring for her home and her son, while also working as a prostitute in her Brussels apartment. Also noteworthy are the unmoving midrange camera placement, the flat monotone of line delivery, spare dialogue, awkward Oedipal mother-and-son conversations. The focus on housework, the confinement of the "action" to one small apartment, and the slow pace confirm film theorist Ivone Margulies's characterization of this film, and much of Akerman's oeuvre, as cinema in which "nothing happens."[18]

But then something does. After tracking the hours in three long days, Jeanne commits an inexplicable, violent act: killing a john (client) with scissors. Is this act an attempt to disrupt (or preserve?) the order of time in which she has been ensconced? As I surmised earlier (Marso 2016a), it might be characterized as a "perverse protest" against patriarchal mandates and expectations. Film scholar Alice Blackhurst cites film critic Elena Gorfinkel's attention to the "cruelties of subsisting in the exhaustion of just being, in facing, time and again, the circumscribed terms of [a woman's] value, a value defined by men, by capitalism, by law," as she concludes that Jeanne refuses these standards to instead become a "luxurious outlaw" (2021, 17). Regardless of viewer and critic speculation regarding what motivates Jeanne's act of violence, the film itself never settles this question, nor does it settle the significance of the orgasm we see Jeanne experience just prior to the murder. All we ever "know" in an Akerman film is what we can observe.[19] What we can observe about this film is Akerman's commitment to explore a different sense of time, space, and desire.[20] What may be most uncomfortable for viewers is not the killing itself but rather the aftermath, when we sit with Jeanne at her kitchen table in silence for seven long minutes before the credits roll. This may be the most anxious and difficult space in the film. In this space and time, viewers are forced to feel time passing.[21] Light rhythmically illuminates Jeanne's unreadable face as a blue neon search lamp swings outside the window.

Akerman's films, and the iterations of her style and themes in contemporary feminist media, are ones that make the everyday and ordinary appear and *feel* strange. This strangeness, what we might call the "mood" of her films, evokes complicated feelings for viewers. Akerman (1983) said she doesn't have an "idea" that she seeks to explore in her films, but instead a "feeling" she tries to express. In an interview, Akerman notes the influence of filmmaker Michael Snow on her work: "the sensory experience I underwent was extraordinarily powerful and physical. . . . I learned [from Snow's films] that a camera movement . . . could trigger an emotional response as strong as from any narrative" (Brenez 2012). Lengthy shots featuring empty interiors, minor gestures, unreadable faces, and seemingly uninteresting household objects invite unexpected feelings as they direct our attention to things we otherwise might not notice.[22] Lack of plot and character development can make minds wander, freeing eyes and ears to be more aware of lighting, any change in expression, sound, or shifts in mood or gesture. Soliciting feeling by focus on detail, space, and mood takes precedence over character, plot, subjective perspective, and narrative closure. In *Jeanne Dielman*, a missed button, overboiled potatoes, an uncovered tureen, and mussed hair become major plot points that trigger anxiety. Viewers do not know whether Jeanne is anxious, but we feel our own anxiety and ambivalence triggered by her actions and comportment onscreen. As I will demonstrate in coming chapters, Akerman's careful work with formal techniques—such as creation of distance and proximity; focus on faces and objects; a privileging of indecipherable scenes, conversations, and actions; and scene duration—can make viewers wiggle, squirm, and possibly want to leave the theater or look away from the screen. These formal innovations combined with often difficult subject matter invite uncomfortable viewer feelings and can culminate in surprisingly emotional viewer reactions.

Akerman's films might be seen as inflected by the surreal, if we think of surrealism with filmmaker Madeleine Hunt-Ehrlich as intensifying the usually unseen horrors and "sordid antinomies of the present" for marginalized subjects, while sometimes "enabl[ing] us to transcend" them.[23] We can think of Akerman's style, too, with film theorist Mieke Bal, as producing what Bal (2013) calls "thinking images." "Thinking images," as Bal defines them, invite viewers into worlds from a plurality of perspectives. Akerman never privileges point-of-view perspective with her camera, but her films nevertheless invite us, with Bal, *to think*. And here, I note, that to *feel* like a feminist does not exclude but, instead, *encourages* thinking! I reject the mind/body, thinking/feeling duality as any feminist should. Akerman's films are intensely cerebral and exquisitely, often painfully, emotional at the same time. They encourage us to question the reality we think we know, to see or hear what we have long missed, and understand that "reality" is itself a construction formed through relationships of power, ideologies, and aesthetics. She heightens the ordinary and the everyday, using her camera to see things we otherwise would not. For these reasons, Margulies (1996) calls Akerman's filmmaking "hyper-realist." Viewing an Akerman film, we are not allowed to forget that there is a person behind the camera, that film is a material medium, and that film can be a collective praxis. Reading Akerman's films as aesthetic objects and feminist project, we can say that women's contradictory and complex experiences under patriarchy are made newly available for critique and feeling.[24]

In this book, I name my own way of thinking about Akerman's distinct style and cinematic lexicon, theorizing her camerawork as an aesthetic form of the labor of mothering. I call this "motherwork camerawork" and "camerawork motherwork" (both orderings of adjective to noun inspired by Akerman's specific camerawork and Black feminist writing on motherwork). Historically and philosophically excluded from the normative identity of "mother," Black feminist thinkers have used "motherwork" to identify a set of techniques and practices. Using this term, we can move away from sorting "good" and "bad" mothers, open space to see the violence and care that are inextricably linked in motherwork, and better notice that motherwork is happening where we otherwise do not see it, such as with Akerman's camerawork. In chapter 1, I read three of Akerman's films that feature the work of mothers and (m)others. I notice how Akerman's camera creates and holds space for viewers to encounter difficult experiences, feel the difficult feelings such encounters invite, and hold them in the space and time of the film. I develop this way of theorizing Akerman's aesthetic style across her oeuvre, and I notice "camerawork motherwork" in the aesthetic style of other filmmakers as well, such as Alice Diop's *Saint Omer* (2022).

Akerman's over fifty films and fifteen installations span from 1968 to 2015. In these pages, I carefully read four of the films (and refer to several others). In addition to *Jeanne Dielman*, I include the thirteen-minute short

Blow Up My Town; a documentary about Mexicans and Americans on the border, *De l'autre côté* (*From the Other Side*; 2002); and her final feature film, a genre-bending documentary in the style of a "home movie," named *No Home Movie* (2015). To the Akerman films, I add feminist films and television series that I read with Akerman as iterations of her cinematic lexicon, even though at first glance, some of them may not appear to fit. The theoretical work I do in each chapter shows that Akerman's uses of camera and sound, and her innovative play with genre, temporality, duration, framing, and color, prompt viewer discomfort (and often confusion), which creates space and time for difficult feelings. Difficult feelings also take pride of place in the writings, and reception, of Beauvoir, the feminist thinker to whom I turn as I think about the significance of the evocation of experience and feeling to move toward feminist transformation.

(and) Simone de Beauvoir

In recent iterations of my feminist film course, I have assigned several Akerman films and their contemporary iterations and asked my students to read the entirety of Simone de Beauvoir's *The Second Sex* ([1949] 2011) alongside them.[25] *The Second Sex* generates almost as much anxiety as the most formally challenging of Akerman's films.[26] Significantly and disconcertingly, Beauvoir's primary and recurring question, "What is a woman?," is never answered in its almost eight hundred pages. *The Second Sex* defies expectations of what a feminist project should be. Beauvoir rejects all preformed knowledge of the existence of feminism's subject (women); she frustrates the naming of a singular origin of oppression; and she eschews the listing of clear and nameable desires, or desired strategies or outcomes for the end of patriarchy. This is profoundly unsettling for students. As the class goes on, the text continues, and the films accumulate, answers to the question "What is a woman?" emerge as a matter of performance, style, and aesthetics, rather than something to be discovered, known, dissected, or even dismantled.

In these and more ways, Beauvoir deliberately frustrates reader desires.[27] But at the same time, and with Akerman, woman-identified readers and viewers are being nurtured. It is as if, as readers, we don't know we "are" women or that we experienced something resembling (or different from, but vaguely familiar to) Beauvoir's account of "girlhood" *until* we read about it in her pages (or see, hear, and feel it in an Akerman film). Beauvoir opens her book by saying she "hesitated a long time before writing a book on woman.... [A]re there even women?" ([1949] 2011, 3). "Does the word 'woman,' then, have no content?" (4). In volume 1, Beauvoir records her research, having read volumes of male-authored science, myths, fairytales, anthropology, history, psychoanalysis, theology, literature, and more. Male authors confidently create images of the "eternal feminine," which veer between the beautiful and the ugly. Studying the language men use to create idealized pictures of the feminine in nature, myth, and life, my students and I notice how attentive Beauvoir is to the power of images.[28] In the first paragraph of the "Biology" chapter, Beauvoir says the word "female" immediately brings to mind several "ugly" pictures: "an enormous round egg snatching and castrating the agile sperm; monstrous and stuffed, the queen termite reigning over the servile males; the praying mantis and the spider, gorged on love, crushing their partners and gobbling them up; the dog in heat running through back alleys, leaving perverse smells in her wake; the monkey showing herself off brazenly, sneaking away with flirtatious hypocrisy" (21). The multitude of images with which women must contend makes a long list: the "virtuous" woman (92); "blessed saint" and "docile servant" (189); the "mother" (190); the "mother-in-law image of decrepitude" (192); the "Virgin Mary" (197); and the "bad women" of Hollywood—"adventuress," "vamp," "femme fatale, 'and "Circe" (207). Decrying how these images affect young women, Beauvoir says, "Through compliments and admonishments, through images and words, she discovers the meaning of the words 'pretty' and 'ugly'; she soon knows that to please, she has to be 'pretty as a picture'; she tries to resemble an image, she disguises herself, she looks at herself in the mirror, she compares herself to princesses and fairies from tales" (293).

Les belles images, a novel Beauvoir published in 1966, describes the effects of "pretty pictures" circulating in public. This short novel eerily anticipates the ways neoliberal conditions of capitalism, patriarchy, and consumerism combine to capture (differently situated) women in their pernicious net to dictate how women should look and act. Circulating like a contagion, images of wealth and beauty promise that more and more beautiful things bring happiness and that there are technocratic solutions to the deleterious environmental and ethical impacts of capitalist glut. Laurence, the heroine of the novel, creates advertising copy (the "pretty pictures" of the title) that manufacture the longing for consumer objects that promises to stave off the abyss of alienation and angst: "I am not selling wood panels; I am selling security, success, and a touch of poetry into the bargain" ([1966] 1968, 28). Assessing her novel in her 1972 volume of her autobiography, Beauvoir sounds almost like a filmmaker: she says that with her novel, she had wanted to "reproduce the *sound*" of Laurence's environment, the "ugliness of [this] world" ([1972] 1993, 122, emphasis added). It reads today as a prescient account of one woman's damaged sense of self in a dystopian future saturated with and dominated by superficial images of beauty. Today Laurence would be cast as an "influencer."[29] Or she might be cast as a character named Jeanne (once again) played by Delphine Seyrig (once again) in a 1986 Akerman film, *Window Shopping* (also known as *Golden Eighties*). Rather than emphasize the "ugliness" of this world, as Beauvoir chose to do, Akerman saturates her images with bright colors, which, in the coda, I will compare with the Barbie pink that Greta Gerwig uses for *Barbie* (2023). *Window Shopping* is a musical set in a shopping mall (we never leave the mall, until the final moments of the film). Characters move from dress shop to beauty parlor to soda fountain singing about love, betrayal, jealousies, and longing for a better life. We see, with Akerman, that "everything is for sale, everything is desirable if beautifully presented in a shop window, if desire is about how one looks, how one presents oneself" (Roberts 2014). This was Akerman's first "commercial" film, and with it, she travels a long distance from the austere *Jeanne Dielman*. Film critic Jonathan Kaplan notices that "Akerman's melodramatic declarations of lost love are siphoned through a repetitive procedure which empties them of their 'truth,' their ability to solicit the empathetic response."[30] We might say that her repetitive and attractive images show how representation is made and how it circulates, something that Beauvoir noticed, too, as she focused her attention on Hollywood and what images can and cannot do.

In *America Day by Day*, a text written almost twenty years before *Les belles images* and around the same time as *The Second Sex*, Beauvoir confesses to her love of movies and her fascination with Hollywood in particular. Cinema gave her a picture of life in the United States: "It was through these Black and White images that I first knew America, and I still think of them as its real substance" ([1954] 1999, 74). Beauvoir was an avid and enthusiastic moviegoer all her life. But she initially dismissed the idea that cinema could have a progressive political impact, not only because of the film industry's tie to profit, but also because she thought that moving images, sometimes "enchanting," sometimes "unbearable," are "paralysing" ([1972] 1993, 177). Viewers of film are held within the grip of Hollywood's profit motive, the movie's narrative, or the director's intention, she surmised. Beauvoir maintained this view for a long time. As late as 1972, she affirmed,

> The potency of images comes from the fact that they provide the illusion of reality, an illusion that I accept in a state of near-passivity. . . .

When I go into a cinema, I leave my actual self at the door; and although my past is certainly there behind me as I react to a film, it is not there as a conscious entity and my only project is to watch the scenes that go by before my eyes. I accept them as true, and I am not allowed to intervene in any way; my praxis is paralysed, and in some cases this paralysis emphasizes the unbearable nature of the pictures, while in others it makes them enchanting. Sitting there in front of the screen I surrender myself entirely, as I do in dreams; and in this case too, it is visual images that hold me captive—that is why cinema awakens *dream-like echoes* in each beholder. If a film affects me deeply, it does so either because it stirs unformulated memories or because it brings unspoken hopes back to life. Sometimes, when I discuss a film with friends—friends whose tastes are the same as mine in other fields—I find that my opinion is quite unlike theirs: the film has certainly touched them or me or all of us in some intimate, entirely personal area. ([1972] 1993, 177, emphasis mine)

Even as Beauvoir worried that cinematic images are too tied to capitalism, and to the director's or screen's control of story, action, and intention, she also saw that cinema can touch each of us in a deep place, stirring "unformulated memories" and bringing "unspoken hopes" back to life. Notice that she doesn't keep these feelings to herself; she discusses the films and the feelings they invite with friends! She often finds that her "opinion is quite unlike theirs, but the film has certainly touched them or me or all of us in some intimate, entirely personal area."

Two texts that Beauvoir wrote explicitly about film should be noted here as well. In 1959, she wrote "Brigitte Bardot and the Lolita Syndrome," and in 1985, Beauvoir wrote the preface to Claude Lanzmann's textual version of *Shoah*. In these essays, she acknowledges that dominant images can be received in more than one way. Though she calls American film directors "Hollywood dream merchants" ([1959] 2015, 116), she also brings attention to the multifaceted sensual and sonorous fields in which cinematic images circulate, and the multiple ways viewers might respond. In the Bardot essay, for example, Beauvoir explicitly acknowledges that cinema can be a force that *interrupts* myth, that undoes the "pretty picture." Even though Bardot (meaning the Bardot myth, the "imaginary creature," not the real person or her characters) is a new iteration of woman as erotic object, Beauvoir says of Roger Vadim's *Et Dieu . . . créa la femme* (*And God Created Woman*; 1956), for example, that at the film's end when Bardot's character is ordered by her husband to return home, "spectators might not believe in the victory of the man and of the social order" ([1959] 2015, 117). The normative picture is a new mythic female creature exemplified by Bardot's "perfect innocence": her tomboy, child-woman demeanor; sincerity; love of animals; and instinctive charm. But when we see Bardot's body moving onscreen, we see her active *desire*, undermining the narcotic effects of the "pretty picture" and becoming disruptive. Beauvoir says Bardot's "body rarely settles into a state of immobility: she walks, she dances, she moves about. . . . [H]er eroticism is not magical but aggressive. . . . [T]he male is an object to her, just as she is to him" (119).

In the very last essay Beauvoir wrote prior to her death in 1986, she introduced the monumental film of her dear friend and former lover, Claude Lanzmann. *Shoah* (1985), a documentary about the Holocaust that does not utilize a single reel of archival footage, is nine hours and twenty-six minutes of interviews with survivors, bystanders, and perpetrators. Beauvoir says of *Shoah* that "the greatness of Claude Lanzmann's art is in making places speak, in reviving them through voices and, over and above words, conveying the unspeakable through peoples' expressions" (1985, iii). Beauvoir's view of what a film like *Shoah* can do may have been influenced by Lanzmann's explicit staging of "remembering" in the film as he returns to sites of destruction to trigger memories and revisit the past anew. In the act of returning to a scene to see what we might have missed, we are witness not only to the "camouflage," like "young forests and fresh grass" (Beauvoir's "pretty pictures"), that hides "horrible realities," but *in that experience* we (viewers) are *moved to experience for ourselves* what happened there, in our "minds, hearts, and flesh" (1985, iii).[31]

(in) the Cinema of Experience

In her *Shoah* essay, Beauvoir seems to say that film can give us access to experiences and memories otherwise unavailable. Note that in volume 1 of *The Second Sex* and elsewhere, Beauvoir debunks the false, mythic weaving of narratives, stories, fairytales, and fables about "Woman" on offer in male theology, science, history, psychoanalysis, fiction, and film. In its place, she does not offer something authentically personal or essentially definitive of women. Instead, it is readers who *discover* or, in some cases, recover, experiences by reading about experiences of others. As in the passage on *Shoah*, moved by Lanzmann's filmmaking, the viewers of the film are "moved to experience" in "minds, hearts, and flesh." This is the work of film feeling, an artistically created magic that can give shape to experiences otherwise unspoken, unnamed, buried, or not even our own.

Beauvoir's quest to discover and share women's experiences proceeds in volume 2 in a distinctly cinematic style.[32] Calling the style of Marx and Engels "dialectical" and "materialist," radical second-wave feminist Shulamith Firestone insightfully notices that because Marx and Engels perceived history as a "movie rather than a snapshot," they did not fall into the "stagnant 'metaphysical' view that had trapped so many other great minds" ([1970] 2015, 4). In other words, Firestone says, they saw the world as process. Likewise, Beauvoir says "becoming a Woman" is a process, a process that might move differently or elsewhere were women alert to their own experiences and feelings in conversation with the experiences and feelings of others. As my students read Beauvoir's accounts of becoming, how these accounts are staged in her text, and how these accounts make them feel, I ask them to particularly notice Beauvoir's attention to detail, movement, point of view, pace, duration, repetition, sound, and so on.

Feminist historian Judith Coffin characterizes the effects of Beauvoir's method as it reverberates with readers in an "exceptionally interesting author-reader intimacy . . . made intimate by the subjects discussed and the dense exchange of ideas, feelings, fantasies, and experiences" (2020, 2). Because our senses are indivisible from patriarchy's ordering of them, getting a "taste" of the lives of others helps us feel reverberations, make comparisons, and build an alternative common sense. An individual's experience is often disjointed or jarring, and it is always, by definition, partial: as Beauvoir puts it, we each experience life as a "detotalized totality" ([1965] 2011, 198). In other words, the world appears whole to us, but it is always partial, only a tiny slice of the total, always changing and constantly in motion.[33] Singular experiences are always oriented in relationship to the structural architectures that shape the bodies and partition the sensible (and not just the visual) for all of us. Her method favors a focus on movement within moments, the open question of historical interpretation, a sense of undetermined becoming that looks more like tendencies, and attention to noncausal and contingent material conditions and opportunities that shape change.[34]

The women and girls speaking from within *The Second Sex* (characters in novels, Beauvoir's friends, passages lifted from memoirs and films) articulate inchoate and multiply different desires for *something else* than what patriarchy offers. What woman-identified subjects have in common is the everyday and multiple ways their freedom is constricted, redirected (into romance, religion, motherhood, for example), or blocked.[35] Engaging in comparison and discussion about these experiences opens us to the often-opaque worlds we inhabit, and it can help us imagine other ways to live. Complaints articulated within *The Second Sex*, often, however, frustrate my students. Why are women so whiny? Why don't they complain *more*? Why don't they do something—leave, revolt, refuse?[36] Are we them? They and we are invited by Beauvoir to compare their and our experiences to those Beauvoir presents, many of which seem outdated, politically incorrect, too embarrassing to say out loud.[37] They are almost unspeakable. But Beauvoir boldly and vividly brings them to life. She describes and appeals to sense experience (taste, touch, smell, sight) to create space for a variety of uncomfortable feelings of identification and disidentification that are evoked in readers. Experiences and senses that had been falsely individualized, considered too private, or rendered unbelievable or unreal in conditions of racialized patriarchy are suddenly available for comparison and conversation.

Beauvoir's archive of experience is an *explicit* appeal to readers, as it asks, "Is this your experience too, or is yours different?" "What do these examples, and the recounting of these experiences, provoke in you?" "How do they make you feel?"[38] Keenly attentive to detail, Beauvoir gathers these details of women's experiences, refusing to leash them to a grand theory. Not everything adds up for her, and it is precisely for *this* reason that her work opens up so many worlds and invites us in. Her existential phenomenological method alerts us to the doubled aspect of all experience: we each experience it singularly, but it opens us to a shared world for critique and reimagining. Mining literature and film for details, she lauds their formal and narrative strategies as the "only form of communication capable of giving me the incommunicable—capable of giving me the taste of another life" ([1965] 2011, 201). Film scholar Kelli Fuery remarks on Beauvoir's use of the detail, quoting from Beauvoir's *Force of Circumstance*: "the practice of well-made plots irritated her because of their artificiality; in her novels she wanted 'to imitate the disorder, the indecision, the contingency of life; I had let my characters and the events in the book sprawl in every direction; I left out all the "necessary scenes"; all the important things happened offstage'" (2022, 220). By "necessary" and "important," she means what is usually considered "major." Like Akerman, Beauvoir attends to what seems (but isn't) minor—small, silent, seemingly incommunicable, or invisible (like Jeanne's housework).

Beauvoir trusts her audience. She says that "a director who wishes to set up a real communication with the audience," "like a good writer . . . will make an appeal to their freedom" ([1972] 1993, 177; see also Marso 2017).

Identifying Akerman as a director who also trusts her audience in these ways, I enlist Beauvoir's view of the reader/text relationship to help me think more about what a cinema of experience can do.[39] Comparing the viewer/screen relationship to that between reader and text is even more relevant today than when Beauvoir reflected on the differences between text and film. Now, personally controlled screens allow us to return repeatedly to a particular scene or image rather than see it quickly pass by.[40]

Beauvoir invites her readers to *experience women's experiences* as an appeal to feeling. The focus on detail triggers reader and viewer feelings precisely because of the way it acknowledges previously uninterrogated, unnoticed, or deliberately ignored or unbelieved experience.[41] Much like volume 2 of *The Second Sex*, Akerman's primary focus is also on the extraordinary but ordinary details of the everyday lives of women. With Akerman, I build on Beauvoir's writings for my cinema of experience because of her interest in and analysis of cinematic style; because she centers the experiences of girls and women both in becoming and defying the norms of "Woman" and draws on experience to do so; and because her writing in *The Second Sex* is itself cinematic in its attention to the singular detail and to life as always in motion. Akerman's films, and her broader cinematic lexicon, sometimes serve as intensified or vivified cinematic examples of Beauvoir's method. But I also carefully attend to differences between Beauvoir's and Akerman's depictions of women's experiences and the significance of these differences. Akerman's style is distinct from Beauvoir's in part because of the singular way she evokes a mood and makes what was ordinary or invisible pop out to us.[42] Akerman famously denigrated cinematic or reading experiences that pass by without the reader's or viewer's hyperawareness of the constructedness of the reading and viewing experience. Akerman reported that she did not want her audience to get lost in the film, to be completely caught up in it, or be so entertained that they forget the time. It is important to her that her viewers *feel time passing*: "You feel the time and space. Usually in a movie, you forget time and space. But that's not my thing."[43]

Reminded by Beauvoir and Mulvey, I emphasize again how politically dangerous it can be to get lost in the aesthetic object, especially when you are *positioned as the object*. But I am attracted to this danger and embrace it in this book! In recent work, Mulvey has revised her claim that female viewers passively absorb dominant images that position them as sexual objects. The male gaze and the cinematic apparatus that delivers it seem less predictable, at least less effective and all-encompassing, when we are attentive to the active minds and bodies that encounter cultural objects. As early as 1992, bell hooks had shifted the conversation within feminist film circles with "The Oppositional Gaze." She insisted that Black female viewers were never passive receptacles of white supremacy and patriarchal power. Black women, hooks notes, always utilized the power of the gaze to "sneak a peek, to stare dangerously," and that, "even in the worst conditions of domination," the "ability to manipulate one's gaze" "opens up the possibility of agency" (116).[44] What hooks doesn't explicitly say, though her work elsewhere supports this view, is that the gaze is simultaneously embodied, somatic, social, and political. Though embedded in fleshed individual beings, and constructed within and emerging from social and political structures of feeling, the oppositional gaze operates best when supported within communities of feeling where experiences are shared, compared, and considered anew as we are held in a cinematic space for feeling like feminists. My argument is that the liberatory potential of feminist cinema is not only in what images show, what they hide, or which perspective(s) the gaze reflects or how we can oppose it.[45] My book aims to show that what is important for feeling like a feminist is the discomforting and dangerous feelings that cinema can invite us to experience and, in particular, that these feelings connect us to others.

Chapter Preview

Contemporary feminist film theorists remain engaged in debates about the male, white, colonial gaze by theorizing how films disperse, shift, or pluralize this gaze in many ways—for instance, utilizing form, sound, image, and theme and inviting both cerebral and embodied reactions to film—and by offering formal readings of films as aesthetic objects, regardless of viewer response. These kinds of film analyses, whether it is their intention to do so or not, add to our collective understanding of how gendered and raced ideals are replicated in media, but also might be weakened via cinematic (aesthetic, technological, formal, narrative) interventions, by viewer responses, and by feminist film analysis. As I have described in this introduction, I add my voice to this literature by exploring how feminist filmmakers use cinematic techniques and formal and narrative strategies to invite viewers to experience women's experiences as an appeal to feeling. My way of theorizing feeling does not assume knowledge (or predict) that any particular viewer will feel any particular way. I am sensitive to the situatedness of lives and notice that oppressive conditions yield a plurality of experiences and feelings in response to them. Feeling is both personal and political, is always mediated, encompasses multiple kinds of acknowledgment and disavowal, and spurs all kinds of dangerous and destructive pathologies and passions. Feeling is a dangerous platform on which to try to build feminist community. Yet I forge ahead.

I claim in this book that there is often a gap between the feelings woman-identified subjects think we are supposed to have and those we may *actually* have. I find freedom and movement in these feeling gaps that create spaces where we are held. What most interests me is that the depiction and intensification of the experiences of woman-identified subjects in film may resonate or generate productive dissonance with the experiences of viewers. By focusing on disjunctive and disorienting feelings, I attend to the immediacy, unpredictability, and individuality of affect—as viewers, we might experience boredom, alienation, fear, horror, joy, anxiety, hope, cringe, laughter—at the same time noting that expected feelings are collectively created. Feminized subjects are taught to desire romance, for example, or to think that mothering is instinctive or natural. Individual feelings we experience in response to a film may or may not be expected, but feelings in response to the cinema of experience that I feature in this book are often surprising, disorienting, and uncomfortable, and can and should be shared and compared with what others are feeling. These different modes of feeling—created expectations, affective impact or individual response to cinematic depiction of experience, and sharing these feelings with others—may be in sync or not, may occur or not. I make the case that the cinematic depiction of experience and the subsequent solicitation of uncomfortable feeling in viewers—held, shared, compared—is feminist film's most transgressive political intervention.

Beauvoir and Akerman are my touchstones here, as I notice how they differently contribute to my thinking on how a cinema of experience produces effects and affects by depicting, inviting, and holding uncomfortable feelings. Beauvoir theorizes how a readership and viewership may respond and take up the recounting of the experiences of girls and women, while Akerman orients my thinking to how alienating or distancing cinematic techniques may enhance not only the depiction of experience but also audience response to it. For Akerman, the invitation of viewer feeling is most intense when neither interiority nor subjectivity is depicted onscreen. I also note that each thinker, in their own way, is occasionally a recalcitrant subject for my project. For example, although Akerman dismissed "feminist," "lesbian," or "queer" as descriptors of her films, I build on her rejection of these labels by asking throughout this book what we mean when categorizing a film as "feminist." And although I am drawn to the way Beauvoir features and explores the experiences of women and girls, she is, at the same time, insufficiently attentive to differences in the lives of women, especially across racial difference and in (post)colonial settings. For some readers, this may disqualify Beauvoir as a "good" feminist thinker.[46] But where Beauvoir fails, I seize an opportunity to deploy her concepts to exceed the limits within which she wrote. One example of this is evident in chapter 4, where I focus on Beauvoir's reading of Brigitte Bardot in Vadim's *And God Created Woman*.

Focusing on how feminist directors utilize cinematic technique, form, and theme to invite discomforting feelings and create what I name as holding spaces in their films, my chapters pair what I identify as feminist innovations in technique or form with particular feelings: camerawork with ambivalence; sound with stasis; expansion of genre with horror; montage and circulation with cringe; and color and camp with plasticity. I treat the films and television in my cinema of experience as distinct aesthetic objects deserving sustained attention, as *more than* merely examples to illustrate my theoretical claims. With these commitments in mind, each of my chapters includes (what can be read as) stand-alone interpretations of the films and television, bookended by and situated alongside a broader account of the political-affective effects of feminist cinematic style.

Chapter 1, "Motherwork Camerawork: Ambivalence," reads three of Akerman's films "about" mothers that span forty years and include her most celebrated film and her final film. Putting *Jeanne Dielman*, *From the Other Side*, and *No Home Movie* together, I argue that Akerman's camera performs an aesthetic form of motherwork by creating spaces where viewers are invited to encounter, hold, and work through feelings, memories, and fantasies about mothers, their work, and their roles. This chapter also links Akerman to Roland Barthes, as Akerman with *No Home Movie* and Barthes with *Camera Lucida* create works that seek to bring their mothers back to them, or for us, to remember and to grieve. Barthes explicitly compares mothers to cameras as he searches for a photo of his mother that will evoke a feeling of her presence. Barthes, Beauvoir, Akerman, and thinkers in the Black radical feminist tradition are put into conversation here about camerawork, motherwork, and Saidiya Hartman's "fabulation," a process of refusal enacted by telling stories about people, events, and desires that official archives previously ignored or erased. The final film I bring into this chapter is the French-Senegalese director Alice Diop's *Saint Omer* (2022), which also poignantly invites the ambivalence viewers feel about mothers with her stylistically and thematically challenging depiction of an inscrutable Black mother on trial for killing her child.

Chapter 2, "White Noise: Stasis," begins with Beauvoir's deft description of patriarchy as a male sensorium—a regime of vision, smell, touch, taste, and sound. This chapter focuses specifically on sound as I begin by showing that Akerman's use of discordant and disjointed sound and silence invites feelings of stuckness, of moving in repetitive loops. Attention to Akerman's innovative use of sound, I argue, can trigger viewer awareness that the white noise of patriarchy might be sleepwalking us through our lives. The chapter's examples, Akerman's *Blow Up My Town*, Emerald Fennell's *Promising Young Woman* (2020), and Michaela Coel's *I May Destroy You* (2020), show how feminist media can help us notice how "women" are made, and trauma is triggered, by the white noise of patriarchy. Ultimately, I show that feminist media can reorient the ears of their audiences to hear like feminists by inviting us to feel, hold, acknowledge, and address the traumas of everyday sexism and worse buried in our psyches.

Chapter 3, "Genre Trouble: Horror," reads three prize-winning arthouse feminist films that I see as adapting key aspects of Akerman's style in the service of gender and genre-bending body horror. Mati Diop's *Atlantique* (*Atlantics*; 2019), Audrey Diwan's *L'Événement* (*Happening*; 2021), and Julia Ducournau's *Titane* (2021) each experiment with horror genre tricks to show horror defined not by jump scares, gore, shock, or survival of the final girl, but as women's everyday experience in our postcolonial, late capitalist, technology- and surveillance-oriented, still patriarchal and sexist world. I choose these three films not only because they experiment with a genre that is known to traffic in misogynist narratives and messages, but because, like their misogynist predecessors, they use cinematic techniques to double down on attention to bodies and feelings. The specific ways these European arthouse films deploy horror genre tricks—hyperrealism, exaggeration, excess, fabulation, or fantasy—capture *better* the feelings and experiences of women under patriarchy than documentaries or what we might consider more "realist" filmmaking. In these films, women's "real" experiences constitute the horror in the genre and are an example of what I name feminist realism.

Chapter 4, "Epistolary Archive: Cringe," features iterations of feminist cringe comedy that I read as love letters to viewers and love letters to a genealogy of feminist creativity. Cringe comedies are another example of (what I call in chapter 3) feminism's visual realisms, so named for doing the feminist political work of bringing women's (horrific, shameful, unnamed) experiences to our senses to focus our conscious attention on them. I read Catherine Breillat's *Romance* (1999) as setting the stage for Joey Soloway's

2016–17 television adaptation of Chris Kraus's book *I Love Dick* (1997), as they each utilize confessional direct address as voice-over or through the circulation of letters. This address to the audience invites subversive affective responses—laughter and cringe. These bodily responses interrupt and humiliate the fantasies of the male gaze, making space to acknowledge the excessive, complicated, and seemingly shameful realities of women's desire. I theorize cringe as an individual bodily gesture that exposes political feelings about collective experience in the intimate spheres of sex, love, and romance. Evidenced by bodily gesture and feelings of cringe, shared laughter and exuberance can bring women's desires into view.

In a short coda (in pink), I read Greta Gerwig's *Barbie*. The explosion of strong feelings in the critical and audience response to *Barbie* is a plastic perfect way to extend my ideas about what feelings can and cannot do, this time not via avant-garde, foreign, or independent film and television, but via a summer blockbuster. *Barbie* was accused of being both too "woke" and too "pink," received intense attention from antifeminists and feminists alike, and earned millions in ticket sales by drawing women and girls to the movies donning Barbie pink clothes and accessories. My reading of *Barbie* positions Gerwig's film in a cinema of experience by showing how it builds on the aesthetic and themes of Akerman's *Window Shopping* and *Jeanne Dielman*. I notice the use of color, artificiality, and the theme of control and lack thereof to argue that *Barbie* invites viewer experiences with gender and aesthetic plasticity in uncomfortable and transformative ways. Maybe most important, *Barbie* invites feelings that help us see ourselves as part of a collective. Feeling linked to other feminized persons can feel uncomfortable and out of our control, particularly when we are positioned in damaging hierarchies and connected through violent structures and institutions. *Barbie* not only envisions parallel worlds existing alongside our own, but also invites us to feel Barbie feeling her way with other women out of these worlds and into something entirely new.

My postscript is called "Invitation(s)." Offering my final thoughts, feelings, and hopes for this book, I revisit the invitation to feeling that a cinema of experience evokes. I locate this invitation as a feminist address in several senses, as I direct attention to the ongoing issuance of invitation(s) to readers and viewers that a cinema of experience makes possible.

1

MOTHERWORK CAMERAWORK: AMBIVALENCE

motherwork camerawork: photos and films of mothers produced by a camera; a way of filming mothers that holds our complex feelings about the myths of mothers and those who have "mothered" us, invites viewers to question and explore normalized "mother" roles, and can create new images of motherwork

ambivalence: the state of having mixed feelings or contradictory ideas about something or someone

FILMS CAN DO IMPORTANT POLITICAL work by complicating stereotypes, representing female subjectivity, and challenging the male gaze. Certain films, because of subject or style or both, do more. As I discussed in the introduction, Chantal Akerman's films frequently elicit strong reactions and stir up deep feelings. Often focusing on ordinary life, her films are stylistically unusual and they touch viewers in surprising but deep ways. In this chapter, I discuss three of Akerman's films—*Jeanne Dielman* (1975), *From the Other Side* (2002), and *No Home Movie* (2015)—that are thematically focused on mothers and that feature camerawork that I claim as an aesthetic form of the labor that is motherwork. To my readings of camerawork as motherwork in these three Akerman films, I add my reading of Alice Diop's film *Saint Omer* (2022), about a Black French woman on trial for killing her daughter.

To add the descriptor *motherwork* to Akerman's and Diop's camerawork, and claim this as an aesthetic and political style of filmmaking, I build on the writings of Simone de Beauvoir as well as Jacqueline Rose, Patricia Hill Collins, Saidiya Hartman, and several other thinkers in the Black feminist theory tradition.[1] Beauvoir and Rose (among other feminist theorists) offer poignant and compelling accounts of the ambivalence that surrounds the myth of mothers as well as the lived experiences of acting as or being a mother, or being the child of a mother. Black feminist thinkers carefully show that the name *mother* is denied to women who do not fit patriarchal, racist, classist (even humanist) norms of mothering, and serves as a disciplining norm even for mothers who do fit the model.[2] Collins chooses a new word—*motherwork*—to create some distance from the normative, as well as sexist and racist, weight of the word *mother*. She says, "I use the term motherwork to soften the dichotomies in feminist theorizing about motherhood that posit rigid distinctions between private and public, family and work, individual and collective, identity as individual autonomy and identity as growing from the collective self-determination of one's group" (1994, 372).

Adopting the term *motherwork* to identify a set of practices, rather than centering normative models of who mothers are, what they look like, and what they do, helps us reject the assumption that women are naturally suited for mothering and that some mothers deserve respect and others do not. Moreover, the multiple forms of violence that haunt not only the work of mothers but also the language and visual figures that most commonly represent this work are front and center in Black feminist writing on motherwork. Hartman, for example, theorizes care and violence together as she seeks to make space for the experiences of Black mothers whose stories of captivity and struggle have been lost to the archive. In *Lose Your Mother*, Hartman asks, "Must the story of the defeated always be a story of defeat? Is it too late to imagine that their lives might be redeemed or to fashion an antidote to oblivion? Is it too late to believe their struggles cast a shadow into a future in which they might finally win?" (2008a, 192). What could it mean to cast a shadow into a future?

Hartman encourages us to disturb chronology and physics as she invites us to create an alternative archive. Naming and following the idea of *motherwork camerawork* in this chapter, I hope to juxtapose a technology used by feminists in the service of freedom—Akerman's and Diop's cameras—to the technologies that tore children from their mothers and mothers from their children—the slave ship, the compass, the marketplace.[3] Thinking with Collins and Hartman, *motherwork* as linked to *camerawork* might help us to create an archive to hold the traumatic loss of mothers who are strangers to us, and it also may help us see more "mothers": mothers who gave birth to us, mothers we claim in a creative legacy, careworkers who are not mothers, and "others" hidden within the word *(m)others*—refugees, fugitives, migrants, the dispossessed, those either disappeared or too visible.[4]

Each film I feature here is focused on nonnormative mothers whose experiences are depicted as both strange and ordinary, never sentimentalized or sanitized. In *Jeanne Dielman*, the actual *work* of motherwork is made newly visible to us and fully elaborated. In *From the Other Side*, Akerman uses shoulder, handheld, and still cameras to film immigrant mothers and families on the US-Mexico border, bringing the mothers and families usually outside Americans' view uncomfortably near. A mix of documentary and fiction, this film reveals the role that nonwhite immigrant "others" play in dangerous myths of American autonomy, gun culture, and exceptionalism, and brings us face-to-face with the hopes and dreams of these (m)others. And in *No Home Movie*, the most emotionally and formally difficult of Akerman's films that I treat here, and the last film she made, Akerman films her own aging mother, a Holocaust survivor, in her Brussels apartment. In this film, the technologies of camera and laptop are central to the negotiation of the mother/daughter bond, the inheritance of trauma(s), and the possibility to affirm a freedom that prizes connection and collectivity.

Finally, *Saint Omer* builds on the readings of the Akerman films I engage in this chapter. The film fictionalizes the real-life trial of a Black mother who kills her child, what many consider the worst thing a mother can do. The film also features a Black woman professor who, for her own mostly inscrutable personal reasons, is fascinated by the trial and the mother at the center of it. The professor has intellectual reasons to attend the trial, too: she is writing a book about Medea, the woman of Greek myth who murders her and

Jason's two sons; as we learn later, the professor is pregnant and has a vexed relationship with her own mother.[5] Diop's camera stays focused for long moments on the inscrutable face of the mother on trial. This camerawork, her willingness to attend to the ways a Black mother can become a universal figure who draws our feelings of ambivalence, and the triangulation of the three central female characters all draw me to this film as an iteration of Akerman's distinct style and themes.

I propose we think of Akerman's and Diop's cameras in these films not just as a technological object (an instrument for visualization that can document or represent what we see) but as another kind of orifice. The Latin word *camera* means "chamber," or room. In these films, Akerman's and Diop's cameras are chambers that hold our feelings, rooms where viewers can acknowledge and explore discomforting fantasies and experiences. The motherwork camerawork I theorize in this chapter is a practice of carving out liminal spaces of encounter for characters and viewers to confront difficult feelings in regard to mothers. Motherwork camerawork also includes the creation of cinematic images where previously less visible or invisible practices of motherwork can be seen, heard, felt, and imagined. Thinking of camerawork motherwork in these ways, we can distinguish how Akerman and Diop not only document but also *perform* motherwork, as distinct from another famous search for a mother with a camera.

In *Camera Lucida* (1980), Roland Barthes says the "extreme weight" of the image, the objectifying view of the camera, might be mitigated by "extreme love" (12). I explore his idea of what that love entails in this chapter (and what it extracts from women), noting that in *Camera Lucida*, Barthes explicitly compares cameras to mothers. His essay, which chronicles his search for a picture of his deceased mother, was published after his own too-early death. His search for his mother's photo foreshadows how Akerman uses her camera to document what became the final months of her mother's life, subsequently released as *No Home Movie* following Akerman's mother's death and Akerman's own, by suicide. Comparing these two kinds of camerawork, I argue that Akerman and Diop create holding spaces not just for capture, as Barthes did, but also for freedom. The ambivalence we experience in relationship to mothers and motherwork is arguably avoided by Barthes but is encouraged by Akerman's and Diop's camerawork as a way to feel our way toward new forms of care for each other.

Finding Mothers and Others

I never followed my father's dream, to have a family. I stayed a girl, the daughter of my mother.

Chantal Akerman (quoted in Brenez 2012)

As demonstrated by Joan Scott in *The Fantasy of Feminist History* (2011), irrational and unconscious fantasies play an outsized role in how historical and political narratives are shaped and reproduced, in how we interact with the world and each other. It comes as no surprise that fantasy, desire, and fear dominate our expectations and assumptions concerning mothers. Mothers are our first human contact and are cast as the absolute *other*. Mothers are simultaneously powerful sorcerers, insignificant vessels, and ultimate caretakers. Mothers create and nurture new beings; their work reminds us of our vulnerability and dependency; the presence and actions of mothers destabilize the border between self and other. Mothers are present at the birth we can't remember, and they remind us of the death we want to avoid. Simone de Beauvoir says that mothers are domesticated *precisely because* of this proximity to death and life, a proximity that makes them seem scary, strange, and much too powerful. Sitting right alongside the comfort of mothers *as home* is the uncanniness of *(m)others* as unfamiliar and dangerous—the cyborg, the replicant, the two-in-one of the pregnant belly. Too close and too far, both familiar and estranged, mothers complicate the borders we try to draw between ourselves and others, our independence and our needs, the mythological and the real.

In a book called *Mothers: An Essay on Love and Cruelty* (2018), Jacqueline Rose bluntly reports that mothers are put in the impossible position of being responsible for the cruelties of the world and expected to repair them, too.[6] This ubiquitous (in)visibility of mothers in their twinned role as virtuous caretakers or dangerous usurpers puts visibility *itself* into question as a credible method, and care into question as a quality we should seek in mothering, lest we simply reproduce patriarchal visions of how mothers look and patriarchal mandates for what mothers do or fail to do. So how do we look and what do we hope to find? Trying to answer these questions, this chapter could be narrowed to focus exclusively on the politics of looking, who sees what, how, and in which situations; the relationship between viewer and vision; and how the frame that captures what we see and don't see is determined.[7]

Barthes explores these questions by considering how certain photos, their framing and their details, affect him, as a way to ask more generally about the power of photography as a medium. In his essay, he confides that he hopes to find a photo of his recently deceased mother that will reanimate her and puncture (wound) him. Noticing a link between photos of his own mother and the ability or inability of photos to produce and capture moments in time, and to bring the dead back to life, Barthes notices that cameras *mimic* mothers: they reproduce, but they also distort. Barthes says the magic of the camera, which is making something absent present, is akin to the magic of the mother's body. She makes something absent present, too, by producing a person out of her body. Barthes doesn't comment on the gendered and raced politics of reproduction and its distortions, but instead sometimes repeats these same gender and race dynamics within his essay.[8] Speaking of the camera as a mother, Barthes says, "A sort of umbilical cord links the body of the photographed thing to my gaze: light, though impalpable, is here a carnal medium, a skin I share with anyone who has been photographed" (81).

Laura Mulvey's foundational work on cinema showed that dominant narrative structures replicate the objectifying gaze of cameras to encode pleasure within a specifically *male* gaze (even for female viewers).[9] Much earlier, Mary Shelley had warned us about the dangers of technophilia harnessed by men.[10] Shelley's Doctor Frankenstein was grieving his own mother when, like Barthes, he turned to a new technology for mortal remediation. He harnessed technology for male reproduction: he created a human, using the power of nature (a bolt of lightning!) to produce his offspring. Sometimes grief moves us to *become* the lost object, not just to mourn it. Such male-motivated forms of reproduction and their use of technology precisely for these purposes should give us pause.

When we look with Shelley, Mulvey, Akerman, and Diop, we may see that, like Doctor Frankenstein, Barthes's gaze is too romantic and too male. And both give too much power to the apparatus to which they turn for control. What about technology harnessed by women? Instead of Barthes's umbilical cord, we might embrace filmmaker Agnès Varda's: "For her 1976 documentary 'Daguerréotypes,' an allusion to the Paris street where she lived, she powered her equipment with an electric cord plugged into her home, limiting her range to its length.... She called it a 'new umbilical cord'" (Dargis 2019). Akerman and Diop also show us how to use cords and cameras differently.

Never birthing nor caring for children, Akerman nevertheless does motherwork with her camera. In figure 1.1, a photograph taken on set while filming the 1980 short film *Dis-moi* (*Tell Me*), an episode for the French documentary television series called *Grand-mères* (Grandmothers), we see a young Chantal with her huge camera. In the film, she interviews three elderly women who lost their mothers in the Holocaust. Offscreen she talks with her mother about her own grandmother who died in the camps. She begins, "Tell me, Mom, what memories do you have of your mother?"[11] The question situates her within a matriarchal genealogy, but at the same time she films with her back to the baby picture off to the right of her head.[12] We are immediately put on notice that she will not be reproducing in a normative (biological) fashion. Her head joined with her camera, Akerman looks like a stranger to this domestic space. In the short film, when Akerman is separated from her camera to sit at kitchen tables or in the living rooms of her subjects, she seems uncomfortable. Invited to eat, she picks at her food, and returns, gently but insisting, to her questioning. When we look at the picture taken on set, although foreign to the domestic space, Akerman appears at ease when fused with the camera.[13] Her head is pressed to a hard apparatus, an apparatus enveloped by a quilted soft cover, but with a thin, pointy penile projection. Gender *and* species are hybrid, we might even say cyborgian, in this photo.[14] Could we call her a cyborg mother? Something we will say for certain by the end of this chapter is that the camerawork she does is a kind of motherwork as it is a form of care performed for others. Moreover, Akerman's camerawork makes space for others, like Diop, to do the kind of motherwork I specify here with *their* cameras.

Unlike Barthes who looks through photographs to find one that might bring his mother to life for memory and comfort, or Doctor Frankenstein who, also grieving the loss of his mother, harnesses generative power to create his offspring, Akerman *joins with her camera* to do motherwork *for us*. It is important that Barthes is interested in photography, and Akerman is a filmmaker; that Barthes searches for his mother after her death, and Akerman films her mother prior to hers. These are key distinctions in medium, timing, and method. But what underwrites these differences is this: Akerman's cinematic practice puts into question shared cultural meanings around mothers and motherwork, while Barthes's search for photographs assumes and reinforces conventional perspectives. Akerman's camerawork challenges conventions of mothering by creating encounters onscreen and off that make the familiar newly strange, bring what is far away unbearably

1.1. Chantal Akerman with her camera, filming *Dis-moi* (*Tell Me*) (1980). Photo by Laszlo Ruszka/INA via Getty Images.

close, and establish the distance necessary to open a space for examining the feelings wrought from relationships that are always too close. Sometimes, as we will see in *Jeanne Dielman* and *Saint Omer*, these encounters and feelings precipitate violence, and they remain unexplained.

Jeanne Dielman, 23, quai du Commerce, 1080 Bruxelles (Chantal Akerman, 1975)

As noted in the introduction, *Jeanne Dielman* is an uncomfortably long film in which it is famously claimed that "nothing happens."[15] We witness three days in the life of a mother (Delphine Seyrig), seen doing housework, cooking and cleaning for her teenage son, caring for a neighbor's child, shopping and having coffee outside the home, and having sex for money with men in her bedroom.[16] The great majority of the film takes place in three airless rooms.[17] Near the end, Jeanne appears to experience an unexpected orgasm with one of her clients, calmly takes scissors from her dressing table, and stabs him as he is lying on her bed. Then she returns to the dining room table. For the last seven minutes of the film, we watch Jeanne sitting at the table as night encroaches in the darkening room, her face lit by a rotating blue street lamp.

In the very *first* minutes of the film, framing Jeanne in close view, Akerman's camera holds not only our gaze but also our confused feelings as we watch Jeanne start to boil potatoes in her kitchen (duration: 1 minute, 50 seconds), greet a john at the door, disappear into her bedroom to service him, and then receive his money and bid him adieu (1 minute, 18 seconds). She then deposits her cash into a pot on the dining room table and returns to the kitchen to drain the potatoes (1 minute, 15 seconds). Next, she removes the towel from the top of the bed, opens the bedroom window, takes the towel to the laundry basket, and returns to the bedroom to shut the window and smooth the bedcovers (46 seconds). We continue to watch as she takes a bath (scrubbing every part of her body; 3 minutes, 53 seconds), partially dresses, and then totally scrubs the bathtub (1 minute, 43 seconds). She gathers the tablecloth and dishes from the kitchen and sets the dining room table (2 minutes, 2 seconds). She greets her teenage son and sets out dinner. These habits continue for the three days that the film chronicles, interrupted only by small noticeable and troubling changes in routine, such as a missed button on Jeanne's robe, mussed hair, or overboiled potatoes.

Akerman scrambles our expectations for story and narrative by engaging her camera in defamiliarizing techniques. These include the duration of single shots; the filming of empty spaces combined with frontal shots at midrange; the use of carefully placed static cameras as well as handheld cameras; alienating exterior tracking shots that are juxtaposed to intimate engagement with almost touchable figures; silence interrupted by disorienting sound, and so on.[18] These methods put what is usually hidden directly in our view. Women's work, suddenly hypervisible, demands that we experience the monotony of three consecutive days in Jeanne's life constructed in segments of "real-time" tasks (see fig. 1.2). But it is not *only* monotony: as the film stretches on, Akerman's camera invites us into a sensual world where we can almost feel the crisp sheets, we can almost smell the freshly brewed coffee, and, with Jeanne, we take pleasure in her pleasure at completing her tasks well and punctually. Likewise, we are filled with anxiety when any small thing goes wrong, when Jeanne fails to put the lid on the pot in the center of the dining table after depositing her money from her sex work, or she forgets to turn off the lights when she leaves a room. Watching Jeanne, we gain enhanced awareness of Jeanne's (and our own) relationship to inanimate objects and an order that creates her situated identity as housewife, mother, and prostitute. But this order also creates opportunities for sensual

1.2   Delphine Seyrig as Jeanne Dielman, peeling potatoes. *Jeanne Diel-*
man, 23, quai du Commerce, 1080 Bruxelles (Chantal Akerman, 1975).

enjoyment, too, for her and for us. The objects, routines, and expectations
hold Jeanne captive, but they also make room for discomforting feelings
and unexpected pleasures on the part of viewers.

Jeanne's encounters onscreen provide a holding space for viewers as we
experience a range of feelings: boredom (when will she finish peeling the
potatoes?); relief (as she completes a task); anxiety (when she fails to do so,
or her timing is off, or she doesn't finish combing her hair or misses a button
on her robe); cringe (as she answers her son's probing, Oedipal questions
about sex); confusion (did she have an orgasm with her client?); surprise (as
she suddenly murders this client); and so on. The camerawork deliberately
provides a space for viewer feelings because Akerman's camera *refuses* to give
access to Jeanne's feelings.[19] Akerman's camera frustrates any expectation
that we will follow Jeanne from room to room. The camera stays in place as
Jeanne moves.[20] Jeanne's flat affect, monotone voice, and conversation that
is always too much (when Jeanne talks to her neighbor at the door, or her
son's monologue from his bed) or too little (huge stretches of silence) leave
her feelings opaque to viewers. The range of feeling generated by the film
(boredom, anxiety, cringe, confusion, and so on) are not Jeanne's but *ours*.
Naming them, I do not mean to anticipate or determine what any particular

viewer may feel. I instead want to indicate how the scenes and our feelings as we view them are ours and not Jeanne's, *and* they are surprising: quotidian while strange, available although distant; these feelings tap into ambivalence about mothers, mothering, motherwork, femininity, autonomy, and home.

From the Other Side (Chantal Akerman, 2002)

While in *Jeanne Dielman*, Akerman brings to our attention what is invisible because it is too close to us, in *From the Other Side* she investigates what is too easily manipulated or becomes distorted because it is too far away. When we bring the work and experiences of disappeared mothers close, this film shows, the acknowledgment threatens our sense of self and autonomy, and it threatens, too, the ideological investment in freedom as an individual experience, best enjoyed when we are unconstrained and unburdened by the existence of others. In *From the Other Side*, Akerman takes her camera to the US-Mexico border that separates Agua Prieta, Mexico, from Douglas, Arizona. Doing so, she brings to our view the lives and labor of immigrants—people whose work and existence white Americans, and even some feminist thinkers, prefer not to acknowledge. She interviews Mexicans and Americans on both sides of the physical border to gauge not just the geopolitical but also familial, psychic, cultural, and social registers.

From the Other Side was first presented in 2002 as a video installation in Kassel, Germany, at the art exposition Documenta 11.[21] It featured eighteen projection monitors, two video screens, and a live feed to the Mexican border.[22] The film version, which is the one I focus on, opens with an interview with a young Mexican man in a doorway, talking about the disappearance of his brother. Like all of the interviews, it is conducted face-forward with a static camera: "My name is Francisco Santillán Garcia. I'm twenty-one, and I was born here. I live here with my mother" (see fig. 1.3). We hear Akerman off-camera softly but directly ask questions in Spanish: "Would you like to live in the US?" "Once I did," he answers. "Before my brother left, I was going to go. . . . I asked 'Who goes? You or me?' He went and look what happened to him." Francisco continues to tell the rest: how his brother's group ran out of water and the "coyote" left them in the desert. They started to walk but instead of going out of the desert they went deeper into it. "That's how they got lost," he says.

From the Other Side is a documentary of sorts, and the story recounted is true.[23] But Akerman departs from the conventions of documentary, as we will see in a moment. She is not particularly interested in producing a

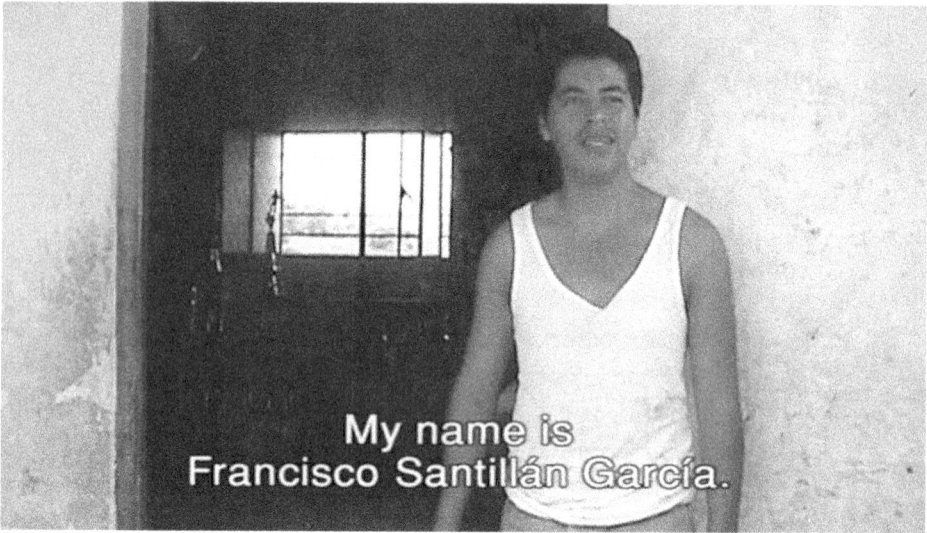

1.3 "My name is Francisco Santillán Garcia." *From the Other Side* (Chantal Akerman, 2002).

realistic or representative picture of the situation on the US-Mexico border, as politically instructive as that might be. Instead, she stages encounters onscreen that hold us in a scene, a moment, or a place to trigger complex feelings. This recurs between the film and viewers as well. The best word for this moving beyond the real and into fiction is what Saidiya Hartman calls *fabulation*, the "dreams of what might be possible if you could escape the house of bondage" (2019, 17). In *Wayward Lives, Beautiful Experiments*, Hartman studies police briefs, charity reports, newspaper articles, and photos to find young Black women in Philadelphia and New York, to create what might have been possible for them through fabulation.[24] She carves a free space for the future out of cramped and cruel worlds, from photos taken to capture young Black girls and Black women. In other words, she finds something in photographs different from what Barthes looks for; where they seem to offer capture, she springs them into release. Fabulation expresses the potential wishes, dreams, or hopes of persons and subjectivities absent from the archives (such as the dreams and wishes of Black women and girls) to make room for freedom in spaces of captivity.[25]

In the last minutes of *From the Other Side*, we hear one such story. As I learned only later when reading about the film, this story is not real. It is Akerman's invention, her fabulation. We hear Akerman as voice-over, as we see images of moving traffic at night as if we are in one of the cars ourselves, along a seemingly endless highway.

David doesn't know how but his mother survived. Or how she ended up in Los Angeles. She must've done odd jobs on the way. Must've slept outside, in barns or parks. We know she worked at a gas station. In a diner. Often as a cleaning woman. She left a trail from town to town. And even in Los Angeles. In Los Angeles, after a while we lost her because the money and the letters stopped coming. It was to find her that David crossed over himself. She was a waitress, one day she didn't come. She was a cleaning woman, one day she didn't come. She said little, did her job. She was polite but somber they say. She was missed especially by the kids. She never stole. The landlady told David: she lived here, she left. She left her coat. I kept it just in case. But she never came for it. Must be back in Mexico. It's been four months now, and I don't know why but I can't rent her room. Maybe it's her fault. She must have left behind an atmosphere or a spell. I have nothing against her, and she nothing against me, or the room. Why she left I have no idea, none at all. She left the rent money and her coat. No note, nothing. She didn't have much. I wasn't around so that's when she left. I can't say much about her. We weren't close. And I'm easy to get close to. But she saw no-one, man or woman. Once I was going to Mexico. I asked her for some good places. She just shrugged. She sort of mumbled something. I didn't catch it. Then she went to her room. There's nothing to say about her. She always left the same time, came back the same time. Hardly went out again. Sundays, she must have gone to the beach. Because Sundays there was a little sand on the steps. Sometimes she went out to smoke. I don't like smoking inside. She'd wander down the block, smoking. She was thinking, but about what? That I can't tell you. She always looked neat. You could tell she ironed. Down the cellar, there's a washer and dryer. The tenants can use them, so she did. She ironed in her room. She ironed with the radio on. I could hear it. Once she blew out the fuses. I told her not to listen with the lights on and iron. But it wasn't her. A radio practically uses nothing. Anyway, a little later she went. Either to Mexico or elsewhere. At times I think she's dead. But that's my dark side. She's not dead. She's in Mexico or elsewhere but I can't say where. I never saw her again. Well, once I thought I did. I'm not sure it was her. It was near here down by the

It must've been a mirage.

1.4 "It must've been a mirage." *From the Other Side* (Chantal Akerman, 2002).

boulevard. Lots of Mexicans there. I was driving. When I got closer there was no one there. It must've been a mirage.

In Akerman's fabulation, we see a lonely highway (fig. 1.4). True to the moving images of the cinema, the highway moves as the immigrants move, always moving, trying to disappear. And, yet, a picture emerges from the small details, and David's mother becomes more than a mirage. Akerman tells the story of this lost mother by adding up insignificant details, small observations, tiny facts. She was missed especially by the kids; she never stole; she left behind her coat; she mumbled; she left sand on the steps; she always looked neat (like she ironed); and she went outside to smoke. She ironed with the radio on, and once she blew out the fuses. Akerman repeats the (imagined) words of David's mother's landlady looking for his mother: "There were lots of Mexicans there," and you couldn't tell "if it was her."

Akerman's story of David and his mother is a cinematic fabulation, a method of refusal that allows her to move beyond the conventions of documentary to get at truths otherwise obviated.[26] Sometimes the subjects share their stories, at other times the voice-over (Akerman's own voice) takes responsibility for the story. Each perspective, however, is never presented as a necessarily realistic or complete representation. With fabulation, Hartman and Akerman counter a world vision that claims we can know the "other," or that names that other as a threat, enacting structural and grammatical violence in that naming, knowing, picturing, and capturing.[27] In *From the Other Side*, this kind of capturing is depicted as racialized, patriarchal, and buttressed by institutional religion. For Arizona residents, the outside/outsider/alien is cast as the enemy in what they call "the daily war." For example, a speech Akerman films at a border agent's funeral mythologizes the power of a Holy Father who puts *His* faith in fathers, nations, and borders, but who is also capricious, unreliable, who doesn't always step in to help in time or in the right way.[28] This scene is followed by an interview with Sheriff Larry Dever of Douglas, Arizona. He reports that one of the key things people in the area (rural Arizona) value is the right to privacy and ownership of property, without the intrusion or control of anyone, whom they will shoot if need be.

While fabulation makes lost mothers in *From the Other Side* more visible to us, Akerman's traditionally "realist" images, like those of the desert and the border wall, also move us, but differently. Here we notice that Akerman's camerawork does something very different from what Barthes says cameras can do. Looking for his own mother, Barthes searches for the *punctum* of an image, that small detail that pierces him. But it only pierces *him*—another detail might jump out at someone else, or none at all in which case the photo cannot do its magic of making present what is absent. This detail, the *punctum*, is contrasted with *studium*, the shared cultural meaning that locates the photo for all of us. Because *studium* (we might think of it as the background) is presumably the same for all of us, we don't really notice it. It passes by, escapes our motivated attention. Barthes insists that the *studium* is transparent, even uncontroversial, but we cannot predict what will break through as *punctum* for any individual viewer.

We have already seen in the example of David's mother that Akerman makes Barthes's *punctum* (the small detail) available to all (she left sand on the steps, she always looked neat), while *studium*, by contrast, does not have a commonsense shared meaning. In *From the Other Side*, the *studium* might be the conventional border wall or the desert, as these are background for many scenes. But not for Akerman. Akerman puts everything in our view up for questioning. Importantly, she explicitly refuses the assumption that her situating backgrounds (the border wall and the desert) have the same meaning for all. Her interviews with residents from Agua Prieta and Douglas demonstrate this very point: the desert and the wall do not mean the same thing for those on opposite sides. The border and the desert are shown to be not only physical, but also psychological, material, and agentic. Fantasies about the border and the desert create relationships, realities, and states of mind that go beyond the marking of national geographical space, and these fantasies give the lie to any claim for "accurate" representation of any of the parties themselves. These representations are shown as clearly unable to be disengaged from the political, cultural, and social context. Akerman interviews Mexicans living on the border, Mexicans trying or who have tried to come to the United States, Mexicans who have lost family members who tried to cross. And on the other side, she interviews residents of Douglas, Arizona, border officials in Douglas, and a Mexican official living in Douglas. Separating these interviews are the images of the physical border. These "realist" shots, placed as "cuts" between interviews with Mexicans and Americans, upend Barthes's idea of *studium*.

As the *studium* is examined and upended, so is the *punctum*. Although *all* the people on camera are strangers to the film's audience, Akerman seems to assume that her viewers are already somewhat familiar with the fears and fantasies of the Douglas, Arizona, residents. What is significant about her interviews with the Arizonans is their willing expression of ugly assumptions and fantasies about Mexicans and their lives. Akerman's camera does not draw our attention to any *punctum* that would make them singular individuals.

The residents of Agua Prieta, in contrast, speak about their desire to find better lives, reunite with family, and escape violence and poverty. As they speak about their lives on the border, their fantasies, fears, and hopes about crossing, or who crosses and why, Akerman's camera draws our attention to more than one *punctum*, and we notice small and singular details about each person. We become aware of gestures, physical attributes, ways of speaking. With attention to these details, dreams and hopes also become vitally, sensually, emotionally present for viewers. Viewers may also notice that though the border and the desert exist as physical spaces that separate, the two groups of people on either side of the desert/border are inextricably connected. Any possibility to live without capture (physical for Mexicans, psychological for Americans) depends on how we imagine and treat those on the "other side."

A long segment near the end of the film shows another realist image that could be mistaken for *studium*: infrared footage from US helicopters, which is being viewed (seemingly in real time) by US border agents. There are shouts of triumph (we assume from the border agents) when the images,

1.5   Crosshairs. *From the Other Side* (Chantal Akerman, 2002).

which looked like white blobs on a black screen, come into focus to clearly reveal a single-file line of people walking through the desert. These images look shockingly like drone footage (see fig. 1.5).

By this time in the film, we have met several people who have tried to cross the border, some whose family members disappeared or died in the desert, some who still dream of crossing despite the dangers. With this context, and the film's attention to personal detail, through Akerman's camera reflecting the drone footage, the fuzzy white blobs have become, for viewers, people with sorrows, joys, families, and material needs. And suddenly, the multiple and ambiguous uses of technology are legible. Cameras used by border agents surveil and capture, but mediated through Akerman's technique of camerawork motherwork, these same images become a vehicle for making lives, longings, dreams, and struggles newly felt.

No Home Movie (Chantal Akerman, 2015)

Documenting yet another genocide—of Native Americans—in the novel *There, There*, Tommy Orange has a mother say to her son: "The internet has a lot to offer, but they'll never make a website that can take the place of your mother's company" (2018, 76). This novel is, in part, about how there can never truly be compensation for Native American land, the stolen mother. I note, too, that this character loses his actual mother. Is this how Akerman felt after losing her mother?[29] That technology could not take her mother's place, even though, as Mulvey notes, film "preserves the living presence of human figures, often long dead, through the film machine" (2006, 10).

When the mother in *There, There* says technology can never replace a mother, Orange debunks the delusion that freedom could ever be possible outside of encounter, that it could ever be possible without some version of home (even "no home") that we might embrace or against which we might struggle.[30] As film scholar Anna Backman Rogers remarks, "Technology, which is predicated on function and purpose, throws into relief the nature of human existence that exceeds notions of utility and reductive meaning" (2019, 85). We might notice, too, that the title of Orange's novel, *There, There*, captures the ambivalence not only about technology and its uses, but also about human relationships that Akerman conjures in her films. "There, there" points us to multiple sites of motherwork (as in "there and there!") while also speaking the repeated words of maternal comfort ("there, there, it will be better soon").[31] The novel's title could be the mantra of Akerman's camera-work motherwork in *From the Other Side* and as repeated in *No Home Movie*.

No Home Movie is simple and stark.[32] It features Akerman's mother, Natalia Akerman (sometimes referred to as "Nelly"), filmed by static cameras positioned around her Brussels apartment and, in other scenes, by Akerman's handheld (sometimes shoulder-held) camera.[33] The elderly, declining widow goes about her days, sometimes eating, sometimes sleeping, sometimes talking with her daughter Chantal in person or via Skype, or talking, eating, and interacting with her caretaker, Clara, and with Chantal Akerman's sister, Sylviane. While a tragic history clearly weighs on the family, there is little direct talk of the horrific events Akerman's mother must have suffered and witnessed, other than during two scenes at the kitchen table. In these scenes, Akerman prompts her mother to answer questions about the family's lapsed practice of Judaism, about her mother's and the family's escape to Brussels from Poland, how they were subsequently discovered and forcibly deported to Auschwitz. Mostly though, the film records her mother's day-to-day habits as she nears the end of her life. There are extended shots of Natalia eating and sitting at the kitchen table, and her movements into empty rooms. Several stretches feature objects and rooms alone, no people in the camera's view. We notice furniture, laundry, plants, dishes. We see the empty kitchen, empty dining room, empty corridor leading into the

1.6   The desert. *No Home Movie* (Chantal Akerman, 2015).

kitchen. This is an example of *studium* rendered as *punctum*. Viewers feel Natalia Akerman's absence even before she is gone.

No Home Movie also includes long tracking shots of the desert, and it opens with an uncomfortably long, unbearably disturbing, over four-minute-long shot of a tree in a desert. One might assume this is the Israeli desert, given the film's origin as an installation of images on desert and mother, which premiered in Jerusalem. But for us, thinking about *No Home Movie* with *From the Other Side*, the desert on the US-Mexico border comes to mind as well (see figs. 1.6 and 1.7).

Akerman's film editor, Claire Atherton, says, "The images of the desert created a distance, which is always so important in Chantal's work, not to be stuck to the emotion. The images of the desert are an elsewhere—they are not linked to a particular location." And yet, as counterpoint to what Atherton says, we *can* locate them, *there* and *there*: Israel and the US-Mexico border, linked to past and current genocides, and in Israel's case, both. But for Atherton, the images are not geographically specific and instead refer to grief. She says, "We didn't know at that moment that this film would be so concerned with the question about what it is to be close and to be far" (quoted in Margulies 2019, 17).

This is the pain Barthes feels in *Camera Lucida*, a grief he tries to mitigate with the magic of the camera, but it fails him. The camera offers up a resem-

1.7   The desert. *From the Other Side* (Chantal Akerman, 2002).

blance that eludes and does not satisfy: "Resemblance refers to the subject's identity, an absurd, purely legal, even penal affair. . . . Likeness leaves me unsatisfied and somehow skeptical (certainly this is the sad disappointment I experience looking at the ordinary photographs of my mother—whereas the only one which has given me the splendor of her truth is precisely a lost, remote photograph, one which does not look 'like' her, the photograph of a child I never knew)" (102–3).

Noticing the difficulty of knowing his mother, especially in her appearance as object, Barthes indicates that cameras make knowledge of mothers simultaneously possible and impossible. Like Barthes, in *No Home Movie* Akerman struggles with her camera to see her mother, keep her present, make her speak, enchant her, know her, remember her, unearth and acknowledge her past, re/present her anew (see fig. 1.8). What Barthes does not notice is that one reason it's so difficult to capture the essence of a mother is because the mother role mandates that mothers be fantasies of someone else, unseen, disappeared, doing their work—and especially their aging—in the shadows. One of the things Barthes admits to having most admired about his own mother is that he never knew her to make "a single observation" (69). She was (and remains) an object, not the subject. There is a deep subjectivism in Barthes's musings on photos of his mother and

1.8 Natalia Akerman in her kitchen. *No Home Movie* (Chantal Akerman, 2015).

even though he seeks to find her, it is only to find her in *his own* gaze, for his memory. He wants to capture her for himself rather than free her for us, to reproduce her for his own pleasure. Were he to free her, she would appear like the aspiring immigrants in *From the Other Side*, brought to life by humanizing detail and wise, sad, or ironic musings. When Barthes finds his mother in the Winter Garden photograph, he refuses to share her with anyone else. The photo is not reproduced in *Camera Lucida*, an entire book about photos and about the search for his mother! We might conclude that Barthes keeps his mother's photo hidden to not objectify her.[34] But at the same time, readers are denied even the possibility to try to see her, to somehow have her touch *us*. Sacred, she disappears. Profane, she circulates. These seem to be Barthes's only options. But Akerman offers a third: fabulation as cinema, camerawork as motherwork.

We can contrast Barthes's refusal to show us his mother with how Akerman uses technology to do motherwork. Instead of only capturing her mother for herself, Akerman holds her mother in the camera's gaze for her own and our view. She wants to *share* her mother with us, with the world; she wants her to be seen in all her moods, desires, contradictions, and ambiguities, in her aging body. Seeing through/with Akerman's still cameras positioned around the apartment, we become intimately familiar with the textures and feelings of this domestic space, and Natalia Akerman's ghostly trace becomes piercing not just for Chantal the daughter, *but for us, too.* We are invited into their relationship to see that Akerman's mother *is her camera* (her reflection of herself, both truthful and distorted), and her camera *is her mother* (the other who mediates but also makes possible her encounter with the world).

If we know of Akerman's mother's death shortly after these scenes were filmed, and then Akerman's own death by suicide just as the film was being released, viewer experience of Akerman's camera's already intense attention to her mother in *No Home Movie* is further intensified.[35] Akerman's mother is filmed as at once a vulnerable and powerful, dangerous and alluring, distant and proximate, intimately known but also mysteriously unknown and unknowable primary other. Her tragic past and her aging body are beyond the comprehension and control of the filmmaker daughter; the daughter's work and travel schedule are beyond the will of the mother; and the world's dangers are beyond the control of both.

Holding their relationship in view, and inviting viewers' own complex and ambivalent feelings about mothers and motherwork, Akerman's camera holds and mediates multiple encounters at once. It mediates the relationship *between* mother and daughter onscreen, making it possible to view each other when they are apart, making it possible for Akerman to record her mother's last days, to try to capture her enduring appearance in a world from which she is about to disappear. These moments hold our feelings, too, as they conjure a complex mix of ambivalence, anxiety, alienation, guilt, love, and anger. In a society so permeated by erasure of mothers, and the desire to erase and ignore these feelings, the quest to use technology to give flesh to her mother's image is itself a remarkable event. True to this complex set of feelings, viewers of the film are witnesses to frustrations and gaps in communication and connection as Akerman the daughter is able to almost but not quite *see* her mother, as her mother only partially sees her, try as she might.[36]

In poignant scenes, multiple cameras vie for attention as mother and daughter try to connect, and then say goodbye, over Skype. In one image from these scenes, Natalia Akerman says, "Your camera, every time" (see fig.1.9). In a second image, we see a laptop sitting on a desk with an abandoned toothbrush to its right (see fig. 1.10). In both images, Natalia Akerman's face is fuzzy or indecipherable. In the second image, we can also notice a little box in the screen's lower right where we just barely see Akerman with her camera on her shoulder. She is looking at her mother while filming her mother, and viewers see all this at once.

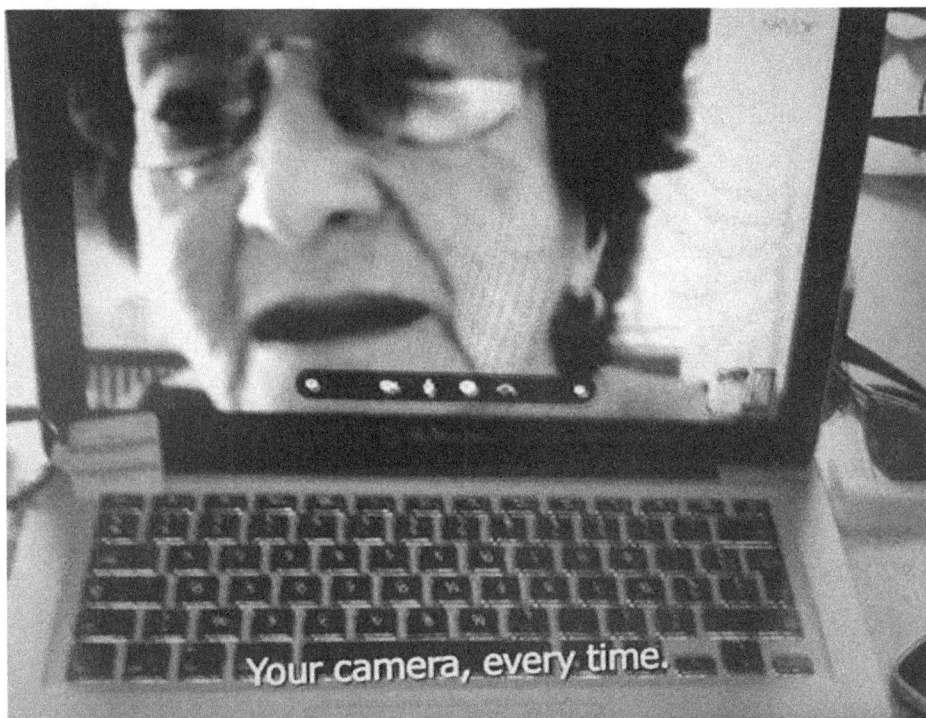

1.9 "Your camera, every time." *No Home Movie* (Chantal Akerman, 2015).

There is always the gap, always the struggle in the hold as it acts to capture and (potentially) free, at the same time. Staging freedom as always and only relational, holding us in difficult spaces, Akerman's camerawork motherwork chips away at other powerful holds: the myths of castrating mothers, dark and dangerous (m)others, the myths of easy relationship, of connection without sacrifice, of full autonomy and unmitigated individual freedom. As reflected in these two images, we see Akerman's laptop and cameras doing this complex motherwork as she navigates the distance between mother and daughter, filmmaker and viewers. The top of Natalia's face looks at her daughter, and Natalia's face looks out at us captured by Skype and by Akerman's camera, but fuzzy and too huge because Natalia is too close to the screen. The conversation is extended again and again, with several goodbyes, more declarations of love, touching of hands onscreen, and then a new topic ("Bye Mommy"). It is heartbreaking for them to break the bond, to break away from the cameras that both connect and separate them, and it is both heartening and heartbreaking for viewers to witness.

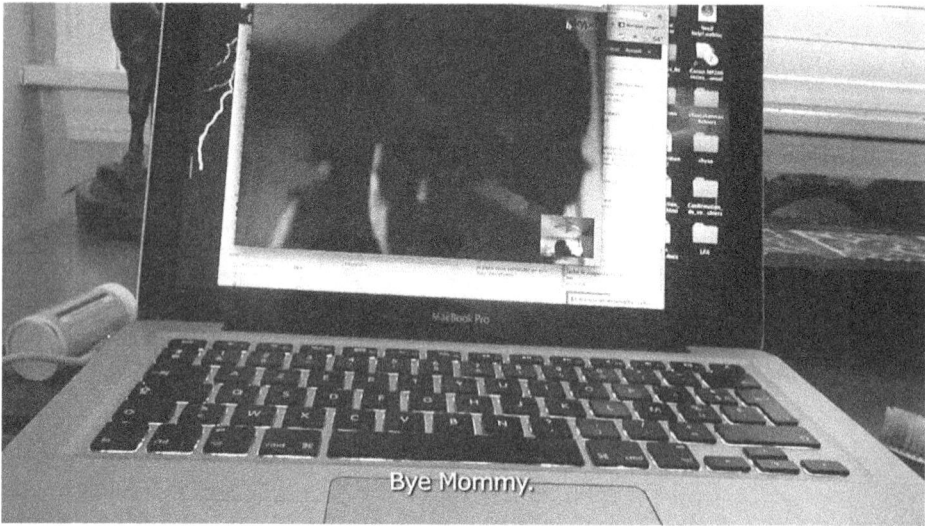

1.10 "Bye Mommy." *No Home Movie* (Chantal Akerman, 2015).

Of this conversation, Akerman herself says that to her eyes it looks "like a love affair between us." She is looking, as we are looking. Your camera, every time. Bye Mommy. To be witness to these conversations is almost perverse: intense and overwhelming, incestuous and invasive.

Each time in the film when mother and daughter use Skype, Akerman's mother asks her why she is filming, to which Akerman replies, "Because I want to show that there is no distance in the world."[37] But, of course, there is distance, alienation, the gap: maybe what Akerman means is that her mother is always with her, a primal bond that can be broken but never eradicated. One thing we can say more certainly is that from this closed-in, small-world space, viewers see that Akerman has limited control: over her camera (can she make it represent the truth?); over her mother (can she capture her truth?); over the outside world (the mother ages and becomes more fragile as the film progresses; her past and present are marked by her experience in Auschwitz). As Akerman tries to make her mother appear to us, she is gradually, all too quickly, disappearing from the world. The mother is lost, the daughter left behind. Neither the internet nor a photo nor a film can take the place of the company of a mother. But Akerman's film gives the lie to this somehow. She shows how technology can do motherwork. Is Akerman's laptop (her camera) what Barthes would call "a sort of umbilical cord link[ing] the body of the photographed thing to my gaze"? (81).

Saint Omer (Alice Diop, 2022)

In my reading, Akerman's camera does feminist motherwork by inviting us to reckon with feelings about mothers, reproduction, violence, care, family, absence, and loss. The *punctum* in the photo of Barthes's mother, in contrast, evokes feelings for him *alone*, and the *studium* remains uninterrogated, or worse. Making photos of her own mother and grandmother available to readers of *Ordinary Notes* (2023), Christina Sharpe compares the *punctum* she finds there with Barthes's inability to see beyond the "ordering structures of white supremacy" (184n123). Sharpe says, "He [Barthes] would never consider nor see the beautiful, elegant life as deeply Black" (185n124). Akerman's camerawork motherwork shifts both *punctum* and *studium*, making them available to us in new ways, and like Sharpe, reimagines both what counts as subjective and what is considered universal. As we know from Beauvoir, Rose, Hartman, Collins, and others, heavy with patriarchal, racialized, and capitalist significance, the figure of the mother (and *how* she is figured, which we can now call the *studium*) triggers feelings about mothers in general and about our own mothers and our own mothering. Each of these—always constructed in both photo and film in regard to framing, mise-en-scène, characterization, and so on—requires our political attention and conversation as we compare and evaluate these feelings. This is the motherwork that feminist camerawork can do.

Senagalese-French director Alice Diop's *Saint Omer* deepens my thesis that, building on Black radical feminist theory, we can call Akerman's camerawork an aesthetic act of motherwork, and locate iterations of her style and practices in the work of contemporary feminist filmmakers. Doing so, we see how certain styles of filmmaking and the way themes and character are featured onscreen can invite the feminist feelings of viewers. Diop's film is especially relevant in this chapter on motherwork for several reasons: (1) it features a Black mother on trial for murdering her fifteen-month-old daughter; (2) the film is based on actual events from 2016; and (3) remarkably, the Black mother at the center of this film becomes a universal figure. Diop presents her as opaque, but still legible and even sympathetic.[38] Diop went so far as to use transcripts from the trial in the mouths of her actors—but she fictionalizes them or, we may better say, following Saidiya Hartman, she fabulates them, an aesthetic effort toward repairing the damaging projection of Black women as unfit mothers, erased from cinema and history. Rather than see this Black mother through the white male gaze, as we typically would, instead, we see, hear, and feel her in a triangulated space occupied with two other Black women: the mother who has traveled from Senegal to Saint Omer for the trial; and a Black female professor who travels from Paris to Saint Omer and attends the trial for research purposes, which immediately reveal themselves to be personal, too.

Diop has said that training the camera on a complex Black woman for the length of time that she does so was a "political act": "It was also a way to show a Black woman in a way that I had never seen shown before" (quoted in Zuckerman 2023). Anticipating and channeling the feelings of viewers, the professor in the film finds herself emotionally drawn to "feeling like a feminist" as she realizes her ambivalence about *her* mother and *her own* pregnancy are not just hers alone. Diop talks about the flow of feelings encountered on set by the actors and film crew in this way: "It brought up such personal and private emotions. . . . The majority of the crew were women, and while we were shooting, it was as if we were in this collective psychodrama. After every scene we'd cry about our own lives. Technically, I couldn't tell you how we did it, because their performances aren't technical. I created a space for the actresses where they could summon forth their own personal ghosts safely and send them back to the attic when the film was finished" (quoted in Girish 2022).

There is no doubt that we often need to send our feelings "back to the attic" just to get through the day. But, as I insist in this book, bringing these feelings to the forefront by inviting them through techniques utilized in feminist filmmaking is itself a political act. It is precisely these discomforting feelings that become our invitation to feel like feminists, as they demand that we reckon openly, and in conversation with others, about what feeling like feminists could mean for rethinking the way we live. I try to show in these pages that this is the most important political contribution that feminist film makes.[39]

To my knowledge, Diop does not cite Akerman as an inspiration, but the feminist director Céline Sciamma compares the experience of watching *Saint Omer* to what it must have been like in 1975 to watch *Jeanne Dielman*. Sciamma is quoted as saying, "One finds oneself in front of a cinema poem—Alice's language, in the history of the language of cinema to which it belongs, but also in her own history, is dangerous and radiant" (Zuckerman 2023). Diop does credit as inspiration the famous documentary filmmaker Frederick Wiseman, known for his oeuvre of more than forty films about what happens to people in American institutions like hospitals, schools, juvenile courts, city halls, and so on.[40] Several of Diop's films are documentaries that feature marginalized populations, and like Akerman (and Wiseman), Diop treats her subjects not as political objects for interrogation but as universal subjects whose stories must be told and whose lives should be centered.[41]

Diop's most recent documentary, called *Nous* (*We*; 2020), received critical notice from many quarters for her caring attention to the lives of her subjects by creating spaces of deep intimacy through long takes and camerawork that respects the dignity and opacity of her subjects who inhabit the *banlieues* of Paris and are mostly recent immigrants. Her films are praised for "creating an archive of stories we haven't been listening to," attending to "memories that haven't been memorialized," and bringing our attention to lives that "have gone unrecorded and unattended" (quoted in Choudhury 2022). Asked about a filmmaker's "duty of care," Diop said the following: "For me, it's a form of ethics. It's the central ethic of my practice as a filmmaker. And it's not a contractual obligation. It's [my] relationship with ethics, with respect, and with the awareness of having the power to configure the stories of people's lives. Knowing that having a camera and looking at others [through it] is a form of power" (quoted in Choudhury 2022). Diop includes home video of her own mother (who died when Diop was seventeen) in *Nous* and in *Saint Omer*, and says of this radical act, so like Akerman's: "What my filmmaking seeks to redress is the invisibility, the absence, the silencing, the marginalization [of certain people] and to place at the center of the shot bodies who have been historically and politically pushed to the margins of dominant forms of representation. For me, the act of repair is already there in what I put at the heart of my films, in the centering of my mother's body in *Nous*. I interrogate the absence of certain narratives but more than that the absence of a will to even readdress what has been absented" (quoted in Price 2023).[42]

In the first moments of *Saint Omer*, we see a French-Senegalese professor named Rama (Kayige Kagame)—whose character, I learned from what Diop has said in interviews, is loosely based on the filmmaker herself—lecturing in front of a large classroom on *Hiroshima, Mon Amour*, the 1959 film directed by Alain Resnais (director of the 1956 Holocaust documentary *Night and Fog*) with a script by Marguerite Duras. *Hiroshima, Mon Amour* is about many things—memory, nuclear disaster, an affair, and an unknowable woman at the center of it all.[43] As Rama talks about the Duras script, she shows her students a PowerPoint image of shaved heads of French women who were said to collaborate with German soldiers during Occupation. These women, we immediately understand, are like Duras's characters—guilty but also victims.[44] Asked about this opening, Alice Diop says:

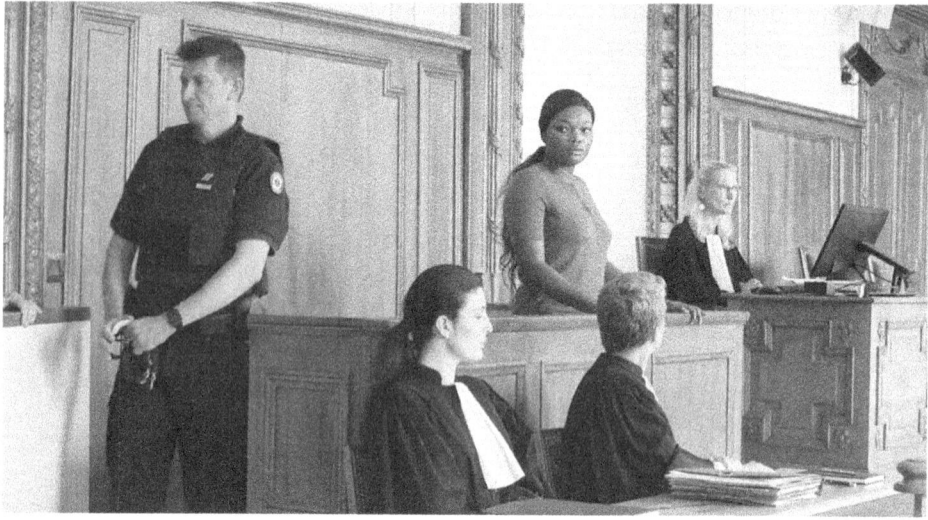

1.11   Madame Coly in the courtroom. *Saint Omer* (Alice Diop, 2022).

The choice of text also gives us clues about what kind of writer Rama is and what interests her about Laurence Coly [the woman on trial in *Saint Omer*]. Her course insists on the necessity for Duras as a writer—and for Rama as a writer—to examine the taboos of female characters who have committed acts that are reprehensible, but with the ambition to make them into heroines to be heard and truly listened to, if not absolved. The way the film looks at Laurence Coly is precisely what Duras does with her fraught women, who are victims and at the same time guilty. Rama's lecture contaminates the whole film; it provides an axis for how we view it. (quoted in Girish 2022)

Our inability—as viewers, readers, fellow citizens—to know the motives and inner feelings of Laurence Coly (Guslagie Malanda), when we might too easily condemn these feelings or claim to know her, is a central emotional and political theme of *Saint Omer*. Because Rama is writing a book about the Medea myth, and we later come to understand, because she has an ambivalent and vexed relationship with her mother, and because, as we also later learn, she herself is pregnant, she is drawn to the case and the person of the accused Senegalese immigrant called "Madame Coly" throughout the trial (see fig. 1.11). One important thing we come to know about Laurence Coly, and that she shares with Rama, is that she is an intellectual. Trained by her mother (Salimata Kamate) to speak perfect French and use impeccable manners, she presents as an enigma—a Black female immigrant who is extremely intelligent, pursuing a PhD by studying a philosopher of language, Ludwig Wittgenstein, known for asserting that words in themselves are inscrutable and only become comprehensible within context.

Two of the many beautiful things about this film that encourage my comparison of Diop's camerawork and technical choices with Akerman's are Diop's long takes during the trial (she reports in interviews that some are as long as twenty minutes), in which we are fixed on the face of Laurence, the face of Rama, the face of Laurence's mother, and the looks between the three; and her use of "home movie" footage in the film, which serves as snippets of memory from Rama's perspective.[45] The patience of the camera "give[s] an intensity to what is seen and heard, and allow[s] spectators the opportunity to change their minds, to move from one idea to another, to move from one life to another," as Diop puts it (quoted in Girish 2022). Interspersing the trial with what sometimes looks like snippets from home movies, and sometimes are framed as Rama's memories, we glean that Rama's relationship with her mother is laden with sadness, silence, an inability to communicate, and her mother's inability to show care. In one of these clips, Rama's mother washes a bowl behind the young Rama and then sets her breakfast on the table in front of her without a word or even a glance. Rama is always closely watching her mother, but her mother barely looks at her. Some of the dialogue in these clips is in Wolof, and viewers are not offered subtitles. Wolof-speaking viewers will have access to the dialogue in these scenes, while other viewers experience the discomfort of not knowing what is being said or communicated.

Coly's guilt is not a question in the trial, but she maintains her innocence. Like Medea, we know she is guilty, but we do not know, and cannot understand, why she killed her child. She herself does not know. When she is questioned by the judge (Valérie Dréville) in the first moments of the trial, Madame Coly says she does not know why she killed her daughter, Lili, and she hopes the trial will provide the answer. Through the process of insistent questioning by the judge, her own attorney, and the prosecuting attorney, and testimony by witnesses, Laurence sometimes blames witchcraft for her actions as we learn about her difficult circumstances. She came to France to escape pressures from her parents in Senegal and find freedom, but, cut off from her entire social life and without a job or options, she moved in with an older white man, the father of Lili, who hid her from his family. Feeling her world closing in, for some unknown and unknowable reason (unknowable even to herself), she takes Lili to the sea and leaves her there to drown.

The emotional intensity of the film is due to the motherwork of Diop's camerawork. Viewers see Madame Coly through the eyes of Rama who herself is awash in all the ambivalent feelings evoked by the incomprehensibility of Laurence's actions; the inscrutability of her composure, facial movements, and bodily gestures; her willingness to blame sorcery for her actions although this contradicts her training as an intellectual; and the passing back and forth of these charged emotions between the two women. Diop recounts that there is a scene where Laurence looks directly at Rama and Rama smiles: "It's funny, because technically the scene wasn't hard to shoot, but emotionally it was very hard on the actress who plays Laurence, Guslagie Malanda. She didn't want to look at Rama. I don't think she herself knows why. She didn't want to smile, she didn't want to look at Rama. She wanted me to stand in Rama's place. It brought up such personal and private emotions for both the actresses" (quoted in Girish 2022).[46]

Camerawork Motherwork

For Barthes, the miracle of the camera is its capacity to capture one's mother on film, to stop or bring back a different time and space, but only for the viewer who feels the personal *punctum* (only for the singular individual) and shares a "universal" (patriarchal, white supremacist) sense of the *studium*. The miracle of Akerman's and Diop's cameras is to be able to hold an image, a scene, a space for a difficult feeling or feelings for all of us, thereby releasing both *studium* and *punctum* from their patriarchal and anti-Black, anti-Mexican, antidifference moorings. Photographs and films about mothers, as motherwork camerawork, are a suitable place to anchor camerawork motherwork, as mothers always inspire feelings of ambivalence. To find and acknowledge our many kinds of mothers, our difficult relationships with them, to examine the work mothers do, and to create new worlds and new senses of ourselves in these new worlds, we must hold the ambivalent feelings of frustration, capture, violence, struggle, anxiety, anger, relationality, and love in one place, all at once. Akerman's and Diop's inspirational camerawork *as* motherwork and motherwork *as* camerawork does not mean we assume a loving gaze; in fact, at times, it is quite the opposite. Think of the drone footage, the long shots of the desert and the wall, the severity of the frontal view when Akerman films interviews, or Diop's focus on the eyes of Madame Coly when she says she has no idea why she killed her daughter —

seeing these images, with the *punctum* we feel the sting, and then in the duration of the shots, we feel the long burn of displacement, exile, disconnection, dislocation, and grief.

This distance, and the acknowledgment of the gap, is as central to Akerman's camerawork as the tender gaze. We are held by Akerman's and Diop's cameras in a mix of complex feelings, as the titles of the films signal the warning to not get too close, even as we are specifically located by place-names: *Jeanne Dielman, 23, quai du Commerce, 1080 Bruxelles*; *From the Other Side*; *No Home Movie*; *Saint Omer*. Though Akerman and her mother spend time in the Brussels apartment, and though they Skype when not physically together, there is no fusing of beings—we sense Chantal's restlessness and boredom. Akerman's mother's frustration with Chantal always working highlights, too, how the camera signifies differently for each of them, representing perhaps two kinds or aspects of motherwork—the immediacy her mother desires and the mediated motherwork Akerman performs with her camera. We can sense that Akerman wants to spend time with her mother but she is also bored and frustrated, and she wants to get back to work! We also can see the distance Rama intentionally and unintentionally creates between herself and her own mother, and we clearly see, through the home-movie footage, that this primary relationship haunts Rama and heightens her ambivalence and worry about her own pregnancy.

Inspired by the tradition of Black feminist theory, I have located camerawork as an aesthetic kind of motherwork detected in Akerman's and Diop's films by directing our attention to the work of nonnormative (m)others and focusing on the several forms of violence done to them, and that they do to others. Oriented this way, viewers are invited to experience our difficult feelings around mothers, their work, their power, their vulnerability, and their inevitable and unbreakable attachments to us. Most important, we are encouraged to attend to the worldmaking possibilities of several forms of motherwork, but specifically the form I name as camerawork motherwork.

The images and the feelings they evoke are indelible: Natalia Akerman on Skype trying to "see" her daughter Chantal and Chantal trying to "see" her mother; the Mexican boy telling the story of his lost brother; the scrolling LA highway onscreen while we hear the story of David crossing to "the other side" to find his mother; Jeanne peeling potatoes at her kitchen table and sitting silent and unmoving in her dining room; the unnamed desert and its single lonely tree; the long border wall snaking through the desert; Madame Coly's eyes; Rama's penetrating gaze as she scrutinizes her own mother and then Laurence Coly. These images and spaces, made even more powerful by sound, framing, and duration, become chambers that invite and hold our complex feelings. Joined with their cameras, Akerman and Diop are cyborg mothers. Within their films wherein motherwork camerawork and camerawork motherwork is featured, we learn new ways of paying attention, of sitting with ambivalences and tension, of undoing patriarchal and anti-Black iterations of *studium* and *punctum,* and of better caring for each other and the world.

2

WHITE NOISE:
STASIS

white noise: noise containing many frequencies with equal intensities; mansplaining, catcalls, derogatory language, harassment,
the constant hum of racialized patriarchy

stasis: a feeling of inactivity or stuckness; or, in response to
trauma, frenzied and repetitive thinking or behavior that goes
nowhere; feeling caught in a loop while moving

I ENDED CHAPTER 1 by suggesting that Chantal Akerman and Alice Diop
might be thought of as cyborg mothers who use their cameras to invite our
feelings about the ambivalence surrounding mothers, motherwork, and the
impossible roles and expectations identified for mothers within racialized

patriarchy. In this chapter, I begin with Simone de Beauvoir's writing in *The Second Sex* ([1949] 2011) that details how the dominant male sensorium of taste, touch, sight, smell, and sound reinforces patriarchal norms, expectations, gestures, and habits to shape the lived experiences of girls and women. Out of Beauvoir's description of this sensorium, I focus especially on sound in order to prepare the way for my reading of how certain feminist films and television creatively bring audience attention to the aural effects of patriarchy.

I will argue that the sounds of patriarchy, which I name collectively as noise, serve as a background track that orients promising young women onto paths and into scripts that limit the promise of freedom and growth for feminized persons. I highlight the word *promise* here because one of the films discussed in this chapter is Emerald Fennell's *Promising Young Woman* (2020). As I began to work with this idea of promise, however, I realized it is a key term for Beauvoir too. We might characterize what Beauvoir is doing in *The Second Sex* as charting how the desires and direction of girls are almost always interrupted and tragically redirected toward the patriarchal promise of romance, marriage, and children. The promising young women of Beauvoir's oeuvre, girls who are gradually, but still rudely, introduced to a male sensorium, might have been doing (and thinking about) lots of other things, but the noise of patriarchy points them in only one direction. Girls sometimes feel these exposures to the male sensorium as just the way things are, and they try to quietly and obediently absorb the sounds of patriarchy. Sometimes these noises and experiences are felt as violent shocks that seem to rip them from the time/space continuum.

The collective "noise" that forestalls the promise of young girls is so ubiquitous that we often hardly hear it anymore, or we try to close our ears in subconscious defense against its sometimes soft, sometimes loud, always constant thrum. To correct for Beauvoir's inattention to the racialized dynamics of patriarchy, I add the modifier "white" to indicate that the noise I have in mind belongs not just to patriarchy but also to white supremacy. Notably, though, white noise also signifies the registers of sound that lull us to sleep. Dismissed as compliments, humor, all good fun, or the way things *are* (boys will be boys, white men will be white men), the white noise of patriarchy not only consists of gaslighting, harassment, body-shaming, and the constant threat of sexual assault but also is delivered as compliments, praise, and the lovely soundtracks accompanying romance, weddings, and the promise that children will fulfill our hopes or redeem our desires. Sound resonates, and it has an affective resonance in our bodies in ways that do not always register consciously. White noise sleepwalks us through life but significantly impacts the way our ears turn toward or away from certain desires and paths. What we take in of this noise, consciously and unconsciously, and in both its ugly and beautiful registers, can keep us stuck in repetitive and static loops that reproduce racialized patriarchy. But it might be otherwise.

This chapter asks us not only to listen carefully but also to be open to ambivalent and disavowed feelings invited by media examples where women characters are shown in a state of repetition or suspended motion (stasis), even though we see them thinking and moving at a sped-up pace.[1] Using technical tools of their art—camerawork, sound, genre, image, montage, color—directors of feminist film and television intensify and exaggerate what Beauvoir documents as lived experience under a male sensorium, inviting viewers to see and hear different things, and to see and hear the same things differently. I begin with a reading of Akerman's very first film, the short *Blow Up My Town* (1968), made when she was only eighteen, very much a promising young woman herself. The film is suggestive of trauma, while Emerald Fennell's *Promising Young Woman* explicitly centers trauma as a theme. Michaela Coel's television series *I May Destroy You* (2020) also explicitly thematizes trauma, here of two kinds: an inability to remember or identify a traumatic sexual encounter, which becomes linked to an inability to create, or to fulfill creative promise.

These examples all use sound in creative and unexpected ways. Discordant sounds and silence are most evident in Akerman's *Blow Up My Town*.[2] Observing the use of sound in Akerman's short film situates us to be able to detect how sound is deployed in the more popular film and television that follow. We will see that my examples each record white noise but also alert their audiences to how promising young women might begin to attune ourselves to different frequencies. Might there be more encouraging sounds, signals, voices, or music? Perhaps these are on a lower or a different frequency, or perhaps if we are trained to listen, we can pick up different cues. Invited by feminist film and television to notice the white noise of patriarchy, viewers might be better able to open their ears—though sound does not only enter our bodies this way—to listen to experiences in the voices of their sisters. Can we, *how* can we, wake up and change the tune?

Woman Is a Man-Stringed Instrument

We will recall from the introduction that in volume 1 of *The Second Sex* Beauvoir chronicles what men say about "Woman." Called *Facts and Myths*, the first volume is divided into three parts on destiny, history, and myth.

Theologians, historians, scientists, writers, artists, politicians, psychoanalysts, anthropologists—all the male experts—each get their chance to mansplain. What we learn is that "Woman" is an ultimately incomprehensible creature with multiple contradictory traits—she is virgin and whore, mother and concubine, comfort and chaos, peace and danger, nature and artifice. The social agreement is that she exists to please men and she must be controlled. Beauvoir quotes from Honoré de Balzac, who says, "Woman is a lyre which only yields up its secrets to the man who can play upon it skillfully" (Beauvoir [1949] 2011, 397).[3] Jules Guyot's *A Ritual for Married Lovers* (1859), also cited by Beauvoir, emphasizes this point in the distinct language of sound: "He is the minstrel who produces harmony or cacophony with his hand and bow. From this point of view woman is really a many-stringed instrument producing harmonious or discordant sounds depending on how she is tuned" (397n11).[4]

In volume 2, *Lived Experience*, Beauvoir documents multiple and diversely experienced ordinary and extraordinary moments in the lives of countless girls and women. She disregards any distinction between high and low culture as she capaciously gathers information by turning to every source possible: her own life, biographies, trashy novels, conversations with friends, literature, Hollywood and avant-garde films, and even the male-authored sources she consults in volume 1 that are now read for dissonant voices. Presenting to readers the results of her wide-net search, she directs our attention to the way that patriarchy invades the senses, ordering and disciplining sense perception and bodily comportment. In a typical passage, Beauvoir remarks that a young girl feels the encroachment of patriarchy "in her flesh" ([1949] 2011, 335). In childhood, the young girl is often "bullied and mutilated," but her future passivity is not *fully* embodied. Upon puberty, "the future not only moves closer; it settles into her body; it becomes the most concrete reality" (342). This invasion reads like horror: "The hand that takes and that touches has an even more imperious presence than do eyes" (335).

The young girl's senses are always attuned to the "imperious presence." As Beauvoir explains, "There is this knee in the cinema pressed against the girl's, this hand at night in the train, sliding along her leg, these boys who sniggered when she passed, these men who followed her in the street, these embraces, these furtive touches" (332). She continues: "She cannot prevent his presence from haunting her" (334). At first, the girl revolts: "She begins to feel a certain disgust for her father; she can no longer stand the smell of his tobacco, she detests going into the bathroom after him; even if she continues to cherish him, this physical revulsion is frequent" (334). She both wants to be desired *and* revolts against these feelings; conflicted and confusing desires "come from this very complexity the girl feels in her flesh" (334).

Although Beauvoir often describes patriarchal expectations and demands as enveloping and circling around women's bodies, using words like "pressing," "sliding," "sniggering," and "furtive," she also often employs the language of penetration, of piercing, shock, disruption, and tearing: "The idea of being *pierced* by a man is horrible," Beauvoir says a "young girl told [her] one day" (335). Several passages describe the physical violence of the first heterosexual experience, but the language of shock refers not just to physical but also to psychosocial experience. What W. E. B. Du Bois would call "double consciousness" is vividly described by Beauvoir: "'At thirteen, I walked around bare-legged in a short dress,' another young woman told me. 'A man, sniggering, made a comment about my fat calves. The next day my mother made me wear stockings and lengthen my short skirt, but I will never forget the shock I suddenly felt at seeing myself *seen*'"(321).[5] It is not an exaggeration to say there are hundreds of passages like these in the second volume of *The Second Sex*. Recounting a variety of incidents in multiple voices, Beauvoir shows that patriarchy is an affective and sense-making system that intersects with and is amplified by racial and class taxonomies.[6] This sense-making system is created by and echoed in the voices and behaviors of men and many women. It is reproduced in language, touch, vision, and sound. Imprinted on individual bodies that habitually reproduce its values and material effects, it resonates throughout the social body.

The soft side of the patriarchal sensorium described above are the promise and accoutrements of romance, marriage, and children—a house in the suburbs or a gorgeous loft in the city, beautiful clothes and jewels, the feminine leisure time desired by "trad wives"—all offered on silver platters to promising young women as compensation for the theft of their freedom. The stories, myths, fairy tales, romantic comedies, feel-good Hollywood movies, "meet cute" set ups, and the burgeoning industry of reality television romance shows are all examples of another kind of white noise. Both kinds—the shocking and the alluring—shape the desires of young women to orient them toward futures that betray their promise to do otherwise than fulfill patriarchal roles.

Unwilling to betray the promise of freedom, Beauvoir attunes us not only to hear this noise as betrayal, but also to listen for sounds of resistance. Can feminist cinema make and keep a promise to promising young women? Nonsynchronous and antirealist sound effects help viewers notice the white noise of patriarchy, and this reorientation, or training our ears to hear differently, can spark new imaginative possibilities for solidarity and action. Separating sound from image, shifting from an "objective" or "realistic" soundscape to a soundscape wherein sonic events are disclosed to a particular situated subject, using music in ways that intrudes on rather than seamlessly flows with a scene, the surprising use of silence, and so on—all of these direct our attention to the sounds around us and alert us to the possibility of listening for other, previously unnoticed, sonic cues. Or another way to put it: unusual or initially strange sonic landscapes can reveal how lives have been limited or compromised, but also show that potential for freedom might yet be redefined or built anew. Via sound's resonance within the holding spaces created in feminist film and television, audiences might experience women's experiences as an appeal to individual and shared feelings. We see this most explicitly in the cinematic lexicon of Akerman, and she will help us notice it elsewhere, too.

Blow Up My Town (Chantal Akerman, 1968)

Blow Up My Town introduces viewers to what might be the outcome of one young woman's promise having been thwarted, interrupted, stuck in a loop, or broken. In its thirteen minutes, we see eighteen-year-old Akerman (the director doubling as actor) enter an apartment building, and then her tiny kitchen, to begin some exaggerated housework—cleaning, cooking, polishing of shoes.[7] But the apartment only gets dirtier. After she frantically eats, cleans, and dances, moving maniacally from thing to thing, task to task—table to cupboard to mirror to stove—she turns on the stove's gas, awkwardly positions her body over it, and blows herself (and presumably, her town) up in an explosion. Is this action the result of some jarring experience(s) or a profound alienation? We will never know.[8] Viewers of *this* promising young woman, dead by suicide at the end of the short, are not invited to accompany her on any journey where we might learn the source or meaning of her actions.

Along with several films Akerman made in the 1970s, *Blow Up My Town* is "renowned for its combination of formalist rigor and feminist thematics" (Hegarty 2017, 149). It intentionally does not invite the audience to experience the subjective inner life or the situating material experiences of the promising young woman in the frame.[9] As we saw in chapter 1, Akerman's films often eschew focus on the subjectivity and situation of characters, and invite viewer feeling instead by strange, unexplained actions, innovative camerawork, and a surprising use of sound.[10] Using different techniques

2.1 "SAUTE MA VILLE." *Saute ma ville (Blow Up My Town)* (Chantal Akerman, 1968).

than Beauvoir uses in volume 2 of *The Second Sex*, Akerman's films nevertheless similarly evoke and hold the embodied feelings of viewers as Beauvoir does for her readers. Akerman's visual and aural style is so disorienting and peculiar that most is left unknown (but not unfelt).

The first image of *Blow Up My Town* (in French, titled *Saute ma ville*) is a black screen. We hear tiny peeps of a female voice, quickly drowned out by the sounds of a train and industrial noise. The black screen disappears and we see a tall apartment building surrounded by what looks like an industrial work zone with the large words "SAUTE MA VILLE" (see fig. 2.1). As "la, la, la, la, la, la, la, la" sing-song sounds begin, competing with (but losing to) the sounds of construction, the camera pans over many tall buildings. When Akerman enters the frame, she looks hurried, determined, maybe frenetic. She is a small figure with a hat, dwarfed by trucks and tall buildings around her, carrying flowers. Once inside the building, she gathers her mail, the "la, la, las" becoming more intense. She pushes the elevator button repeatedly and then rushes to the stairs as her humming gets more intense, faster, and much louder. We watch the elevator moving ever upward. The camera focuses mostly on the elevator, not following our young woman, but we sometimes catch glimpses of her rounding a bend in the stairs, all while the humming "la las" and "da da dums" sound crazier, louder, and more intense.

Once inside a tiny kitchen, she sits at a small table, and the humming becomes a whine. We hear her lock the door, we hear a church bell chime just once, and a clock starts to tick loudly. Soon we notice a very loud whisper of a word that sounds like "skichy," repeated three times, as she throws some spaghetti into a pot on the stove. She then steps on a stool to tape the top of the front door as we hear humming and she bites into an apple. We hear the crunch. We notice every time sound *is* synced to image, as in the crunch of the apple when she bites it, when she throws her apartment keys to the floor and we hear them hit, as she unrolls the tape and pulls it across the cracks of the doorway. In most instances, the sound seems to make no sense, although sometimes we hear a familiar sound, for instance a ringing bell as she takes the pot off the stove, which makes us retrospectively realize the clicking sound was a timer. She sits at the table and shoves spaghetti into her mouth and drinks the last of a bottle of wine. All this while a less frenetic singing, loud sighs, and some laughing are heard, but the sounds are always as voice-over, never coming from her mouth. The singing gets louder and more distressed, almost like yelling, as she fills a pot, tapes more of the door, and our attention is drawn to a cat as we hear its meow. Several times the frenetic and anxiety-producing sound is broken by a sudden and long silence, unlike any kind of silence we are used to. This silence is not employed to enhance narrative intensity, or at least not in any way the viewer can easily identify. Instead, we might wonder whether the film's sound has suddenly broken or, if watching at home, whether YouTube is still working![11]

At the five-minute mark, the "housework" gets more exaggeratedly ridiculous and counterproductive. Items are thrown out of the cupboard, powdered dishwashing soap is sprinkled all over the dishes, water is splashed everywhere. Now donning a raincoat and headscarf, the young woman mops up all the displaced random items from the cupboards across the floor into a chaotic mess. This sequence unfolds mostly in one of these long silences, interrupted only by the sound of the items being kicked across the floor and the splashing of a bucket of water against the wall. The most famous scenes of this short are Akerman sitting on the floor to polish her shoes, as we hear vigorous brushing of her lower legs and her shoes, and then brushing even more vigorously, then silence again. More silence as she sits and leans against a radiator, and then the humming/singing begins again as she turns the pages of a newspaper. Over the insistent humming, young Akerman peers at her reflection in a mirror. As she begins to tape the window shut, the sound of tape releasing and sticking seems deafening in the otherwise silent frame.

She next retrieves her flowers from the cupboard and then we hear harsh and ugly laughter as she smears cream and makeup on her face, dancing. Visual perspective shifts, and we see her dancing through the mirror's reflection (fig. 2.2). The laughing starts to sound almost like the end of an orgasm as the young woman smears indecipherable words on the mirror with her lotion-covered fingers. She strikes a match; we hear the words "bang, bang"; we see a balloon pop; she takes a lit match to the gas stove; we hear the gas flowing; she holds her flowers. Finally, young Akerman positions herself limply over the stove, head resting on top, right arm draped over the side, left arm holding the flowers upside-down (fig. 2.3). We watch this image for a distressingly long twenty-eight seconds while we hear the gas flowing. A loud bang, screen to black, ten loud explosions, and then the "la, la, las" begin again with a more cheerful lilt, and Akerman speaks out the credits in voice-over.

Precisely because Akerman refuses to construct any point of view for her character—as we have seen, she intentionally does not privilege her character's line of sight, hearing, or voice—thus frustrating any adoption of the character's point of view by viewers, the disruptive and asynchronous use of sound and image calls attention to itself. If the gaze is overdetermined, as we learned from Laura Mulvey in 1975, might sound open a way for viewers to have our own feelings and experiences in response to a film? Rather than adopt what we think are the feelings of the young girl, we are left alone (or with others in discussion) to grapple with our reactions to seeing this young woman take her life and blow up her town, not knowing the reasons or context. Maybe she is a feminist resister. Maybe she has absorbed the white noise of patriarchy all too well and is despondent as a result. Maybe she is a victim, or maybe a heroine for other young women who will start blowing up all the towns, burning it all down. As viewers, the thirteen minutes we spend with her might be received as trauma, puzzle, assault, emotional jolt, example, or invitation.

Cut loose from conventional narrative and a "realistic" soundscape (or what we might call "male" common sense), *Blow Up My Town* refuses the male sensorium, jolting us out of the sleepwalking induced by white noise. The audience is left to reflect on our own feelings of confusion, disorientation, and possibly antagonism.[12] As one critic has recently said of Akerman's use of sound, "Recurring sound-image figures . . . contribute to a vivid, visceral reception experience and a complexly layered sense of time" (McBane

2.2 Akerman, playing unnamed young woman, dancing. *Blow Up My Town* (Chantal Akerman, 1968).

2.3 Akerman, playing unnamed woman, slumped over stove. *Blow Up My Town* (Chantal Akerman, 1968).

2016). As my students have noted, these thirteen minutes feel long and uncomfortable. Feeling this discomfort, we are prompted to look around, to ask questions—Do you hear what I hear?

Promising Young Woman (Emerald Fennell, 2020)

Like in *Blow Up My Town*, in *Promising Young Woman* we hear before we see. In this case, we hear the Charli XCX song "Boys," which features the refrain "I was busy thinking 'bout boys," with the echo "boys, boys" repeated, for a triple dose of "boys" as we see the pelvises of men moving on a dance floor. Director Emerald Fennell includes "Boys," alongside several easily recognizable pop songs in her soundtrack, prompting one commenter to note its "girly escapism" (McHenry 2021). However, for those who are schooled by Akerman and now attentive to the use of sound in film, we notice that the pop songs do not match the visuals. While upbeat pop music delivers lyrics wherein young women "think 'bout," "dream 'bout," and their "heads spin 'bout" boys, we get ugly visuals of the disgusting boys and men on offer. Sooooo many men, like a fraternity party. These frat boys have aged badly. They were likely never very appealing but now they wear their ugly insides on the outside. Why would we think 'bout, dream 'bout, get our heads in a spin 'bout *these* boys?

Instead of replaying tired "meet cute" narratives of the romantic comedy, starting from its opening scene, Fennell's film uses sound as a wake-up call that delivers some hard-learned lessons about patriarchy. Hard lessons are not strangers to the heroine, Cassie (Carey Mulligan), whose best friend, Nina, we learn later, was raped at the medical school where they studied together and then died by suicide. Cassie blames herself for not being there to stop the rape and has devoted her life to a pedagogical journey of teaching men that the women whom they harass, torment, sexually abuse, and rape are not just sex objects, but instead living, thinking, breathing, sometimes violent humans who will seek justice.

Two versions of white noise—the pop music mantra reaching the ears and echoing on repeat in the psyches of too many young women ("I was busy thinking 'bout boys") and the "locker-room talk" of men about women—vie for attention in the opening scene. As the song echoes ("boys, boys, boys") the camera zooms in on three particular men, one Black, two white, all of whom appear to be in their early thirties, chatting at the bar about the unfair restrictions of the #MeToo era. The very first words we hear are "Fuuuuck her, fuck her, this is how business is done!" This comment refers, we suspect, to a complaint by a female colleague about doing business on the golf course. One of the boys says, "It's just a round of fucking golf. You'd think we were taking clients to a strip club." "Which we can't even do anymore after the Christmas party last year," another chimes in. When one of the men notices Cassie sitting with legs spread, head lolling about, alone on a red couch, looking completely drunk or conked out, they all turn their attention immediately to her. "She's kind of hot," one says. "Yeah, a hot fucking mess," replies the other. "She is just asking for it!" PTSD ensues as we recall the vile language that former boy-in-chief Donald Trump defended as "locker-room talk" when the 2005 *Access Hollywood* tape was released: "I wanted to fuck her"; "I moved on her like a bitch"; "When you're a star, they let you do anything"; "Grab 'em by the pussy, you can do anything!"

Living in the United States in the early twenty-first century, the boys have some reason to hope they might score with a promising young woman like Cassie whom, sleep-walking to the ubiquitous tune of misogyny's white noise, has come to the bar, partied too hard, and might be persuaded to go home with one of them. The designated "good guy" of the three (Adam Brody)—the one who half-heartedly tells the other two that making deals on the golf course maybe could exclude their women coworkers since women are not allowed in the club—says he will "check on how [Cassie] is doing," as the other two make lewd gestures. Cassie barely speaks, answers his questions monosyllabically, sometimes only groaning or gesturing with a thumbs-up. He offers to help her get home—she says she has lost her phone and thus cannot call a car—but on the way, he suggests they go to his house (which they are conveniently passing) for a nightcap. Cassie doesn't say yes, but she doesn't say no either. She ends up on his bed, close to passing out (fig. 2.4). He kisses her face (she doesn't kiss back), fondles her body, gets visibly excited, and begins to remove her underwear. Cassie mumbles, "What are you doing?" repeatedly, softly; he mumbles back "Shush, it's okay. You're safe," as horror music is introduced.

Just as he gets her underwear off, murmuring an appreciative "mhmmm, your body!," Cassie suddenly opens her eyes wide, timed in sync with a loud horror chord. The horror music speeds up, discordant stringed instruments sounding frantically. Cassie pops up to a sitting position, stares into his eyes, and loudly demands, "I said: What are you doing?" The "good guy" looks back with a look of terror, and the title, *Promising Young Woman*, appears onscreen. "We are the weather girls, and we got news for you!" The familiar sounds of the Weather Girls' "It's Raining Men" are the soundtrack to Cassie's haughty barefoot strut as she repurposes the stereotypical "walk of

2.4 Cassie with a "good guy." *Promising Young Woman* (Emerald Fennell, 2020).

shame." What looks like blood drips from her body, but then the camera pans up. We see that Cassie holds her high heels in one hand, while with the other she gobbles a hot dog, ketchup dripping (fig. 2.5).[13]

This triumphant walk is interrupted briefly by more white noise, this time directed right at Cassie. Unlike the sounds of the men talking that invited us to listen in on "locker-room talk," this scene's use of sound is utilized so that we experience its harm from Cassie's point of view. The music of "It's Raining Men" gets softer and retreats into the background as Cassie is called to attention by the catcalls of three construction workers: "Why don't you give us a little smile, huh?" Cassie stops and stares back, her piercing gaze disorienting the workers. "What the fuck you staring at?" they insist. "You can't take a joke?" "Hey, fuck you, then!" "God Bless Mother Nature. . . . She's a single woman, too!" the Weather Girls sing as Cassie returns to eating her hot dog. Horror music returns as the camera focuses on the pages of a book in which Cassie is keeping a count. Lists of men's names and several series of five-tally marks have accumulated on the pages.

This pattern of luring and teaching men goes on, with its repetition of trauma, until viewers are offered brief relief as a "meet cute" romance interrupts Cassie's nightly routine.[14] A former med school classmate (yet another notable nice guy sort, explicitly signaled by casting Bo Burnham) wanders into the coffee shop where Cassie works. Despite Cassie's suspicions of all men, she softens to his goofy charm and the two hit it off. One scene where the two dance and sing in a drugstore to Paris Hilton's "Stars

2.5. Cassie strutting her stuff. *Promising Young Woman* (Emerald Fennell, 2020).

Are Blind" has all the trappings of romantic comedy. We are *almost* lulled into a comforting slumber by this romantic (non)sense. But after not too long, sound plays a different role, interrupting Cassie's smooth return to the male sensorium. The sound of the new boyfriend's voice, captured on tape, wakes Cassie (and us) up, as it confirms that he was present at the gang rape of Nina. Not *only* his voice: his *laughter*. His laughter is sonic evidence of not only his presence but also his complicity.

Near the end of the film, as a haunting and slowed-down instrumental remix of Britney Spears's "Toxic" plays, Cassie dresses as a stripper to exact her revenge at the bachelor party of one of Nina's rapists.[15] Cassie intends to etch Nina's name on his body but is instead killed by him, smothered by a pillow, in one of the most prolonged and difficult-to-bear scenes of murder in conventional cinema. At the point where the rapist successfully positions the pillow over Cassie's face to smother her, an uncomfortably long, intense period of silence pierced only by small peeps from Cassie (ten seconds that seem much longer) ensues until we hear an elongated scream that doesn't seem to come from Cassie and could just as well be Nina. Stringed instruments provide the music of horror as the rapist's rapid breathing and his repeated demands to Cassie to "stop fucking moving" and "this is your fucking fault!" hit our ears as they are meeting Cassie's ears. A full three minutes go by before we see Cassie's limbs go fully limp, her squeaks stop, and he takes his knee off the pillow on Cassie's face. The rapist's tortured breathing never stops, and he cries when it is over.

The next morning, the rapist and his buddy burn Cassie's body in a funeral pyre. It looks like they might walk away without consequences, but Cassie, ever a Cassandra, had anticipated her own murder as one possible outcome, and she demands to be heard beyond the grave. One of Cassie's appeals is sonically very familiar and timed to arrive as strikingly asynchronous. Viewers likely take special pleasure in hearing the familiar "ding" of Cassie's former boyfriend's phone to indicate a text message coming in as he mingles at the wedding party of the rapist. He sees the message is from Cassandra Thomas ("You didn't think this was over yet, did you?"). Her text, delayed to arrive just at this moment, denies synchronicity of life and experience. And just then, too, Juice Newton's "Angel of the Morning" begins. The music, this time, syncs with the visuals: "I'm old enough to face the dawn." Of her choice of songs for the film, Fennell says, "I wanted it to be a highly female soundtrack. I wanted to use pop music, particularly pop music by people like Britney Spears and Paris Hilton that isn't generally taken seriously. I think in general, that's a nasty, undermining thing of our culture to designate what's good and what's not" (quoted in Rosen 2020). And what's justice, and what's not? In other words, Fennell changed the sensorium by not only reinvesting in the cultural capital of the low, the girly, but also having promising young women get their due. The film ends with the rapist led away from his wedding in handcuffs while Juice Newton's 1981 hit plays on.

I May Destroy You (Michaela Coel, 2020)

In Michaela Coel's *I May Destroy You*, Coel acts in the central role as Arabella (Bella), a hip, young Black writer whose extremely successful first book (*Chronicles of a Fed Up Millennial*) was printed from her popular blog and has turned her into a celebrity among certain demographics in London. In the very first episode we learn that she is currently under contract for a second book and has a sometime boyfriend in Italy who distracts her from writing. Her London friends support her dreams, but their lively presence and invitations to have fun also divert her from her goals. Or maybe Arabella is stuck because she simply feels too much pressure to deliver on (the promise of) her talent. But then, an event: a roofie-induced rape threatens to undermine her confidence, snatch away her promise for real, and undo

2.6. "I MAY DESTROY YOU." *I May Destroy You* (Michaela Coel, 2020).

her sense of self. From this point forward, the recurring sounds that play in the soundtrack of Arabella's mind position her as stuck in the repetitive time of trauma. We hear the noises of trauma from Arabella's perspective—men's voices of excitement in the bar; the clinking of shot glasses together and the cheer "eyes, eyes, eyes, eyes, eyes"; the silence of the bathroom stall where the rape occurs; the sound of her head hitting the toilet; the thumping and grinding of the rape; and the confusing hum of traffic as she stumbles out of the bar. Although many things are still to happen and Arabella will make new discoveries about herself, her friends, and new forms of solidarity along the way (there are twelve episodes from twenty-five to thirty-seven minutes each), the quest to turn off these sounds and escape this traumatic loop is *I May Destroy You*'s most significant narrative thread (see fig. 2.6).

While the sounds of trauma that recur throughout the series mostly leave us confused and in the dark with Arabella, the musical soundtrack is employed to provide clues that give depth to the characters. Created by twenty-seven-year-old Ciara Elwis, who, in consultation with Coel, chose mostly African diaspora–inspired music, the soundtrack matches each character with certain music. Each friend of Arabella's faces their own distinct challenges as they navigate sex, love, work, and life, and each is accorded their own perspective on their shared social life. Elwis says that the soundtrack

2.7. Arabella and Terry. *I May Destroy You* (Michaela Coel, 2020).

is meant to open up spaces of ambiguity for each character and for the series as a whole and that it is deliberately not intended to tell viewers how to feel (Ugwu 2020).

Although several objectively bad things happen to Arabella throughout the series, and she is challenged and often surprised by what she is constantly learning about sex, friendship, Black identity, feminism, and the possibilities for solidarity with those unlike one's self, Arabella responds with humor, curiosity, and tenacity. As I read it, *I May Destroy You* both introduces viewers to the damages of the soundscape of white noise and shows one woman's determined effort, with the significant help of her friends, to rouse herself out of its stasis-inducing loop (fig. 2.7). Because Arabella has support in her life, people whom she can ask, "Do you hear what I hear?," she is able to orient herself beyond the white noise playing on repeat, and seek out and grab other cues.

Nevertheless, unwelcome memories—sound and image—haunt Arabella and come to her unbidden, at surprising moments. Not knowing how or by whom she was drugged, how or when she was raped, she actively hunts down clues to re-create the night and discover what happened to her, all while also trying to finish her book.[16] We come along for this ride, as we continuously have our assumptions questioned, wondering what is true, what makes sense, if we can believe what we see and hear. Positioned by point-of-view phenomenological experiences of the individual characters, viewers are exposed to the world differently when different characters are onscreen: Arabella; her gay Black friend, Kwame (Paapa Essiedu); her Black girlfriend, Terry (Weruche Opia); and a white former schoolfriend, Theo (Harriet Webb), take turns to disclose their worlds to us. Each has different experiences, often of the same event. *I May Destroy You* thus sets up a perspectival narrative along with specific phenomenological sensory experience of events by different characters that asks viewers to hear and look at the same events from yet another vantage point, never resting in certain knowledge.

The twelfth and final episode of *I May Destroy You* offers three alternatives for revenge, reparation, and repair in the aftermath of Arabella having suddenly put everything together to remember the identity of her rapist (a white man named David, played by Lewis Reeves). Our sonic and visual senses are engaged in each possible ending, but viewers can never quite trust what is happening because, like previously, we keep getting new versions of the same event. At the end of each scenario, Bella rearranges the notes stuck on her bedroom wall that are constructing the storyline of her book. She seems inspired after each episode to arrange them anew like a director rearranging a storyboard.

The different scenarios begin with Arabella and her white male roommate sitting in their garden, listening to birdsong. In each except for the last, Arabella says she has to depart the garden and its birdsong to do her "bar watch," waiting for her rapist to emerge so she can extract a version of revenge. In the first version, Arabella adopts the playbook of Cassie, but goes further and exacts eye-for-an-eye revenge. In the second, David is taken away by the police after he reveals to Arabella that he is himself a victim of abuse. The third is the most surreal and most reparative, and the sound of a bird is a marker for moving the narrative from one potential outcome to a better one. In this last one, David says his name is Patrick, and Arabella and Patrick make out, both consenting, in the toilet stall, and the next scene cuts to Arabella's bedroom. Their lovemaking is tender and ends with her on top in the typically male role as they both climax. They wake to the sound of the bird, and she tells him to go.[17]

Each narrative ending could be seen as a critique and supplement to the others. With only five minutes left in the series, a fourth scenario threatens to begin, with the same exact early details of the others, but this time either the bird chirps more loudly, or Arabella hears it differently. The roommate had always commented on the bird ("That is such a loud bird!") but this time, Arabella seems to hear it, and responds, "Hmmm...I wonder where it's coming from." Then she suddenly decides she doesn't need to go to the bar this time. It is as if the birdsong spoke to her and she can hear something new: she is free to exit the repetitive time of trauma and enter the time of promise. Cut to a point in the near future, signaled by the sound of a clock ticking and the patio filling with new growth. Terry enters Arabella's bedroom, and Arabella gives her a gift, her completed book, with the dedication written to Terry: "Your birth is my birth; Your death is my death; This book is dedicated to Terry, my best friend."[18]

Do You Hear What I Hear?

When Beauvoir uses the word "promise" in *The Second Sex*, she most often is denigrating the compensation offered to young women for their freedom being stolen by the demands of female destiny. For example, discussing requirements for clothing and comportment for young girls when playing ("posture is imposed on her, stand up straight: don't walk like a duck; to be graceful, she has to repress spontaneous movements"), she says the "girl can compensate for boys' superiority of the moment by those promises inherent in her woman's destiny, which she already achieves in her play" ([1949] 2011, 296). In her adolescent daughter, the "mother sees the promise of a prosperous future; friends envy and admire the one getting the most masculine admiration" (341). "Young beauties are promised a glorious future" and take "pleasure in a masochism that promises extreme conquests" (305). Society and patriarchal family make these (false) promises, a return on strict compliance to patriarchy's rules. But sometimes hard reality breaks through via experience. "Seeing life as a promise of decomposition demanding more unending work" (476), the wife feels that marriage "does not guarantee the promised happiness" (519). From her "narrow and petty existence, she escapes by dreams"; "she promises that the future will take revenge on her mediocre existence" (352).

This chapter asks a question: Can feminist cinema make and keep a promise to young women? The "dreams" that offer escape for Beauvoir's promising young women in today's feminist media landscape become so much more than just escapism. With the help of technical tools and radical cinematic lexicons, feminist directors are able to exaggerate, intensify, and vivify the experiences similar to those that Beauvoir chronicles in *The Second Sex*. Invited into the experiences of other women as viewers encounter them onscreen, new encounters invite viewers to compare them to their own. Beauvoir anticipated this possibility, giving a much more positive cast to what (different) dreams can do in a passage from *All Said and Done* that I quoted in the introduction: "Cinema awakens *dream-like echoes* in each beholder. If a film affects me deeply, it does so either because it stirs unformulated memories or because it brings unspoken hopes back to life. Sometimes, when I discuss a film with friends—friends whose tastes are the same as mine in other fields—I find that my opinion is quite unlike theirs: the film has certainly touched them or me or all of us in some intimate, entirely personal area" ([1972] 1993, 177, emphasis mine). Viewers might hear what characters hear and see what they see and, thus, get a situated female perspective; or, using distancing methods inspired by Akerman, viewers might be jolted out of expectations for realism and enter a hyper-realistic, radically strange, and out-of-sync, out-of-time perspective. Either way, suddenly, what might have felt like individual alienation, loneliness, and repercussions of trauma are disclosed in experiences that have happened to others, too. Suddenly we are invited into a collective. We have company that we didn't even know was out there.

I cannot help but think what might have been different for Akerman's young woman and for Cassie had they, like Arabella, had friends to whom they might turn to ask, "Do you hear what I hear?" The lyrics of the song that opens *Promising Young Woman*, "Boys," are about promises not kept. The promises kept are the ones to patriarchal expectations (busy thinking 'bout boys), but the broken ones, named in the song's lyrics, too, are to "my girls":

> But I was busy thinking 'bout boys
> Boys, boys
> I was busy dreaming 'bout boys
> Boys, boys
> Head is spinning thinking 'bout boys
> In every city I got one with different ringtones
> Flying from L.A. all the way to Puerto Rico
> My girls are calling me asking me where I'm at
> Didn't hit 'em back.

"Didn't hit 'em back" and thus could not ask them, "Do you hear what I hear?" "Do you hear what I hear?" is an appeal from the screen to the ears and feelings of the audience. We do not and will not hear exactly the same things, situated so differently as we always are. The question "Do you hear what I hear?" does not measure the accuracy of any sound or make certain that all ears have been represented. Although the bird loudly sings in the garden each time Arabella leaves to do her "bar watch," she doesn't hear it until the very last scenario. We might speculate that it is Arabella's willingness (much like Beauvoir who turns to her friends to discuss films) to turn to *her* friends that makes the difference. Arabella compares her own experiences to theirs. They see her trauma and validate its existence, and it is *this* encounter that allows her to break out of the repetitive time of trauma. Only then can she hear the bird, free herself to write, and move to the time of promise. Sadly, neither Akerman's unnamed woman nor Cassie had a chance to hear the bird's promising song, even though that bird might have been chirping the entire time.[19]

Asking each other what we hear, and how we might act in response, opens up new possibilities for relation, resistance, and solidarity. Understanding the necessity of community to change the tune and engaging the method of fabulation discussed in chapter 1, Saidiya Hartman identifies and names "black noise" as a "dangerous music of open rebellion" (2019, 283). To detect *black noise*, Hartman fabulates a "riot" from the turn of the twentieth century by 265 inmates, city girls from Harlem, the Lower East Side, Chinatown, and the Tenderloin, being detained in the country "for moral reform" at a Bedford Hills, New York, prison.[20] To those who can't quite hear, or hear in concert with girls and women, black noise sounds like "a din without melody or center" (283). But Hartman characterizes it as "sonic tumult and upheaval . . . resistance as music . . the free music of those in captivity, the abolition philosophy expressed within the circle, the shout and speech song of struggle" (284).[21] We can also think with Jayna Brown in *Black Utopias* (2021), who enlists Afrofuturists like Sun Ra and Octavia Butler, musicians like Alice Coltrane, and philosopher Henri Bergson to make contact with the other worlds that are possible within the time and space of our own. Brown builds on Bergson's insight in *The Creative Mind* (1934) that nothing prevents "other worlds . . . from existing in the same place and the same time" (2021, 9).[22] Brown hopes to locate "practices, real and imagined, through which we access other realms—planes of material reality and consciousness . . . that are with us and around us, like electricity or sound waves" (9).

Hartman's black noise—discordant, "a din without melody or center" (283)—resonates with Akerman's soundtrack in *Blow Up My Town* while Brown's search for other sounds, other worlds, existing within our own limited perception of time and space helps me think about Arabella's hearing of the bird's song that she never heard before, even though it was always singing. Building from these tools of feminist theory and criticism, we might see technologies of feminist cinema as inviting the possibility that we can tune in to the white noise of patriarchy; wake up, create, and respond to better noises, black noises; find other worlds and possibilities within our own; and sound our resistance via collective refusal.

3

GENRE TROUBLE: HORROR

genre: a category of artistic composition of literature, cinema (or gender), characterized by similarities in form, style, or subject (or bodily) matter

trouble: difficulty or problems

horror: an intense feeling of fear, shock, or disgust

I NOW TURN TO RECENT films that take up some of Chantal Akerman's stylistic techniques to interrupt, stretch, or surprise film's genre expectations—in this case, horror. The films I discuss reinvent horror by focusing on what should *really* scare us. The feelings they invite arise from viewer encounters with women's collective experience rendered through discrete moments in the lives of characters. Importantly, each also offers a glimpse of old worlds dying and a new world coming into being, explicitly signaled at the end of each film.

Genre means "gender" in French, the overlap of the two words pointing to the original pernicious classification of humans into two complementary types arranged in a hierarchy. An innovator of the genre and gender of philosophy, Simone de Beauvoir corrects for its male abstractions by moving to women's lived experiences in *The Second Sex*. Her archive is an *explicit* appeal to readers, as Beauvoir seems to ask, "Is this your experience, too, or is yours different?" "What do these examples, and the recounting of these experiences, provoke in you?" "How do they make you feel?" Or, as I asked in the last chapter, "Do you hear what I hear?"

Akerman is also an innovator of genre. As we have already seen, Akerman's cinematic style is impossible to neatly categorize: her films have been seen as structuralist, hyperrealist, modernist, and avant-garde. What especially attracts me to Akerman's films is the way they bring our sensory attention to bodies onscreen and to our own bodies and feelings as viewers, even and especially as she refuses to work exclusively through narrative, character development, and the obvious ways of connecting the dots to narrativize lived experience. Viewers often find it *hard to name* the feelings stirred up by her pacing and long shots, the still camera, the middle-distance camera (positioned at her height), claustrophobic framing, repetition, disjointed or disorienting sound, unexplained lingering on single objects or faces, refusal of the shot/reverse-shot sequencing, and so on. The films are felt to be profoundly moving by many viewers even though her techniques often establish and maintain a critical distance between viewers and characters. As was evident in my readings of *Jeanne Dielman, From the Other Side, No Home Movie,* and *Blow Up My Town,* Akerman's films often feature opaque characters who wrestle with their desires and destinies; forms of resistance or action that are compromised and thwarted, rather than brave or exemplary; and aesthetic and narrative choices that invite complex and uncomfortable feelings for viewers. Encountering these characters and their confusing and strange experiences onscreen, we are asked to acknowledge, recognize, and work through social and political aspects of what appears as individual experience and feelings, such as ambivalence about mothers and motherwork, and what it feels like to be stuck in repetitive loops mapped by and within a patriarchal sensorium.

In my three readings in this chapter, three prize-winning, feminist directors take up key aspects of Akerman's style and put them in service of gender- and genre-bending body horror.[1] I explore Mati Diop's *Atlantics* (2019), the first film directed by a Black woman to compete for the Palme d'Or at the Cannes Film Festival, winning the Grand Prix; Audrey Diwan's *Happening* (2021), which won the Golden Lion at the 2021 Venice Film Festival; and Julia Ducournau's *Titane* (2021), winner of the 2021 Palme d'Or for director.[2] These films experiment with genre to pinpoint horror's source in women's experiences of patriarchal, colonial, racial, and capitalist forms of exploitation.

What Is Horrible?

As just noted, the three films I study in this chapter each won a major international prize that recognizes their status as high art. I will be reading them as horror, a "low" genre that shares a rung with pornography. To think about horror and the avant-garde together is not itself new. Film scholars have long noticed features that the two share. For example, in *Cutting Edge: Art-Horror and the Horrific Avant-garde* (2000), film scholar Joan Hawkins explores ethics and the politics of taste in "low" horror and "high" art to show that "art horror" and the "horrific avant-garde," because of their status as art and avant-garde, are able to steer clear of ethical debates that circle around the "low culture" genres of horror and pornography. Hawkins notes that three prevailing features of twentieth-century avant-garde aesthetics are also often present in pornography and low horror: "the breaking of taboos surrounding the depiction (and performance) of sex and violence, the desire to shock the bourgeoisie, and the willful blurring of the boundary lines traditionally separating life and art" (2000, 117). Reading the figure of the "pontianak," a terrifying female vampire ghost, in popular Southeast Asian film, Rosalind Galt also points out the crossover between what is seen as "trash aesthetics" and the "low cultural spaces" of horror with European art film (2021, 12). The pontianak, Galt convincingly shows, reflects anxieties around gender, race, religion, and nationalism. Film scholar Adam Lowenstein tracks a related but different boundary crossing that also anticipates my concerns and insights in this chapter, that between horror and the everyday. In *Horror Film and Otherness* (2022), Lowenstein reads how the figures of political "others" appear as transformational figures in horror films. In a chapter on gender and a chapter on race, Lowenstein reads "feminine horror" and "race and horror" films as exemplars in portraying female and African American experiences. My readings here build on these studies, but one important difference is that the films I select as examples of horror for this chapter are not categorized as horror, even as they play with and expand horror's genre conventions.

The way my films specifically traffic in genre conventions to qualify as what I'm calling "feminist horror" is also different from the way scholar Anna Backman Rogers makes the case for Sofia Coppola's *The Virgin Suicides* (1999) as a "feminist hauntology" (2019, 28). She classifies *The Virgin Suicides* as "a horror film from which all signs of horror are eradicated" (30). The bodies of the Lisbon sisters in Coppola's film represent experiences of abjection, fetishism, and self-abnegation, all rendered through gorgeous images.[3] In the films I choose, in contrast, horror is not hidden underneath the surface of beauty. Horror genre tricks—hyperrealism, exaggeration, excess, fabulation, or fantasy—are intentionally employed, but used to convey the experiences of girls and women within racialized, postcolonial, and patriarchal worlds as themselves *specifically* and straightforwardly horrific. When we categorize these films as horror, and we highlight the mechanisms the directors use to depict character experience *as horrific*, we can see how the genre and gestures of horror better capture these experiences of women-identified subjects than documentary or what we might consider more "realist" styles of filmmaking might be able to do. In these films, women's "real" experiences constitute the horror in the horror genre.

The films I see posing the question "What is horrible?" experiment with a genre that is known to traffic in misogynist narratives and messages, and like their misogynist predecessors, they use cinematic techniques to double-down on attention to bodies and feelings. Bodies onscreen wait, sweat, brood, experience anxiety and humiliation; they are possessed by others against their will, eyes blacked out and absent; they are disciplined and straightened, told what to do and say, and tested for evidence of compliance; they are tossed and lost at sea, flung up limp on the beach. Bodies are bloodied and violently killed; a young woman aborts her baby in a toilet as the umbilical cord dangles between her legs in one very explicit scene; in another, a woman dies giving birth to a child that is part car, part human. In reaction, and not expecting horror, some viewers might squirm, feel ill, get offended, turn away, maybe even walk out of the theater or turn off the computer, dismissing events and the character responses to events as excessive, inappropriate, gross, and hard to believe. Viewers might feel angry, manipulated, or annoyed. Others, however, might feel validated or "called" by these same characters and events. In my readings, the film as aesthetic object and the embodied viewers who encounter this object both matter profoundly.

Remarkably, these films, and their play with genre that makes me call them feminist, bring to mind (and bodies) the lived experiences of women under patriarchy far more accurately than what film realism or more accurate or diverse representation can deliver. They capture experience and transform our feeling and thinking about that experience in ways that cannot be matched by expansion of our knowledge base to include the individual lived experience of women unlike us, with whom we do not share identities or situations. Using cinematic techniques that I identify as "Akermanian," and specifically deployed to amplify spectator feelings, they exaggerate and intensify the collective nature of the diverse experiences of individual women to which Beauvoir brings our attention.

Atlantics (Mati Diop, 2019)

French-Senegalese director Mati Diop is no stranger to the film world. She is the niece of Djibril Diop Mambéty, the Senegalese director of *Touki Bouki* (1973), known for his unconventional style depicting the lives of ordinary Senegalese. Before becoming a director, Diop was an actor; her most well-known role is as the daughter of Guadeloupian actor Alex Descas in Claire Denis's *35 Rhums* (*35 Shots of Rum*; 2008). Film critics have noticed that Mati Diop's cinematic style seems to be in conversation with Akerman's, even though Diop has never (to my knowledge) explicitly made this connection. Her short film, *In My Room* (2020), has been compared to Akerman's first feature film, *Jeanne Dielman*, and to Akerman's last film, *No Home Movie*. But maybe *Dis-moi* is another interlocutor for *In My Room* as both feature intergenerational female conversations. As discussed in chapter 1, Akerman's *Dis-moi* (*Tell Me*), also a short, was one segment in an omnibus French television series about grandmothers. Diop's *In My Room* is also one of several in a series, this time commissioned by fashion house Miu Miu with the directive that their clothing be featured. Several important feminist directors— Agnès Varda, Miranda July, and Lucrecia Martel, to name three—also directed short films for this project.[4]

In Diop's film, *Miu Mui Women's Tales #20*, Diop herself plays the main character.[5] She is in COVID lockdown (in the fall of 2020) and takes the opportunity that isolation offers to view recorded interviews with her grandmother Muji, who, we learn, lived alone in a Paris apartment for twenty years. Diop had interviewed her grandmother as she was losing her memory just prior to death, a circumstance that has invited the comparison to Akerman's *No Home Movie*. As we saw in chapter 1, *No Home Movie* similarly chronicles Akerman's mother's final months in her Brussels apartment, where Chantal spends large swaths of time with her, or, when away working, she Skypes with her and films their interactions.

Diop's apartment is almost the entire set for the aptly titled *In My Room*, but her camera sometimes scans the windows to glimpse cityscapes and to catch private moments of other isolated individuals in "their" rooms. The staging of conversation between granddaughters and grandmothers, mothers and daughters, speaks thematically to the significance of genealogy and inheritance of trauma, intensified by technical cinematic choices that Akerman and Diop share in common: limiting vision and movement to one room; using the patience of the camera's unmoving gaze to hold difficult feelings in that space; and the trust in viewers that such a patient camera reveals. These distinct and unusual themes and technical choices bring Diop and Akerman together as they explore their own experiences, compare them with the experiences of their grandmothers and mothers, and implicitly ask viewers to attend to these experiences, too. Diop's style in *In My Room* repeats features of the cinematic lexicon we see in her earlier feature film, *Atlantics*: a rejection of linear narrative and frustration of generic expectations; the centering of mostly opaque characters; the invitation of difficult feelings.

Set in Senegal, the story of *Atlantics* centers on Ada (Mame Bineta Sané), about whom we know little, and Souleiman (Ibrahima Traore), about whom we know even less. What we do know about Ada is that she is in love with Souleiman, a construction worker who, early in the film, sets out on a rickety boat to Spain with several other disgruntled men who have been denied their wages, and so they risk their lives to try their luck elsewhere. The journey is tragically aborted as Souleiman and the other migrants drown at sea. Ada's parents have promised to wed her to an older, successful man (Omar, played by Babacar Sylla) whom Ada shows no interest in and treats with disdain. Throughout the film, Ada engages in small but accumulating acts of refusal to comply with the life she is expected to embrace after Souleiman's death. And then a shift: after the death of the workers at sea, the story moves into a genre that looks a lot like horror. Their girlfriends (with the important exception of Ada) become possessed by the spirits of the dead migrants, their lost boyfriends. The young women rise from their beds to gather in the night and demand the men's past-due wages from the corrupt builder of luxurious skyscrapers at the edge of town. In the meantime, the bed of Ada's fiancé, Omar, is mysteriously set on fire during their engagement party. A young detective assigned to investigate these crimes, and who investigates

Ada as a likely culprit, also becomes possessed by a spirit who later turns out to be Souleiman. Possessed by Souleiman, the detective (Issa, played by Amadou Mbow) makes love with Ada in the final scene.

The emotional and political power of *Atlantics* seems to sneak up on the viewer, as the narrative takes surprising turns and some of our political and emotional expectations are frustrated or made to wait. The first scenes with the men demanding their wages seem to promise a political story; the next scenes between Ada and Souleiman seem to promise a love story. Or if we think of them together, the film's early focus on the men's stolen wages, their arguments with the boss, and then Souleiman and Ada's kisses and conversations on the beach suggest that the political scenes will blend with the love story to create an interwoven narrative about young love in the afterlives of slavery, set against conditions of late capitalism, postcoloniality, neoliberalism, the migrant crisis, and misogyny. But there will be even more to this story.

Our first glimpse of Ada is through the eyes of Souleiman. Separated by a passing train, the two stare directly at each other in short gulps, each seeking the eyes of the other between the train's moving cars. It is as if viewers are already being warned that there are fast-moving, powerful, and seemingly unstoppable forces between them: capitalist greed, the demands of patriarchal family, the lure of other shores, and a quest for better lives. Diop's Ada knows what, or at least *who*, she wants—she wants Souleiman—but we learn her desires not through dialogue but through comportment, gestures, and facial expressions. We otherwise have no access to her thoughts or perspective, and Diop refuses point-of-view camerawork. Ada does not refuse patriarchal expectations deliberately, but she eludes the grasp of those who seek to control her by staying just barely out of their reach. Her refusals accumulate to become something that looks like an alternative. When her fiancé's parents force her to undergo a humiliating virginity test in a doctor's office (she passes—her hymen is intact), Ada submits but with a calmly focused stare. Throughout the film, Ada emits a cool air of detachment from outdated customs. But she does not embrace the modern either. When her rich fiancé gifts her a rose-gold iPhone that he acquired in Italy, Ada accepts it indifferently. Later on, she trades it for a functional, inexpensive flip phone on which she hopes to receive messages from Souleiman's spirit. In the end, Ada refuses to marry and has her first sexual experience with the detective, Issa, whom she believes is possessed by the dead Souleiman.

In addition to combining politics, romance, and horror in one film, Diop also defies genre expectations regarding how to represent African migration. Most films about African migration are realist and focused almost exclusively on men. *Atlantics* departs from realism and centers one young woman in love, in connection and community, sometimes fighting against but other times in sync with family and other young women.[6] Even more surprising is the turn the film takes from romantic entanglements infused with and situated by political realities, to a supernatural imaginary where female bodies become possessed by the ghosts of their boyfriends. We may wonder if we have seen this film before, or at least this *move* in a film before. The female body as an always open, thus vulnerable, hostess—for alien babies, unwelcome penises, and other invaders—is familiar cinematic territory. Female hosting in archetypical horror amplifies not only the ever-ready permeability but also the strangeness of women's bodies. But the hosting in *this* film is very different.

Diop's choice to move into horror, in particular, bodily possession of the young women by the spirits of the young men in the second part of the narrative (fig. 3.1), intensifies the strange but real experiences of the characters and invites viewer feelings about these experiences. Linking the presence of spirits with ubiquitous, gorgeous, threatening, and sublime images of the Atlantic Ocean, itself a character in the film, Rosalind Galt says, "Diop's film understands these spirits as a form of anticolonial realism, capable of rendering visible the affective depths of the Atlantic Ocean: they bespeak the ocean's unimaginable archive of Black death, as well as envisioning beauty and grace in contemporary Black life" (2022, 97).[7] Viewer feelings that might arise when encountering the "real life" conditions of the Senegalese in the film (outrage, concern, empathy, anger) turn to dread, prickly body horror, and confusion as the dead boys' former lovers start behaving like zombies. Black-eyed, fevered, sweating, rising from their beds to engage in unplanned collective rebellion, the young women behave like Euripides's bacchants. They are possessed by the lost boys, like the bacchants are possessed by Dionysus. The girls could be seen as *merely* doing their bidding, but Diop's style and story suggest that we should consider other possibilities.[8]

Questioned about the choice to move from a narrative of political critique to a form of supernatural horror, Diop retorts that the distinction drawn in this case between real and fantasy itself is a problem. She insists that the supernatural imaginary in this film *is* the real. In an interview with Dennis Lim at the 2019 New York Film Festival, Diop explains that Senega-

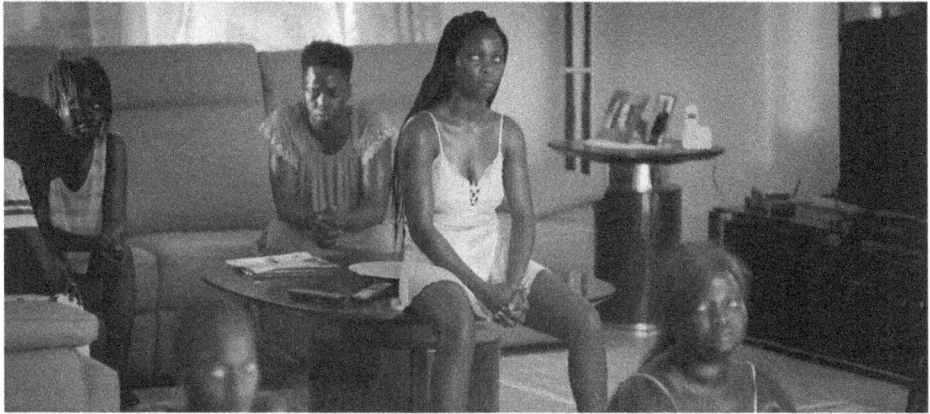

3.1. Zombie girlfriends. *Atlantics* (Mati Diop, 2019).

lese do not encounter the film as a fantasy—it depicts their life, everyday reality, lived experience.[9] In Senegal, she argues, the "frontier between visible and invisible, reality and fiction, death and life, is very, very different."[10] Although Diop admits that her choices and narratives are indeed influenced by gothic tales and gothic romance, hers is a story about ghosts, haunting, and possession that is *not* generic, that is rooted in a *very specific* social, economic, historical, and political reality.[11]

This history is rendered cinematically by Diop with rich attention not only to characters and narrative but also to color and mood. Diop and her cinematographer, Claire Mathon, captured what Mathon calls "Dakar's very ghostly atmosphere" by using cameras and color that highlight, for example, a circling green laser beam featured in the nightclub scenes where the young women gather with their boyfriends prior to their departure, and then gather again, when possessed, to wait for their men; the "clairvoyant" night scenes of a very dark Dakar; and the "humidity coming off of the ocean that gives one the sensation that even the cars are sweating at night."[12] Mathon (2019) adds that they wanted spectators to "feel the materiality of dust, humidity, and the sea spray." The combination of the French and Wolof languages; the haunting music (a mix of classical and African, arranged by Fatima Al Quadiri);[13] the lush color palette of green, orange, and blue; and the camera's movement from the sometimes ominous and sometimes calling waves of the ocean all set the backdrop for the love story as an interiorized romance trying to protect itself from harsh, cruel, and indifferent, but somehow also magical, conditions.

3.2. Ada and Souleiman/Issa with green lights. *Atlantics* (Mati Diop, 2019).

Near the end of the film, the group of possessed girls, acting like Bonnie Honig's bacchants who take back the city,[14] collect the stolen wages of their boyfriends from the corrupt capitalist developer. And then they insist on one more thing: looking at him with their collective blank eyes, they demand that he dig their graves. They chide the developer as he picks at the hard ground: "Look, he doesn't even know how to dig! That's real work!" "Every time you look at the top of the tower, you'll think of our unburied bodies at the bottom of the ocean." Some of the possessed girls continue to stare at the digger; others move off to the side, alone, contemplative. The moment feels like justice, or at least the beginning of justice born from collective consciousness and the payment of long-overdue reparations.

The film then cuts to Ada in the bar, framed by luminous dancing green lights, standing to meet Issa who comes to her possessed by Souleiman. Issa becomes Souleiman as he approaches and embraces Ada. Magically, they are three in spirit, two in flesh, circled by the green lights (fig. 3.2). They move in a tight circle, embracing, kissing, luminous. Issa is kissing Ada, then Ada is kissing Souleiman; back and forth the bodies sway, morph, become one, two, three. We see the dancing green lights, tender and slow lovemaking, accompanied by the low and lovely sound of African instruments. The Atlantic Ocean appears through the window, the sound of the waves reminding us of those lost just the other day, as well as long ago. Always beckoning. "I knew you'd be back," Ada murmurs. "It could only be you." Through Issa's body, Souleiman and Ada defy the borders of genre, capital, nation, body, and death itself to consummate their love. Against a shimmering image of the sun setting over the Atlantic Ocean, Ada says in voice-over, "I'll always taste the salt of your body in the sweat of mine."[15] And then Souleiman's voice: "How beautiful you are. I saw you in the enormous wave that consumed us. All I saw was your eyes and your tears. I felt your weeping dragging me to the shore. Your eyes never left me. They were there, within me. Pouring their light into the depths."

The morning arrives with the ocean framed by the open windows of the bar, where Ada and Issa have now made love, where the girls and boys used to meet to dance and talk, where the girls first learned the boys had gone "to sea," where the girls learned the boys had perished, and where the girls gathered when possessed. We next see that one of the girls who had been part of the burial scene has arrived safely home, loose bills tossed all over her bed and spilling out of her open hand. Issa reports to his boss that "the case is closed," as he delivers the security footage showing that he set the bed of Omar on fire. Ada awakes in the bar, stretches, starts to dress, and in voice-over says, "Some memories are omens. Last night will stay with me, to remind me of who I am." She then turns sideways to look into a mirror, her image reflected as speaking directly to the camera: "And show me who I will become: Ada, to whom the future belongs" (fig. 3.3).

Happening (Audrey Diwan, 2022)

Featuring female hosting of a different sort, Audrey Diwan's *Happening* tells the story of an unwelcome pregnancy and a nearly unattainable and extremely painful abortion. Like *Atlantics*, *Happening* doubles down on body horror but defies genre conventions. *Happening* is Diwan's second film; Lebanese and French, she was previously a producer and writer, and for this film, she adapted French writer and Pulitzer Prize winner Annie Ernaux's memoir (2001) sharing the same title. In the film version, the horror arises from Diwan's unflinching gaze on the intimate and invasive experiences of an unwanted pregnancy. Everyone around the young protagonist in *Happening* turns away from her pain, looks elsewhere, and refuses to help her. But forced to bear witness, viewers might begin to feel their way into trau-

Ada, to whom the future belongs.

3.3. "Ada, to whom the future belongs." *Atlantics* (Mati Diop, 2019).

matic memories of their own; into situations they have heard about but couldn't possibly imagine; or into ones that they never dared imagine, but now can.

Happening documents roughly two months in the life of a young working-class student, Anne (Anamaria Vartolomei), as she tries to procure an illegal abortion in France in 1963. The film opens to a black screen, and we hear only a girl's voice say, "Can you help me?" Then we see Anne and her friends getting prepped in front of a mirror, the "help" required to adjust a bra, to prepare for fun, dancing, the feel of freedom as the young women go out on the town. This help from her friends stands in direct contrast to what happens later in the film when, finding herself pregnant, Anne's desperate pleas for help fall on deaf and unwilling ears. Her plea to the first doctor to "Do something!" is met with staunch refusal: "You can't ask me that. Not me, not anyone." Her plea to the second doctor—"I want to continue my studies! It's essential for me!"—is drowned out by the doctor's interest in whether Anne knows a boy he knows at her school, a "remarkable young man" who will "go far." This doctor then commands her, "Leave!" but Anne insists, begs, "Help me!" To get her out of the office, he prescribes a pill that he says will "help her menstruate," but Anne learns later that she was deceived, and the pill strengthened the embryo. She also begs for help from friends, but everyone feels the weight of potential criminal charges. Anne asks a male friend who "knows a lot of women" whether he has information on where to get help, and although he eventually puts her in touch with a woman with an address, he first refuses: "Stop. No. Stop it, Anne!" When Anne persists and follows him home, he tries to rape her since "there's no risk if you're pregnant." She shows her belly to her best friends and demands, "What do I do?" One friend says, "It's not our problem"; the other friend later tells Anne she, too, has had sex but just was luckier than Anne because she did not get pregnant. She says she was "ashamed, but the desire was stronger."

Diwan foregoes using Ernaux's words as voice-over or backdrop in order to situate the film not safely in the past, but as "happening" now. The director insists that the film is not meant to be experienced as documentary or as history. It does not inform us about competing political ideologies, structures, and laws around reproductive rights. Diwan hopes instead to get at the truth of one young woman's experience through her body. She says, "As Annie Ernaux puts it in her text, she wanted to touch the truth of her memories. So I really tried to capture the way the truth of the instant is perceived in the body" (quoted in Elkin 2022).

The sensors of Anne's pregnant body (and ours, as viewers) are attuned to anxious waiting. Here we might recall the words of Beauvoir, that waiting is what women do, or are said to do. The egg "waits passively for fertilization" ([1949] 2011, 28); when in heat the female "waits for the male" (35); women are asked to wait for suffrage (142, 145) and any form of political agency; merely an "axillary" to man, "woman is the one who stays in place, who waits"—"I am she who remains and stays and who is always there" (242). The young woman, "locked up in a tower, a palace, a garden, a cave, chained to a rock, captive, put to sleep: she is waiting," waiting for her prince to come, for her future to arrive (305); a woman's youth is "consumed by waiting," "waiting for Man" (341). Later in life, the mother, too, waits, not *always* passively but unable to be heard or seen by the common sense of man, she "endures, complains, cries, and makes scenes" (309). The mother "waits for [her children's] return anxiously"; she "waits for her husband urgently"; and then, in both cases, she must "ward off the disappointment of a presence that does not satisfy the expectation of her waiting" (514). Even women's work, amid the hustle and bustle of capitalist demands, remains defined by waiting: "All the time they are doing their marketing, waiting in lines, in shops, on street corners" (479); housework is laden with waiting: "waiting for the water to boil, for the roast to be cooked just right, for the laundry to dry" (481).

Beauvoir observes that women's waiting becomes so much an integral part of their comportment and being that "one's eyes no longer perceive, they reflect; one's body no longer lives; it waits" ([1949] 2011, 370). Here, in Beauvoir's prose, the woman's body is turned into an object: "it" waits. Anne first waits for her period, noting its nonarrival in her diary. After the pregnancy is confirmed and she seeks a solution, we wait and watch *and feel* with her as Anne sees and feels physical evidence of the unwelcome being growing inside her: her protruding belly in the mirror, her tightening trousers. A bright and motivated student who embodies the hopes of her working-class parents, Anne continues her studies but gets increasingly distracted. Her supportive but unknowing mother is played by Sandrine Bonnaire, the brilliant star of Agnès Varda's 1985 *Sans toit ni loi* (*Vagabond*), reminding viewers of another desperate young woman whose promise, like the characters in chapter 2, has been somehow stolen. Bonnaire's vagabond, Mona, values her freedom and independence first and foremost and does not directly seek help from strangers she meets on the road, but Varda's staged interviews with those who had "seen" or met her, however, show that she is mostly denied her humanity (one example: "Female drifters are all alike—they loaf and chase men").[16] Time runs out for Mona, and at the end of the film, she is found frozen on a road in the countryside of southern France.

Viewers are poised to worry about Annie's future, too, as we experience time as always running out for her. Ernaux says of the film, "I was immediately plunged back into those days of waiting for a period that never came, which felt like a kind of silent, incredulous horror, back in the days when abortion was absolutely forbidden, when we hardly dared utter the word" (quoted in Elkin 2022). Anne's body morphs and changes; viewer anxiety builds. Film titles announce the passing weeks—three weeks, four weeks, five weeks, seven weeks, nine weeks, ten weeks—as Anne's ordinary life continues but she becomes more and more desperate. She tries to abort on her own with a long skewer, but it doesn't work. Finally, she gets a lead to a back-alley abortionist whose first try fails.

The *New York Times* film critic Manohla Dargis (2022a) says of the film, "As five weeks turn into seven and Anne's belly swells, 'Happening' becomes an existential thriller." Hearing Ernaux's words—that waiting for her period felt like a "silent incredulous horror"—leads me to reclassify the film as less thriller, more horror. Diwan wants us to feel the horror with Anne, to feel its immediacy. Diwan's stated intention is for the spectator to *directly* identify with Anne, to feel her body's changes, to feel her waiting, her anxiety, her desperation: "The idea was to focus on her body and not the setting. I asked myself: how can I film this so that we're not watching Anne, but rather *become* her?" (quoted in Elkin 2022).

Some have harshly criticized Beauvoir for her accounts of pregnancy and maternity, the "becoming" of the pregnant woman, in *The Second Sex*, saying, for instance, that they are full of "withering condemnation" (Richardson Viti 1999, 114). It is certainly true that Beauvoir documents these experiences in writerly terms that are so vivid that readers can almost feel them (as horror? as excitement? as anticipation?) in their own bodies. Her chapter on "The Mother" brings the visual, the imaginative, the narrative, and the sonic experiences of pregnancy and motherhood to our feminist senses. But first she begins with eleven pages on abortion. In these pages she talks about the hypocrisies and cruelties of the politics and ideology structuring abortion policy in France in 1949 (none of which is recounted in *Happening*). Later she records the feelings, and in particular the worries and bodily changes, women experience when they learn they are pregnant, and then when they become mothers. Eschewing all the trappings of Hallmark and Hollywood, Beauvoir helps us feel the real.

When Beauvoir begins to recount her stories of women's experiences with pregnancy is the moment the chapter resonates most powerfully with Anne's experience of body horror: "The fetus is part of her body, and it is a parasite exploiting her"; "she possesses it and she is possessed by it"; "she feels like the plaything of obscure forces, she is tossed about, assaulted" ([1949] 2011, 538–39). Diwan gets at these feelings—anxiety, ambivalence, anger, fear, resentment, and more—and magnifies them through cinematic techniques. Bringing Beauvoir's method to life with Anne's "becoming," Diwan inspires us to feel like feminists as she draws on and intensifies Beauvoir's style, itself articulated as naming the experiences of "becoming Woman." In Diwan's film, viewer response and feelings arise from camera angle, image, mood, mise-en-scène, and especially sound.

Diwan registers "becoming Anne" most vividly by the use of sound. Throughout, we hear the unmistakable sound cues of horror—low single notes at key moments. The first occurs when Anne visits the first doctor, learns she is pregnant and that the doctor cannot or will not help her, and pronounces "it's not fair!"; the second sounds soon after as Anne stands in her underwear looking at her body in the mirror; the third, in the same scene, when she turns her gaze to her still flat belly; the fourth, also in the same scene, as the camera moves in for a belly close-up. These notes continue at key moments over the entire film.

Diwan's camerawork is unflinching as viewers watch the entire abortion procedure, filmed over Anne's right shoulder as she perches on a table in the abortionist's home. We see the metal instruments, the speculum, a long metal stick, and then a long rubber tube, not from Anne's visual line, but just over her shoulder as Anne twitches, shudders, and squirms in pain. Are we positioned as witnesses? As participants? The only sounds are Anne's staccato breathing and her gasps of pain. Mme. Rivière (Anna Mouglalis), the back-alley abortionist, sternly warns Anne: "Not a sound, a shout, or I'll stop!" Is this a directive to the viewer, too? Don't look away; don't make a sound! Listen, see, feel! Diwan shares how breathing is so central to the film's effect on viewers: "For physicality to exist, you have to use all your senses, so there were lots of things we used to have you feel something—we worked so much on the breathing and use it as music to tell the story" (quoted in Saito 2022).[17]

When the first attempt by Mme. Rivière fails, Anne has to return to try again, knowing it is extremely dangerous to "insert a second wand" and she is risking her life. Just after this second procedure, which viewers are (thankfully) spared from having to watch and hear, Anne starts bleeding heavily. She is in her school dorm, on the bed, and suddenly stumbles to the bathroom stall as horror music sounds, then silence. We hear a very loud "splat," a splash in the toilet water. Another girl comes to Anne's aid as Anne's sweaty face is framed and she asks the girl to get her scissors from her room. Still on the toilet, Anne looks down between her legs where the umbilical cord dangles in plain view. She begs the girl, Olivia, to cut the cord. Anne says, "I can't. I won't be able to. Please!" Olivia does it. This act of solidarity seems like a miracle in a film where solidarity is rare.

But even amid so much ugliness, the film, quietly but vividly, evokes a space of possibility for the sexual desire of young women unencumbered by threat of pregnancy and the "withering condemnation" of others. We can feel the heat and hear the thrum of desire and anticipation escaping the screen that first time Anne and her friends walk to the dance and begin to move their bodies freely on the dance floor (fig. 3.4). In another brilliant scene that wisely avoids any hint of voyeurism, one of Anne's roommates uses a pillow to demonstrate how to get to orgasm. She coaches: "You need to take your time! It can take time!" Taking time for one's pleasure is different from waiting on another's time. The camera fixes on Anne's face as

3.4. Anne on the dance floor. *Happening* (Audrey Diwan, 2022).

we hear Brigitte's breaths come more quickly, get heavier, as she moans and climaxes. This moment was not in Ernaux's book. In an interview for *Screen Slate*, Diwan talks about how she mixed her own experiences with Ernaux's, effectively adding to an archive of collective experiences of young women:

> When you talk about illegal abortion, you've got the [implication of] sexual life. But there wasn't much about it in that book. So I took part of my own experience. For instance, when Anne watches her friend masturbating on a cushion. It's something that happened to me when I was younger. A friend showed me how to do it. I was able to ask Annie Ernaux if it was right for me to add part of my own experience. It was the perfect combination, the best way not to betray the book, and also to be very intimate, and to involve myself in the story, as Annie Ernaux involves herself—not as much, but still to involve myself with my own experience. (Quoted in Scherffig 2022)

After Anne has secured the abortionist's address, she goes to a bar alone, flirts with a firefighter she has met on another occasion, and accompanies him to his house to have very satisfying sex. Before the sex, he asks her why she is sad, and Anne says she suffers from "solitude." With her pleas for help going mostly unheeded, abandoned by country, laws, and mostly by her friends for fear of criminal complicity, Anne is left all too alone.

Not surprisingly, the father of the baby, an older student who makes a fleeting impression in the film and only in the process of their confrontation, also refuses to help after Anne finally, in desperation, calls him and then pays a visit. He demands: "What do you want?" Her reply: "Help! That's what I want!" Of a higher class, with snooty friends to impress, he is unwilling to extend any solidarity to Anne and worries instead that the stench of shame will touch him, too. Being a man, he walks away from it all. There were two moments where it seems that Anne might confide in her professor, and I, as a professor, hoped he would be the sort of person who would actually help. He had earlier told her that "professors can often spot other professors," and he invests in nurturing Anne's intellect, curiosity, and talent. Early in the film, in a large school auditorium, Anne is called on to explain poetic verse. She insightfully notices that the lover's drama evokes a political one—for us, anticipating *the personal is political* cast of the film we are watching. Anne never tells her professor, but near the end of the film, she confirms that she can now fully re-devote herself to her studies, having fought "the illness that strikes only women and turns them into housewives." "I want to write," she declares. The film ends with Anne taking her exams in a crowded class-room. We hear only the sound of her pencil on paper as the screen turns black.

Titane (Julia Ducournau, 2021)

Julia Ducournau's *Titane* is all fantasy and fabulation, but it opens with something that seems *as if* it could be a real event. We see images of hard edges and round whirring discs of gleaming steel and metal as "Wayfaring Stranger" by 16 Horsepower provides the soundtrack. Humming along to the car's engine, in the backseat, is a young girl with a determined face. Her father, visibly annoyed in the driver's seat, turns up the radio to drown her out, as she kicks at his seat and he yells at her to stop. Irritated, she frees herself from her seatbelt; the father turns to grab her, loses control, and the car veers off the road. This is the last (and only) semipredictable or realistic thing that happens.

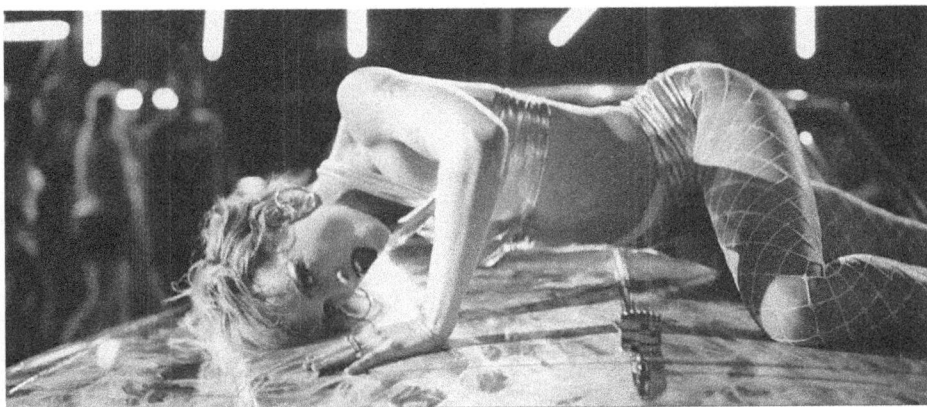

3.5. Alexia as car model. *Titane* (Julia Ducournau, 2021).

The film's narrative is easily followed but totally bonkers. As a result of the car accident, young Alexia gets a titanium plate inserted into her skull. As she and her parents leave the hospital, Alexia hugs and kisses the car. In the next scene, she is grown up and working as a dancer at an auto show where girls and cars merge as objects of desire (fig. 3.5). A fan follows her to her car to profess his love and beg for an autograph and a kiss. Alexia (Agathe Rouselle) pulls him into the car with the kiss, retrieves a thin long needle from her hair bun, and pierces his ear straight to his brain. His insides dribble out of his mouth onto Alexia's shoulder.

Are we watching a feminist revenge film? Alas, this thrilling expectation is shattered when Alexia's next victim is a sister-dancer with whom she has sex. Alexia seems to have no motivation for killing other than a quick and strong irritation that flashes like a red light during potential moments of intimacy. Simply because they are there, she kills all the dancer's roommates and then burns down her parents' home, locking her parents inside. For some of these kills, she uses her trusty hair needle; for others, the leg of a chair (inside her victim's mouth) or blunt and sharp objects that she grabs from around the house. Multiple online zines, articles, and stories document women using knitting needles to kill in horror films and in real life: Alexia expands the repertoire.

What kind of feminism is this (if it even is feminism)? Can we get our feminist bearings from Ducournau's first film? *Grave* (*Raw*; 2017) features a young woman veterinary student who goes from vegetarian to cannibal. The film can be said to be "about" many things at once: hazing on campus, female sexual desire, sister solidarity, racial tensions in contemporary France, and more.[18] But it is clearly a horror film and is usually classified as such. Many spectators get turned off by the body horror of seeing the heroine snack on the finger of her sister or cause car accidents in order to feast on the bodies of the victims. In my feminist film course, I often teach *Raw* with Claire Denis's *Sangre caníbal* (*Trouble Every Day*; 2001), another horror film "about" cannibalism and sexual desire. In class, we discuss the monstrosity of female desire, its dangers, its posing of trouble for rules of gender and racial binaries and the ways we organize and structure our world.[19] But my students are often troubled by resistance that doesn't look exemplary, heroic, or positioned toward building a better world. They would also be likely to react ambivalently to *Titane*'s Alexia, who seems, at first glance, to simply be a sociopathic serial killer, albeit in female garb. Ambivalent feelings on the part of viewers might arise partly from the joy that Alexia takes in killing. Indeed, the apartment massacre is accompanied by joyful music ("Nessuno mi può giudicare" by Caterina Caselli). There are even moments of humor between the scenes of gore. Surprised to see yet another housemate who asks her if the bathroom is occupied, Alexia asks with exasperation, "How many of you are there?" He answers: "There's Cri-cri, Romu, Jiji, and me. Are more coming?" Exhausted, Alexia says, "Hope not!" As she embraces this man who offers her his bed for a nap, Alexia stabs him in the back.

Fleeing a police hunt, Alexia notices her resemblance to a missing boy on a poster in a train station who would now be about her age. She shaves her head, breaks her nose, and tries to pass as the lost boy, Adrian, with his father (Vincent Lindon). Is this film posing genre trouble *as* gender trouble? The father is willfully oblivious to the fact that Alexia is not his son. He refuses a DNA test; he looks away on several occasions to not catch a glimpse of her naked body; and he professes his full belief in her identity as his son, no matter the biological or visible evidence to the contrary.

Over time, Alexia grows visibly pregnant from a sexual encounter with a car after her first onscreen kill. The car "calls" her with its thumping sounds; she gets in the backseat and rides to orgasm. Straps in hands, car lights blinking and the front of the car bucking, both Alexia and the car seem to desperately need the encounter although it is neither erotic nor tender. Later, we see Alexia painfully binding her breasts and her pregnant belly. She leaks black oil from her breasts and vagina; her belly bulges and shifts as the baby grows. Much like Anne in *Happening*, Alexia is horrified by her body's changes. Whereas Anne tried a long skewer, Alexia attempts to kill the fetus with her trusty needle. But like Anne, she fails.

Indisputably, Alexia is a much less sympathetic heroine than Ada or Anne. *Titane*'s violence is so outrageous and untargeted, the heroine's motives so unclear and possibly suspect, that viewers (and especially feminist viewers) have to wonder how the film, or even *whether* the film, interrupts the male gaze. More than most, *Titane* actively resists what we might call the "rules" for feminist filmmaking. These rules specify a film as feminist if it flips the scripts from male to female, if it helps us get inside the heads of women characters, if it helps us understand women's subjectivity and perspectives, or something else. "Problem" films, like *Titane*, expand the conversations, forcing us to think carefully about how art undoes the rules, and can undo us, too.

Consider the Bechdel rule. This is the feminist "test" introduced in 1985 by graphic artist Alison Bechdel in a comic strip named *Dykes to Watch Out For*. In one installation, titled simply "The Rule," two lesbians debate which movie to watch, a perennial dilemma. One says to the other, "Well, I have this rule.... I only go to a movie if it fulfills 3 requirements ... it must have at least two women, who talk to each other, about something other than a man" (Bechdel 1986, 22). The Bechdel rule is a very low bar and yet most movies—Hollywood, at least—fail to pass. The two dykes cannot find a movie, so they go home to make popcorn. *Titane* seems to pass the Bechdel rule when Alexia talks to another dancer, but invariably, just after the talking (not about men, but about nipple rings), Alexia kills her. Does this mean it passes or fails the Bechdel rule?

Perhaps what makes a film feminist is the debunking of what Beauvoir called myths of "the eternal feminine" or the idea of Woman—what could be called the "realism" rule. Although *Titane* portrays the specific perspective of a female character and certainly defies Beauvoir's "eternal feminine," Alexia's murderous and selfish actions, her lack of empathy, her cold and calculating gaze, could just as easily serve to buttress, rather than undo, the Medusa and other female monster myths. *Titane* cannot be classed as realistic, whereas both *Atlantics* and *Happening* open in a semidocumentary, at least more realist, mode before they move into horror. But had either film stuck with a realist style, they likely would not have been nearly as effective in inviting viewers to feel like feminists. As Beauvoir cautions, the reach of documentaries is limited, and "lessons" of didactic films are quickly forgotten.[20]

Some argue that what matters most for feminist film is a woman director and a cast of diverse female characters. The films I interpret in this book mostly meet these requirements, which we might call the "diversity" rule. For this rule, *who* directs the film, who is onscreen, and whether and how the heroine is a role model are key.[21] But the diversity rule fails to capture what is most compelling about a film like *Titane*. The heroine is not feminist, and the narrative is driven by plot and image, rather than by the heroine's subjective experience and point of view. Viewers are *never* invited into Alexia's thoughts, and we are left in utter ignorance about the world from her perspective.

To assess the impact of *Titane* for helping viewers feel like feminists, I think about Akerman's focus on feelings—"I don't have an idea. I have a feeling that I try to express" (quoted in Nelson 2018)—and Catherine Breillat, whose *Romance* (1999), often dismissed as pornography, is discussed in chapter 4. Breillat's images of female bodies in pain, ecstasy, and gross, unappealing yet beautiful excess populate her impressive cinematic oeuvre (see Marso 2024d). Like these filmmakers, and in company with Diop and Diwan, Ducournau is willing to explore the strange in the everyday: to show us our own bodies, soft and hard, that surprise and fail us; that are the source of pain and pleasure, leak strange fluids, grow old or ugly; exceed and break the rules of gender; and are just simply never in our control. Pushing against film's genre expectations, Ducournau pushes against what we think we know about who has power and who is vulnerable, and in which situations; she shows us how we fail to connect in almost every instance and how it is like a miracle when we do so. Recall Ada and Souleiman making love through the body of Issa, defying time, space, and even death.

Most important, we *feel* these things watching *Titane* rather than our coming to know or understand them. At times, it is profoundly uncomfortable to watch, but at other times it is pure joy. Ducournau's images touch our bodies and trigger our emotions. What was hitting my eyes and ears made me cringe, look away, look back, tune out, tune back in, and peek through squinted vision. My skin got a little itchy and I felt sick; my emotions veered from ecstasy to deep sorrow. I mostly didn't understand what I was feeling or why I was feeling it.

One moment of the film was especially moving for me: Vincent (Vincent Linden) and Alexia dance together in the kitchen after Vincent begs her to speak (she does not) when he notices her breasts are leaking (fig. 3.6). Vincent swears he won't hurt her; Alexia runs from the table and Vincent turns on "She's Not There" by the Zombies and begins to dance:

> Well, no one told me about her, the way she lied
> Well, no one told me about her, how many people cried
> But it's too late to say you're sorry

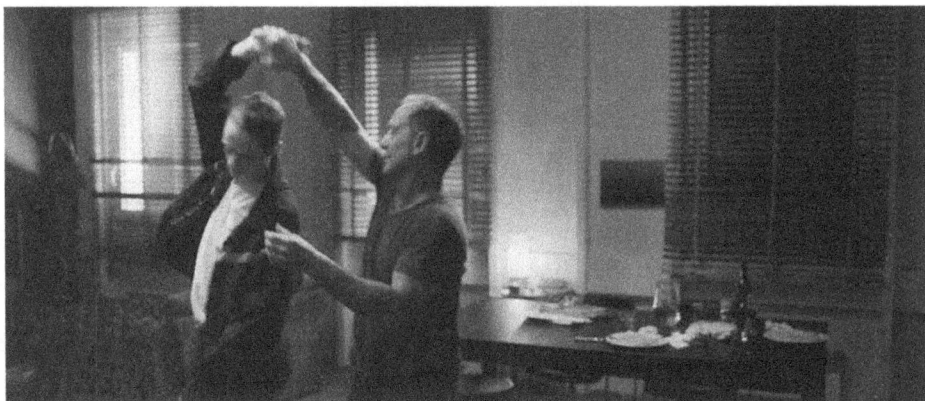

3.6. Alexia and Vincent dancing. *Titane* (Julia Ducournau, 2021).

How would I know, why should I care?
Please don't bother tryin' to find her
She's not there.

The lyrics capture what is so perplexing about Alexia. She lies, she kills, she makes people cry, she hides herself. But to her "father" as "Adrian," she need not say she is sorry, reveal, or explain herself. I read "she's not there" as scrambling the "she" we "expect" to be there. Alexia is someone else, some creature of the next world, but someone Vincent accepts and loves unconditionally. The dancing begins as sweet; it turns to aggression and ends with Vincent on the floor with Alexia holding the needle above him, going in for the kill. A breathless Vincent says, "What's that for? You in a knitting club? Wanna fight? Fight like a man!" But the threatening words belie his behavior. As the music swells, Vincent holds her in a bear hug and says, "Why do you always want to leave? You are already home!" This may be the most transformative father/son scene in all of cinema and literature, breaking every rule written about inheritance, gender, family, and love. And Alexia seems to feel it. From this point on, there is something of a transformation and she is no longer a killer.

The film closes with one of the most vivid and difficult birth scenes in cinematic history (Breillat's scene of a baby's head crowning in *Romance* [which was X rated] is also a contender; another is the dangling umbilical cord of Diwan's *Happening*). Alexia's obsession with cars, and her sex with a car, has caused her pregnancy. Vincent helps her give birth to a car/child, and Alexia dies in childbirth. But Vincent is still alive. He has traveled on his own journey of becoming, and now he is the adopted father to a new kind of being—a car/child with a steely spine—a little future that he will nurture.

Maybe the feminist feeling of this film, especially when thinking about horror and read alongside *Atlantics* and *Happening*, is this: it invites us to feel the possibility, indeed the necessity, of leaving behind the selves we were and are to become something else entirely. This is a fantasy, but one that sharpens our critique of how what and who we are now limits ways of reimagining iterations of a feminist future inside the present tense we are living. We *could* be cyborg beings, with new genres, new forms of kinship. Bearing witness, I felt the dreams of new feminist worlds coming alive inside a film that initially felt like horror.

Feeling Horror Like a Feminist

We tend to think of how gender works in horror like this: the stereotypical male (occupying the assaultive gaze) attacks and sometimes kills a female victim (with the reactive gaze), but sometimes the female victim, in particular, the final girl, fights back. The final girl in slasher films is the last one standing, the one who lives to tell the story, to confront the killer. We might assume that male-identified audience members identify (unhappily? thrillingly?) with the killer and female-identified viewers identify (unhappily? thrillingly?) with the final girl, or the girls who don't survive. But as early as 1992, film scholar Carol Clover argued that gender in the modern horror film, both onscreen and in terms of viewer identification, is much more complex than this schema allows. She says that the formulaic narratives of slasher films, as well as their cinematic gaze, invite male adolescents (slasher film's biggest audience) to identify with the final girl who survives to exact bloody revenge on the killer. In the new preface to the 2015 edition of *Men, Women, and Chainsaws*, her classic book on horror, she goes even further: "Taken together, these films [several types of modern horror] offer variant imaginings of what it is, or might be, like to be a woman—to menstruate and be pregnant, to be vulnerable to and endure male violence, to be sexually violated.... What new-regime horror showed us is that at least some male audiences were willing to make-believe these sensations" (xiii).

Clover focuses her attention specifically on the film's gaze, who is looking at whom, and with whom viewers identify, while also acknowledging that horror's gaze can elicit varied embodied responses, or "sensations," from a range of differently embodied and differently situated viewers.

Citing Noël Carroll, she says that bodily responses such as "shuddering, nausea, shrinking, paralysis, screaming, and revulsion" are common and serve "as a kind of mirror to horror movie audiences" (167). This "mirroring effect," she claims, is one of "the defining features of the genre" (167). In *Life-Destroying Diagrams* (2022), film theorist Eugenie Brinkema says that to assess film in regard to these sorts of effects and affects is to fall into line with a version of what she cleverly calls "neck aesthetics." Brinkema's antiphenomenological, antiexperiential, and antiembodiment perspective sees neck aesthetics—her shorthand to name how thinkers evaluate films that can make our necks feel itchy and irritated—as a critical mistake. Neck aesthetics distract us from close reading of the negativity of negative affect or, in other words, from the speculative possibilities of the text for creating new forms. Committed to what she calls a "radical" (not as in political, but rather as rooted, foundational) formalism, she pays attention instead to design, abecedaria, rhythm, circle, toroid, grid, diagram, and torture.[22] Attention to these forms does not crowd out attention to affect per se but stages their relationship differently.[23]

In contrast to Brinkema's work which deliberately avoids feminist politics as she considers films that speculate on horror and love, Alison Peirse's edited collection, *Women Make Horror* (2020), centers feminism. Each author in the Peirse collection reads horror as a place of potential political change. Several of the authors are attentive to the kinds of feelings, rather than reactive bodily sensations or what Brinkema calls "neck," that horror films invite in their audiences. Peirse cites Kier-La Janisse, horror fan and author, for example, who says, "I gravitate towards films that devastate me and unravel me completely—a good horror film will more often make me cry than make me shudder" (2020, 7). The essays in this collection read horror films made by women *as* horror (i.e., intentionally meant to be included in the genre).

In my estimation of what is going on in the feminist art-house iterations of what I call horror, the directors are not seeking that their films be recognized as horror, nor are they engaging in formal or narrative strategies to irritate or ignite our necks, or to create new forms. What defines horror in my films is not a crazy serial killer, psychoanalytic terror, or the kind of jump scares that viewers thrillingly anticipate. Diop, Diwan, and Ducournau do not add to the genre and its conventions, but stretch and remake it, all the while employing cinematic tricks and techniques borrowed from horror to exaggerate, intensify, and fabulate the everyday experiences of girls and women. Gender, labor, reproduction, family, colonial relations, and what we recognize as human are all interrogated in a presentation of experiences that invite strong, disconcerting, and often confusing viewer feelings.

The "horror" of these horror films is found in the everyday encounters and experiences attended to by directors and brought to our feminist senses as viewers. On the screen, feelings of characters are sometimes apparent, and sometimes obscure or unavailable, but an important effect of each film's formal and narrative choices is to appeal to viewers to *feel through a sensorium* that is normally not available as common sense. As we saw in chapter 2, what is called "common" sense, "generic" sense, arises from, replicates, and reproduces the male perspective. The sensorium in these films reveals the horrific aspects of everyday life and ordinary experiences for feminized, racialized, marginalized, cyborg subjects living within patriarchal, capitalist and commodity-obsessed, worlds. Viewer response might begin with bodily sensation (shuddering, terror, disgust, anxiety), but importantly for me, these sensations themselves trigger feelings of horror rooted in a feminist sensibility and feminist feelings that are often heretofore "lost," or ignored, misplaced, buried. These feelings acknowledge the "real" for our characters onscreen and possibly in the audience, too. They acknowledge and confirm an alternative or dismissed reality grounded in women's experiences.

Feeling like a feminist thus becomes the ground for imagining something beyond, or sometimes within (but buried), what we currently know or can imagine. These films complicate or reverse the gaze, diversify the identities of characters onscreen, and differently *document* or add to the storehouse of women's experiences. But the most significant thing they do is intensify, exaggerate, and fabricate to invite us to feel like feminists.

4

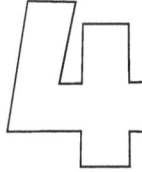

EPISTOLARY ARCHIVE: CRINGE

epistolary archive: a collection of letters

cringe: an inward feeling of embarrassment or awkwardness

THIS CHAPTER LEANS INTO THE EMBARRASSING and confusing feelings invited by "feminist cringe comedies" that frame sexual experiences from the perspective of women.[1] I borrow the moniker "feminist cringe comedy" from *New Yorker* critic Emily Nussbaum (2017) who names a genre that features female fantasies in a comedic register. Comedy can be confusing, even dangerous, and maybe especially so for feminists who are too often said to be humorless and not often "in on" the joke.[2] Think of feminist theorist Sara Ahmed's work on the "feminist killjoy" as a cultural trope, as one example.[3] Just as we might hesitate to explore, much less admit to, what and how something turns us on, we also worry about what makes us laugh, what laughter does with and to our bodies, and how unruly forms of laugher might affect the body politic.[4] In this chapter, I bring what turns us on and what makes us laugh together in my reading of feminist cringe comedies. I explore how cringe comedy invites feelings that course through bodies, letters, and communities of women in the examples I feature.[5]

In chapter 3, I considered genre-bending films that intensify women's everyday experiences by showing them as body horror, or that show that body horror simply *is* women's everyday experience. We see in these films that specific experiences of colonized, pregnant, and cyborgian women are *lived as horror* for characters and felt as such by viewers. Camerawork, sound, color, and music bring these experiences alive for viewers and invite discomforting feelings of "fear, shock, and disgust."[6] What I call "feminist realism" in horror could, I argued in chapter 3, inspire new ways of imagining where the boundaries of the body start and end, what we see as "human" experience, and what needs to change in order for people to thrive and be free. I suggested at the end of the chapter that though some feminist films may fail the Bechdel, realism, and diversity tests, their success in pressing viewers to feel like feminists makes us ask whether we might have to leave everything we know behind in order to create a new world.

The feminist cringe comedies I turn to now stage crises of interpretation over sexualized and raced bodies and turn our attention to the always present deep suspicion of women's claims to credibility and authority. Simultaneously, they brilliantly witness women's subjectivity, visibility, desire, hilarity, wittiness, and creativity. But we proceed with caution. Feminist cringe comedies that explore sexual desire are doubly dangerous, and the reactions I explore—irruptive laughter and the feeling of the cringe—are neither predictable nor predictably feminist. Even the bodily responses provoked by feminist cringe comedies are paradoxical. The cringe positions our bodies and thoughts inward, but laughter opens us to others. To cringe and laugh at the same time is inherently ambivalent. Cringing, we expose our collective investments in gendered and racial fantasies; laughing, we open ourselves us to something new. Within this dangerous territory lies the possibility not only to expose the male fantasy gaze that is too often replicated in visual culture, but also, and for me, more importantly, to feel our way toward something else. Like sexual desire, comedy tests us: "always crossing lines, it helps us figure out what we desire or can bear" (Berlant and Ngai 2017, 235). How should we feel about women's sexual desires under patriarchy, varied and impure and unruly as they are, and made especially risky when made into a joke?

In the two central analyses of this chapter, I read Joey Soloway's adaptation of Chris Kraus's novel *I Love Dick* (1997)—an eight-episode Amazon television series that premiered in August 2016 and was released in May 2017—as a reception (of sorts) of French feminist auteur/director Catherine Breillat's *Romance* (1999). Soloway's *I Love Dick* references several important feminist visual artists in the series via short, unexplained cuts sutured into scenes where we do not expect them. These are, I will argue, little love letters to feminist film and women's creativity that are secreted throughout the series like cuts that make us feel. Chantal Akerman, among others, is one of the directors featured, even though she is known for *not* cutting, for using duration shots that make viewers look for a long time. Breillat's films are not cited or secreted within *I Love Dick*, but I think they should be. Breillat's bold and distinct version of feminist realism—her depiction of everyday sex and women's fantasies—draws my attention and frames my interpretation of *I Love Dick* because of its cringy comedy and because of its epistolary invitations. *Romance* prepares the way to love beyond Dick, we might say. In *I Love Dick*, we see artists willing to explore women's (shameful, shameless) unrecognized feelings onscreen, first as sexual lust and then as creative energy.[7] The sexual lust, seen so visibly, so embarrassingly, in letters written to Dick, might make us feel pretty cringy, but it is tightly linked to a creative feminist energy and feminist aesthetics that, unleashed and uncontrolled, might change everything.[8]

Real Sex?

Becoming a woman really does not seem to be an easy business. At least on the stage that has been set by the fantasies, phobias, and taboos a man . . . has about woman's sexuality.

Luce Irigaray, *Speculum of the Other Woman* ([1974] 1985, 39)

Luce Irigaray says that life's "stage" has always been set (as well as peopled, directed, ruled, judged) by men. Sometimes life's stage is set by reasonable or benevolent men (still they are men), but ugly and malevolent male fantasies, fears, and anxieties always lurk just beneath the surface. As we know from the first volume of *The Second Sex*, male fantasies *are* the real, and as we learn in the second volume, male fantasies shape what is considered true, real, verifiable. Even the "data" of biology is determined by male anxieties and fantasies triggered by the contingency of sexual difference in nature.[9] Male desires permeate what we know of women's desires, as women are constantly subject to a soundscape of white noise and visual landscapes dominated by the male sensorium and touted as reason or common sense. Schooled by Beauvoir, we know that what is considered real, particularly "real" desire, is always a product of fantasy, struggle, interpretation, and politics.

It comes as no surprise that cinematic representation of sex and fantasy from the perspective of woman-identified subjects invite complex feelings for woman-identified (and other) viewers, as well as debate (or outright dismissal) among critics. I position *Romance* as an early iteration of *I Love Dick* partly because Breillat's film oeuvre is famously populated by experiences of sex and fantasy from the perspective of girls and women. Breillat is (in)famous for consistently violating rules about filming unsimulated sex, casting young female actors and porn stars, and courting X ratings.[10] Her films are said to challenge the border between eroticism and pornography. Whether viewers experience the sex as fantasy, as real, as pornographic or erotic, as a combination of these, or something else entirely most often depends on how they see themselves in regard to sexed and gendered identity, what kinds of sex they enjoy or are willing to admit to enjoying, whether they watch porn and which kinds, and what kinds of sexual experiences and which sexual traumas are buried in their psyches. *How* the sex and fantasy are filmed, how and whether sex seems attractive or real for viewers, for *which* viewers, and whether Breillat is an "ethical" filmmaker (a debate I do not find that interesting, and I do not explore) are all issues raised by her films. These tricky questions and intimate feelings, stirred up by Breillat's provocative oeuvre, create a minefield for viewers and critics.

Breillat's films not only ignite, but also recall, debates about what is real and what is fantasy in sex and desire, and why it matters politically. Sounding again Beauvoir's warning that men are the measure for what is real in all things, we remember (with frustration and anger) that women are often disbelieved, doubted, questioned, and said to be unreliable narrators, liars, hysterics, shrews, frigid, nymphomaniacs, and worse. Can we rely on women (as characters, viewers, or critics) to distinguish what *really* happens in sex from what they unconsciously or subconsciously wish for? In the "he said, she said" battle, what *he* said most often prevails. Some still say that Anita Hill must have fantasized the obscene attention of Clarence Thomas. This is a problem with a history. Working with hysterics, Freud traced the cause of their symptoms—that is, the physical problems with their bodies—to an overactive imagination. Here is Freud quoted by Irigaray: "In the period in which the main interest was directed to discovering infantile sexual trau-mas, almost all my women patients told me they had been seduced by their father. . . . I was driven to recognize in the end that these reports were un-true and so came to understand that hysterical symptoms are derived from phantasies and not from real occurrences" ([1974] 1985, 37). Irigaray locates the source of *this* fantasy with Freud himself. Freud, father of psychoanaly-sis, seduces his students, and on and on, and the seduction is covered up by the law known as *the Oedipus complex in women*. Irigaray concludes: "Law organizes and arranges the world of fantasy at least as much as it forbids, interprets, and symbolizes it" (38).

But are men any better than women at distinguishing fantasy from real-ity? If we take our bearings from the writings of antipornography feminist Catherine MacKinnon, who argues that masculinity is dominance eroti-cized and femininity is submission eroticized, we can conclude that men often mistake the sexual violence in hardcore pornography for what women want in sex.[11] In *The Right to Sex: Feminism in the Twenty-First Century* (2021), feminist thinker Amia Srinivasan reminds us that antipornography feminists of the 1970s characterized porn as a "virtual training ground" for male sexual aggression, and that her students today, women *and* men, having been raised on internet pornography, have basically learned *what sex is* through their viewing of porn. And not feminist porn: "the hard-core stuff, the aggressive stuff—what is now, on the internet, the free stuff" (40). While MacKinnon argued that to mistake pornography for sex benefited the dominance that men exert in the bedroom as well as in society writ large, Srinivasan says that some things have changed, at least for some men. One of her male students, she reports, "asked whether it was too utopian to imagine sex that was loving and mutual and not about domination and submission" (40).

Breillat's films reference these debates but do not explicitly comment on or resolve them. She simply films sex and the fantasy of sex from what she sees as the perspective of women and girls, distinguishing the two (sex and fantasy) by using different styles. She films sex in a realist style. By "realist style," what I mean is that she does *not* use sexy or swelling music, fade-away camera movement, soft focus, zoom shots, or other romance-inducing de-vices to film sex. Eschewing technical tricks that add affect and emotion to sex (i.e., that make actual sex look like fantasy), Breillat offers instead the mechanics of bodies and their parts—the erect penis, the limp penis, the vagina, and in *Romance*, she films one result of the interactions of some of these parts—a live birth of a baby. What we see are uncomfortable and awkward maneuverings, periods of preparation and of boredom, the presence of used condom wrappers, used tampons, blood and other fluids—all the stuff that makes sex look gross and difficult. The fantasies she puts onscreen also differ profoundly from what we are used to seeing in romantic comedies or romance genres. They signal "fantasy" by their surrealist and outlandish settings and events—in *Une vraie jeune fille* (*A Real Young Girl*; 1976), for example, one of the fantasies of the fourteen-year-old girl of the title consists of being tied up by the hunky farmhand as he attempts to insert earthworms into her vagina. The fantasies in Breillat's films are always from the perspective of her female characters, and, as evidenced by the earthworm incident, they are often quite funny. Not surprisingly, male-identified viewers often fail to find these scenes funny, and do not find them in any way arousing either. According to the evidence of critics who write on "extreme" cinema and include Breillat's films in this category, male viewers tend to respond to Breillat's aesthetic provocations with indifference, anger, or simple refusal, and sometimes walk out of the theater.

These films certainly stir up a lot of difficult feelings and elicit varied responses based on these feelings, even for feminists.[12] From the perspective of antipornography feminists, Breillat's often philosophical and sometimes funny fantasy scenes of rape, sadomasochism, and female sexual submission unwittingly or too willingly replicate the cinematic male gaze.[13] Other viewers find that the masochism, pain, hunger, comedy, and anger of her female characters resonates with them, and sometimes quite sharply. For some critics, the question of whether and how Breillat is showing us something "real" in the real sex becomes the focus of their interpretation. Eugenie Brinkema argues that "Breillat is unequivocally misread when she is said to show female desire or represent female sexuality" (2006, 152). She says, instead, that Breillat's fascination with the materiality of flesh, particularly of "wet female desire," is a foray not into female desire but instead into the "ontological realism of the image" (149). Brinkema asks, "Why have we ignored this space, Breillat's film insists, this interior female bodily desiring space that could produce such powerful, such erotic, images of its own workings?" (151).

Wherever critics and viewers stand on the questions of what offends, what resonates, and whether Breillat's films are extreme, pornographic, unethical, realist, or feminist, and however differently viewers are situated—politically, socially, sexually, or experientially—almost everyone feels unsettled or confused as the credits roll. I categorize *Romance* as an early version of contemporary cringe comedy not only because of Breillat's focus on real and fantasy sex that evokes the cringe, but also because so much of what she presents as fantasy in *Romance* is flat-out hilarious. Viewers might not laugh, but, always, her female lead *invites us to be in on the joke* by speaking directly to the audience via voice-overs, by sharing her sexual fantasies, and by accompanying her as she experiences (boring, excessive, absurd, assaultive) real sex.

For me, the important question for Breillat that extends to my reading of Soloway's *I Love Dick* is how each depicts the shameful, messy, cringy, unfeminist aspects of women's desire and sexual fantasies, always contaminated by men's fantasies and the male gaze. Bravely showing shame-filled sex *and* fantasy from the point of view of women and girls as cringy, funny, or both, Breillat and Soloway invite the complex feelings of woman-identified viewers. What also interests me as I explore what it might feel like to feel like a feminist in these two cinematic examples is how the willingness to embrace these fantasies by characters and with viewers can permeate, circulate, and spread, contaminating and changing the body politic.

Feminist realism of the sort that I am exploring here mandates that we abandon any search for the "truth" of female desire in favor of exploring, enhancing, and displaying its real-life manifestations, caught between worlds of the male gaze, women's sexual experiences, and women's fantasies. The cringe and the laughter are responses to seeing, hearing, feeling women's everyday sexual experience and their sexual fantasies onscreen. These experiences and these fantasies give voice, via visual and sonic texture and the use of cuts, to the fact that the meaning men make of sexual difference *is* violent, horrific, and extreme. Women's fantasies, often funny, and often surreal and shameful, offer a release in laughter, and maybe a way forward, through complex meanings and readings of the cringe.

Romance (Catherine Breillat, 1999)

Romance is an "institution of intimacy" (Berlant 2000) that is one source of the "cruel optimism" named by queer theorist and cultural critic Lauren Berlant (2011). Or, as Shulamith Firestone said much earlier, in 1970, romance is a "cultural tool of male power to keep women from knowing their conditions" ([1970] 2015, 131). Romance keeps us tethered to heteropatriarchy and the nuclear family. Romance also has a particular kind of aesthetic appearance, accompanied by scripted emotions and feelings that mark these life narratives and their representations. But Marie, the schoolteacher heroine of Breillat's *Romance* (played by Caroline Ducey), does not experience this version of romance with her boyfriend, Paul (Sagamore Stévenin), or with any of the men she seeks out for sexual encounters when Paul refuses to have sex with her and she goes looking for it elsewhere. Try as they might, both Marie and Paul are having a lot of trouble following the script that the patriarchal view of romance has written. It also takes a lot of effort for Paul and Marie to follow the rules of gender that are the signposts for that script. We learn in the very first scene, for example, that Paul must fake his masculinity. We see him working as a model, leaning backward, having makeup applied to his face so he can pose as a matador in a bullring. Once in the ring, he is told to stand taller (up on his toes) and look straight at the camera. The female model is instructed to "look down," to "be a bit submissive to the man."

Marie also seems to have to work at being a woman. She wants Paul to dominate her, to act more like a man, so she can play her complementary female role. Or if he can't summon the energy for that scenario, at the very least she hopes for a response while servicing him. In one sex scene with Paul, Marie diligently works on a blow job as he reclines, head on pillow, one arm under head, looking into the middle distance, unaroused. Tired of sex of this sort, Marie goes looking for something and someone else. The ensuing encounters are confusing and discomforting for viewers. She regularly has S&M sex with her boss (François Berléand); she gets violently raped in a stairwell; she goes home with a man from a bar (in real life, an Italian porn star, Rocco Siffredi), during which she speaks her thoughts as voice-over: "I want to be a hole, a pit, the more gaping, the more obscene it is." This is a cringe-inducing line for feminists if ever there was one.

Marie's desire takes her to some dark places, leads to what looks like debasement and humiliation, and all the while she retains her flat affect, her detached way of observing herself and her absurd situation. She shares thoughts and observations directly with the audience via voice-over. I interpret these as little letters to viewers, even though we mostly do not know what to make of them, what they mean, where they might land.[14] In the first instance of these voice-overs, Paul speaks to Marie from his bed where he stares intensely at a television show featuring male gymnasts flexing their muscles. He says that their sexual dry spell is "not that serious." Marie stares at herself in the bathroom mirror while brushing her teeth, and says to us, "Yes, it is."

Film critic Roger Ebert admits his inability to understand the film's intentions in a review published after its screening at the Toronto Film Festival: "Perhaps it is a test of how men and women relate to eroticism on the screen. I know few men who like it much (sure proof it is not pornographic). Women defend it in feminist terms, but you have the strangest feeling they're not saying what they really think. At a screening at the Toronto Film Festival there was some laughter, almost all female, but I couldn't tell if it was nervous, or knowing" (Ebert 1999). It is interesting to compare the report that Ebert heard "some laughter, almost all female," in the Toronto theater to what Janet Maslin (1999) reports experiencing in the *New York Times*. She says the film is "solemn" and "cerebral." I think it is both solemn and comic, and that this is the point. It invites our cringe. The listless way Marie holds her body and her mostly expressionless face while having various forms of explicit sex is already cringy, made even more so by the thoughts she confides to viewers.

One of Marie's fantasies is sparked by a dehumanizing gynecological exam during which Marie says (to us) she is being treated like a "slab of meat." Nine doctors and interns penetrate her with their fingers in a scene that lasts two minutes and twenty-four seconds. Marie's out-of-body experience is vividly described by the *Guardian*'s film critic: "[As] Marie is examined by a row of smirking medical students, each with their rubber glove, she fantasizes about a row of genteel enceinte matrons being petted by their fussing husbands while their lower halves are candidly rogered by porno stallions" (Bradshaw 1999). The point, Marie shares in voice-over, is that "a cunt doesn't go with a face." The patriarchal message that infiltrates women's fantasy life, here made fodder for both cringe and laughter, is that women are either whores or virgins. In both roles, women are exchangeable, one for the other, and absolutely alike. The men on the porn side of the brothel compare the size of their cocks, while the adoring couples on the other side pretend this isn't happening. Marie surmises that "love between men and women is impossible," as the money shot from the brothel side transforms into the gel being squeezed onto Marie's stomach for her pregnancy ultrasound.

And yet s&m sex with her boss, Robert, takes Marie to new places in her head and her body (fig. 4.1). Robert does his job like a professional, searching for just the right cuffs, gags, and ropes in his toolbox, all the while chatting to Marie and telling her stories. He tells Marie he has deliberately set up his apartment like a stage (we think of Irigaray) to attract women. He laughs and jokes. "Nobody bothers to talk to women anymore," Robert says. But he also says, "The only way to be loved by women is via rape." Marie has a surprising response to this stagecraft and its props. He gently gags her, carefully positions her body into "beautiful" positions, and arouses her by

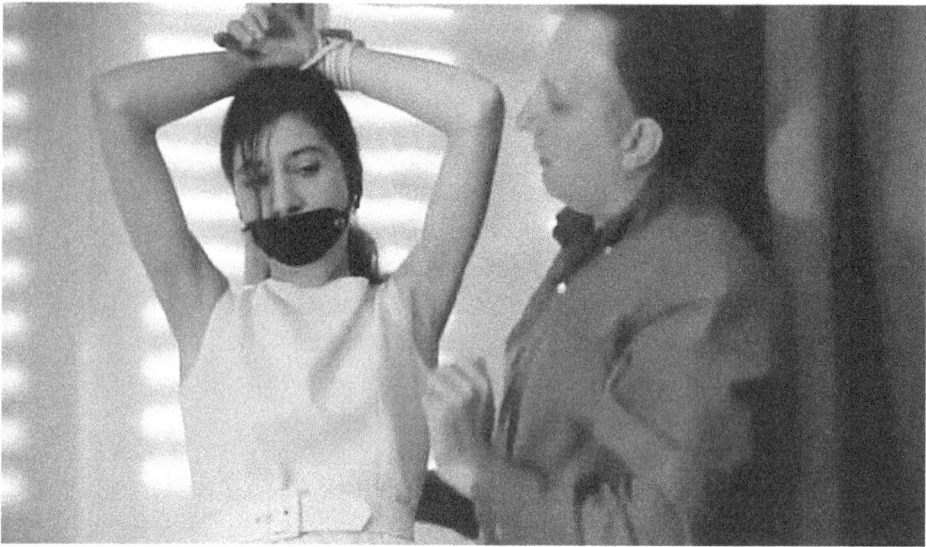

4.1. Marie and her boss. *Romance* (Catherine Breillat, 1999).

putting his fingers in her vagina. When this happens the first time, we see Marie's facial expression change, also for the first time. When Robert examines his fingers, we see the sticky substance that Eugenie Brinkema (2006, 149) calls the "ontological realism of the image."

Marie's complicated feelings, her sexual arousal, being talked to, or all three, have changed the mise-n-scène and the trajectory of her life. "This kind of embarrassment," she confides to viewers, "is desire. . . . It's part of the game." Her arousal in this cringy moment, and especially her surprise and delight at her arousal, moves her away from passivity and toward a complicated embrace of desire and even relationality. "I grew attached to Robert," Marie confides to us. "Tying me up without tying me down was the secret of his ritual. After these sessions, I wasn't gloomy. We giggled. We partied and overate." She discards her all-white costume and wears a red dress. We see the two out to dinner delighting in food and conversation. Just before Robert first walked into her classroom and set their encounters in motion, Marie put the day's dictation lesson on the board: "Everyone had settled for a life that was dull and orderly."

Late in the film, Marie gets pregnant with her boyfriend Paul's baby in a bedroom tryst where she becomes the "man" and screws him. When she voices what they are doing ("I'll be your guy; I'll screw you!"), he knocks her out of the bed. Marie says, "That's how that selfish bastard got me pregnant!" When it is time to go to the hospital, Marie calls Robert to drive and accompany her. Walking away from the apartment she shares with Paul, Marie deliberately turns on the gas. At the hospital, we see very explicit views of the baby's head crowning in the scene that many viewers report as the most upsetting in the film. Just as the baby is placed in Marie's arms, we see the apartment blow up.

This is a radically different ending than the one we saw in *Blow Up My Town*! As we will remember, in that short film, Akerman, playing the young girl, blows up her apartment and kills herself in the process. While viewers cannot know what thoughts, actions, feelings, or trauma may have led to this ending in Akerman's short, in *Romance*, we know that Marie has embraced her own and the viewer's shame to find some version of freedom and to affirm that women's desire, as complicated and shameful as it may be, exists. In the hilarious last scene, we find Marie, decked out in a sexy black outfit, holding her baby at Paul's funeral. We hear her thoughts: "I gave my son his father's name.... If someone up there counts souls, we're even." This is a winning and witty ending, and feminist too. But as I turn to Soloway's *I Love Dick*, I note that though viewers are invited to feel *with* and *as* Marie, her journey is solely an individual one. Film theorist Damon R. Young argues that Breillat's films feature the (collective female) vagina over the (individual liberal) face. Young thus concludes that Breillat's films are "radically incompatible with the liberal view that connects sex to pleasure, to autonomy, to a contractual exchange between equals, or that views it as property of an individual subject" (2018, 59). I see this a bit differently (see Marso 2024d). But we do notice that there is no other woman in the film with whom Marie finds connection, solace, or solidarity. Like *Blow Up My Town* and Julia Ducournau's *Titane*, *Romance* fails the Bechdel test, even as it invites viewer feeling in transformative ways.

I Love Dick (Joey Soloway, 2016–17)

I Love Dick opens with a red screen filled with large white letters: First, "DEAR DICK"; then, "EVERY LETTER IS A LOVE LETTER" (figs. 4.2 and 4.3). Or a lust letter. Chris Kraus (Kathryn Hahn) writes letter after letter to Dick (Kevin Bacon) describing her (shameful, shameless) sexual fantasies in abundant detail. Chris is a frustrated filmmaker who accompanies her older husband, Sylvère (Griffin Dunne), a Holocaust scholar, to Marfa, Texas, where she is called "the Holocaust wife."[15] The Marfa Retreat is a place for writers and artists to "read, write, or think." It's run by Dick, a man whose

4.2. "DEAR DICK." *I Love Dick* (Joey Soloway, 2016–17).

4.3. "EVERY LETTER IS A LOVE LETTER." *I Love Dick* (Joey Soloway, 2016–17).

4.4. Dick carrying a lamb. *I Love Dick* (Joey Soloway, 2016–17).

aesthetic vision and brooding, brilliant, bad-boy personality dominates and structures the town and fascinates its inhabitants and visitors.

When we first meet Chris and Sylvère we learn that Chris plans to drop off Sylvère at Marfa and then travel to Venice, Italy, where the short feminist film she directed is scheduled to premiere. Instead, as soon as she arrives in Marfa, she gets word that her film is out of the competition because of a copyright issue on some music she used. Creatively stymied, she is bored, frustrated, and adrift. But then she sees Dick riding down the middle of a deserted street on a horse, and this gets her artistic (and other) juices flowing. Her fantasy vision is of shirtless Dick draping a lamb over his shoulders (fig. 4.4).

Chris is older than Marie of *Romance* and thus is positioned as even more cringy when she insists on going wherever her midlife libido takes her. Chris's desire (sexual, aesthetic) is supercharged by her fantasies of and about Dick, a man she barely knows and doesn't care to know, at least not in any way other than sexually. As the series unfolds, we witness Chris's sexual obsession and aesthetic ambition merging. Does she want to have sex with Dick, be Dick, replace Dick, obliterate Dick? She takes pride in her letters, and gleefully plasters them all over town.

In the first episode, already smitten, Chris invites Dick out to dinner with her and Sylvère to a restaurant that Dick chooses (it serves "small game"). In response to Chris's (admittedly inarticulate) description of her film work and explanation for being kicked out of the festival, Dick flippantly says to

Chris that desire, "pure want," if she has it, should have been enough for her film to succeed.[16] Chris responds: "If all it took was desire, Dick, there would be a trove of amazing films by women filmmakers." Dick interrupts: "Unfortunately, most films made by women aren't that good. . . . See I think it's pretty rare for a woman to make a good film because they have to work from behind their oppression which makes for some bummer movies." Viewers are treated to a quick series of feminist media cuts by Chantal Akerman, Sally Potter, and Jane Campion that pass across the screen at lightning speed—unexplained, shocking, energizing.

Each of Soloway's eight episodes in the series is cleverly interlaced with image montage of unnamed feminist film and video art, which includes the works of Akerman, Maya Deren, Cheryl Donegan, Marina Abramović, Carolee Schneemann, Petra Cortright, Liz Lerman, Jane Campion, Dimitris Papaioannou, Vanalyne Green, Sally Potter, Naomi Uman, Cauleen Smith, Stephanie Smith and Edward Stewart, and Annie Sprinkle. Many of these images are sexually explicit or sexually suggestive, and they do not seem, at least on first viewing, to add narrative information even though they were carefully chosen and paired to characters and moments (Frank 2017). With these clips, viewers are urged to stop and think about the connections between the narrative and the clips. For example, when Dick says films by women aren't that good, the clips seem to be evidence of female talent. Throughout, the clips bear witness to women's creativity. Perhaps they are Chris Kraus's archive. Perhaps they are, or should be, ours! Like Marie's voice-overs, but here appearing within and creating community, they are love letters to feminist viewers and to feminist film. They might be understood as editorial clips and cuts that make us feel, but what we feel is uncertain and unpredictable.

After Dick's insult, Chris retreats to the women's bathroom to try to regain her composure. We see her look at herself in the mirror in the first bathroom shot; in the second, we see the red background and the white lettering of her letters once again: "DEAR DICK, GAME ON." Game on, but the game is rigged. We recall Irigaray's words about the setting of the stage and Beauvoir's insistence that "the conditions under which woman's sexual life unfolds depend not only on these facts [that women have to struggle with cultural scripts that ascribe shame, passivity, and lack of pleasure to female subjects] but also on her whole social and economic situation" ([1949] 2011, 415).[17]

The first evidence of Chris's desire is a letter, the initial words of what will become an avalanche of letters. Chris begins to pen this letter on her laptop, sitting on her couch in the dark, after this dinner. It is late at night. Sylvère gets out of bed, asks Chris what she is doing, to which she responds curtly, hoping he will return to bed and that she can get back to her project. She says she is writing a short story in the form of a letter and that it is fiction. Sylvère urges her to read it out loud. The letter reveals that Chris has revised what happened with Dick at the restaurant, refashioned as her fantasy version of events. In real life, Dick had acted indifferent to and dismissive of Chris. Dick blithely dismissed Chris not only from the conversation, but also from art, and Chris made a hasty retreat to the "ladies" room. But in Chris's fantasy version, when she abruptly leaves the dinner table, Dick follows her into the bathroom where she is waiting for him like a "stupid girl." "Waiting for him like a stupid girl." This line, paired with what we know from *Romance*, demands an acknowledgment of the role that female masochism plays in the fantasy worlds of women: "I thought you were following me, stalking your prey, I imagined I was cornered, I wanted to be cornered." As Chris reads, we see images of Dick undressing Chris in the bathroom of the restaurant. "I wanted you to be rough," she reads, "so, so rough."

As Chris reads from her laptop, Sylvère becomes erect. He says, "Look at this!," pointing to his crotch, and calling attention to the easy visibility of male desire. If Breillat were filming this, we would see the penis.[18] We don't *see* Chris's desire, were that possible, so we can't know if Chris is aroused or not, what she is thinking or feeling. But when Sylvère jumps on the couch, onto and into Chris, he triumphantly declares that he has the evidence of her desire. "You're so wet," he gloats, as if this were his doing. But is Chris's wetness a response to Sylvère's erection? Or has she turned herself on with her letter writing? We will see in the last episode that when Chris and Dick finally attempt to have sex, Dick, too, finds Chris "so wet," but he, also, is not the (only) reason for her wetness. Sylvère and Chris have a quick fuck, their sexual "dry" spell over, but is Chris's desire satisfied? No. She returns to her laptop! She continues writing her fantasy, revisiting and rewriting the previous night's events.

Beauvoir notes (critically) that Freud concludes, "Woman is masochistic because pleasure and pain in her are linked through defloration and birth, and because she consents to her passive role" ([1949] 2011, 411). In response, Beauvoir debunks the idea that pain is always linked to destruction (it is also linked to the desire to merge, she says) and dismisses the notion that pain plays a larger role in women's erotic life than it does in men's. Beauvoir also cautions us about seeing women's masochistic fantasies as the "truth" of what women really want. "We have seen that most of the time the young girl accepts in her *imagination* the domination of a demigod, a hero, a male, but it is only a narcissistic game. She is in no way disposed to submit to the

WHAT IF WE ALL STARTED WRITING YOU LETTERS?

4.5. "WHAT IF WE ALL STARTED WRITING YOU LETTERS?" *I Love Dick* (Joey Soloway, 2016–17).

carnal expression of this authority in reality" (412). She adds: "The little girl who dreams of rape with a mixture of horror and complicity does not *desire* to be raped, and the event, if it occurred, would be a loathsome catastrophe" (412). We are thus cautioned to note that although fantasies inform what counts as real, and though they permeate our bodies, condition our feelings, and organize our politics, there *is another reality* we can find and confirm were we to acknowledge women's desires. This is feminist realism.

In episode 5, aptly titled "A Short History of Weird Girls," Chris's desires have now spread like a contagion and the picture widens to include a diverse group of women who reside in Marfa. The episode opens with Chris saying that when she walks down the street she investigates the faces of the women she meets and wonders about the history of their desire. She asks, "DEAR DICK, WHAT IF WE ALL STARTED WRITING YOU LETTERS?" (fig. 4.5). What if, indeed. Could we collectivize the cringe? Subsequent transformations ensue because the women of Marfa read the address (the recipients, or addressee, as well as the destination) as mobile. Is Chris addressing Dick, addressing patriarchy, addressing other women? When the women of Marfa see Chris's letters all over town, they cringe, they laugh, and they start to move differently.

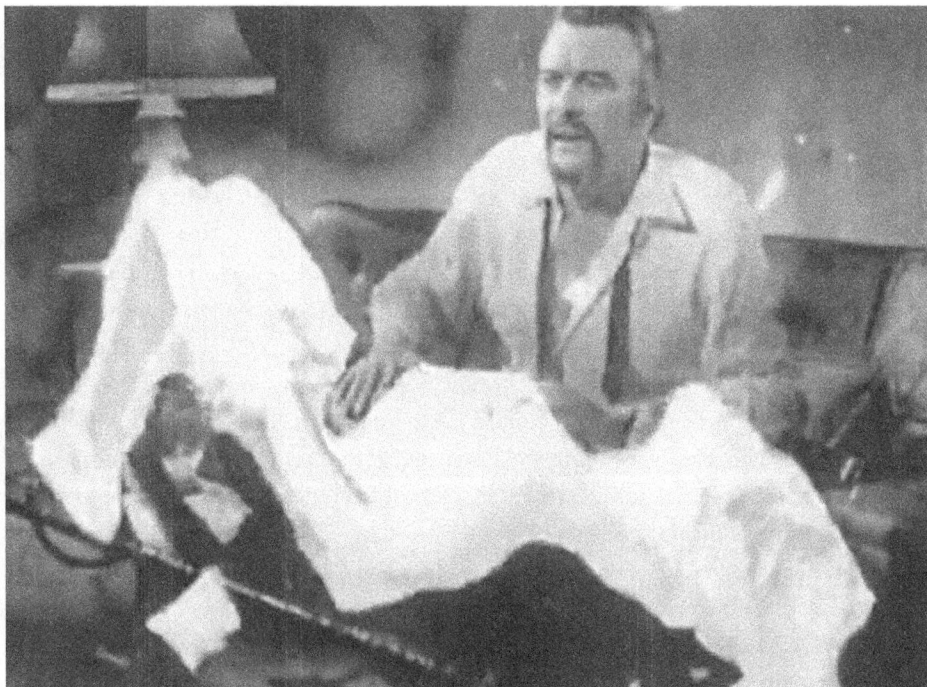

4.6. Clip from Naomi Uman's *Removed* (1999) in *I Love Dick* (Joey Soloway, 2016–17).

This episode includes a clip from Naomi Uman's *Removed*, created in 1999, the year *Romance* premiered. To make the short film, Uman replaced the women in pornographic films with bleach and nail polish applied directly to the film itself. The material result is that the women appear as white bubbles (fig. 4.6). From the perspective of omnipotent male desire, woman has "*nothing* you can see" (Irigaray [1974] 1985, 47). But Soloway's gaze, like Breillat's, veers from the perspective of male desire, and so women see and show *something*. We follow the "histories of desire" for Devon, the butch lesbian who was born in Marfa, lives in a trailer next to Chris and Sylvère, and aspires to be a playwright; Paula, assistant curator of Dick's museum space, who is not given the space by Dick (literally or figuratively) to express herself; and Toby, redheaded academic who is, like Sylvère, a fellow of the institute and works on the aesthetics of pornography. Aesthetically mimicking the Uman clip, the stories they narrate of the histories of their desire begin with each being blotted out by white bubbles. But their desire becomes visible as it is expressed in the telling as letters to Dick (Dear Dick, what if we all started writing you letters?), and simultaneously as love letters to viewers.

Paula, the curator, starts by recalling her love for her mother. She describes it as a love story for her Black mother, who is a feminist activist. Seeing this episode the first time, I hoped (and anticipated) that it might be positioned as an iteration of Akerman's motherwork camerawork: a way for mothers to be *seen*. But the cringe interrupts Paula's (and my own) desires for this particular love story. Spotting a tampon string between her mother's legs, young Paula feels the patriarchal cringe at the sight of her mother's menstruation, and she goes in search of a new love object. She finds Dick. Paula says she is so attracted to him because he leaves his works untitled, leaving an empty space for ambiguity, for "boundlessness." But working with Dick, she now finds the thing that fascinated her—his mysterious aura—in real life means that he will not say yes to any of her ideas, particularly those that involve displaying the work of feminist and Black artists. By the end of the series, Paula takes over the Marfa studio. She fills it with the work of nonwhite and feminist artists.

Devon, who says that her family tries to politely ignore the fact that they (brown folk of Texas) have worked Dick's land for decades, aspires to *be* Dick. She pretends to be him when her cousins want to practice kissing, and she copies his swagger and style. But when Devon sees Dick exiting the bedroom of her mother, she, too, experiences a cringe. While Paula's cringe oriented her toward Dick, Devon's turns her away from him. In subsequent episodes, we see Devon inspired not by Dick, but by Chris. Devon has a breakthrough with her writing; she also acts on her desire for Toby, another fellow of the institute. Though their sexual encounter in some ways mirrors patriarchy's script (Toby wants to suck Devon's "big cock"), it disrupts it, too. By the end of the series, Devon has emancipated her aesthetic ambition. She writes a play that incorporates Chris's letters to Dick; and in another performance piece, she stages a ritual dance performed by the men of Marfa, who start to embrace their feminine sides (see fig. C.7, in the "Coda").

Toby's story betrays her sexual history: the too-often repeated sexual history of the many hysterics who trekked through Freud's offices. Toby's recollection of her childhood implies that her hippie father sexually molested her, but he also owned a coffee-table book of Dick's work: all "massive steel and concrete cock." Toby wants to be an artist, too, and she is inspired by Dick's minimalist and formalist aesthetic. Though her PhD in art history examined pornography, Toby focused on its aesthetics—all shapes and forms—and avoided the politics. And yet, she recalls that there are "five hundred times as many female nudes in art history textbooks as female artists." At the end of her story, after citing Dick's accomplishments and measuring them against her own, Toby announces in her letter to Dick: "You haven't made a piece in nearly a decade. Your time is running out. Dear Dick, we are not far from your doorstep." And indeed, Toby's art goes viral when she sits naked for hours in the oil-rig campsite outside of town to draw attention to the rape of the earth.

Expanding Chris's story beyond her own to those of other women in Marfa, *I Love Dick* highlights the struggles women face to be seen, to have their desire, as well as their art, appear when male desire permeates everything and is seemingly everywhere. One of the challenges presented here is to overcome shame, take up an active stance, and stare back without hesitation, risking fear of failure, refusal, and rejection. This shows a willingness to sit with difficult feelings and transform them in community, and it is much more than a simple inversion: we see with Paula, with Toby, and with Devon (as we see with Chris) that desire itself is transformed and changed by the feeling, hearing, voicing, and visibility of its active presence. *I Love Dick* shows what desire *can do* when women aspire to own it, to feel it, to follow it to wherever it leads, and, most important, to share it! This, in spite of complex, inevitably impure and inappropriate expressions of desire that replace the no-place of lack—a white bubble.

We get several examples from Soloway of what desire can do, in light of and despite its impurity, its contamination by male fantasy and power. In the ending sequence of images for the pilot episode of *I Love Dick* we see Dick from behind as he strips himself naked and submerges into a pool. Is this Chris's fantasy—watching Dick secretly, and from behind? Does it stage Dick's fear/fantasy—the abyss of woman? Could it be both—the saturation of Chris's fantasy by male fear and fantasy? As Irigaray contends, though in the male sexual imaginary the woman is only an obliging prop for male fantasies, "that she [a woman] may find pleasure in that role, by proxy, is possible, *even certain*" ([1977] 1985, 25, italics added). The pool enveloping Dick might be, at one and the same time, the wetness, the infinity, the circularity, inclination, not-one-ness of women's desire, and the "dark gulf ready to swallow him [man] . . . a maternal darkness" of "a cave, an abyss, hell." These words are Beauvoir's in *The Second Sex*, describing the way men think of the "mystery" and "magic" of Woman ([1949] 2011, 166). Man wants to "break the barriers of the self and comingle with water, earth, night, Nothingness, with the Whole" (167). That is Woman's danger, but also her appeal: while she condemns man to finitude, she also "enables him to surpass his own limits" (167). Beauvoir elaborates: "In all civilizations and still today, she inspires horror in man: the horror of his own carnal contingence that he projects on her" (167). Women are trapped by carnal contingence with menstruation as its reminder and remainder: unclean, impure, and cursed. We will come back to menstrual blood and to wetness.

For now, we note that, *like* the dark red stain of menstrual blood, desire is active, not passive, and especially so in this case. Taking the form of an epistolary outburst, Chris's desire bleeds out all over the town, interrupting Dick's aesthetic dominance and seeping into everyone else's veins, too.[19] As mentioned earlier, the first time we see Chris writing on the couch after the fateful dinner, she begins the creative actions that become the funnel for her desire. The products, the letters, undo Sylvère. At first he is turned on by the letters, and Sylvère and Chris's sex life improves dramatically, but when the letters become public, he feels ashamed by his wife's excessive behavior. They also undo Dick, who is made the muse and visibly disturbed by this gender reversal. But they do not undo Chris or the women of Marfa; they experience more of a *redoing*, a wonderful transformation. Chris's *writing saves her*, redeems her, fortifies her, and makes her courageous—in a later episode, we see Chris nail the letters to fences and tape them to walls and windows, sharing her desire with all of Marfa's residents (see figs. 4.7, 4.8, and 4.9). Chris's actions literally paper over Dick's gaze that has heretofore dominated and structured the aesthetic of the town.

To say that women's fantasies subvert from within is to pay attention not to what desire *is*, or what it looks like or what it represents, but instead to what it *does*, no matter what it *is*, where it comes from, or to what or whom it is attached. The end of *I Love Dick* emphasizes female desire, women's bodies, their fluids and fluidity, their pleasures and potential. This is what women's desire *can do*, the series seems to say. Recall, too, that at the end of *Romance*, Marie creates life, she prevails, she moves forward without a man, and she wins the game! (We remember Chris's confident announcement in her fantasy, "Game On!") In the final moments of the last episode of *I Love Dick*, Chris seems about to have her fantasy come true in real life by having sex with Dick. Dick says to Chris, "You are so wet," and he demands that Chris tell him it is *he* who makes her wet. He inserts his fingers in her vagina and pulls them out. Dick's fingers are covered not with "wet female desire" (Brinkema 2006, 151) but with menstrual blood. Dick steps back from Chris and peers at his fingers, looking bewildered and slightly appalled, while Chris tries to remember what day it is to gauge whether she is late or early.[20] Dick hastily retreats to the kitchen to wash his hands clean;

4.7. "Julie" resting after assembling her letters in Akerman's *Je tu il elle*, referenced in *I Love Dick* (Joey Soloway, 2016–17).

we see the blood run down the drain as he scrubs. Alone, Chris looks in the mirror and seems to take stock of the situation. She dresses, gathers her things, puts Dick's cowboy hat on her head, and walks out of Dick's house into the sunset. As blood runs down her legs, Chris holds her head high, leaving the disappointing Dick behind.[21] Building on Marie's individual but expansive journey, Chris's contaminated desire bleeds all over Marfa.

Just prior to this final scene, the penultimate montage with all the women in the series is suffused with pure joy: Paula fantasizes what the gallery will look like filled with feminist, Black, queer, Latinx, and all kinds of norm-challenging and form-challenging art; Devon gathers the men of Marfa to dance a ritual of healing and love in which Sylvère enthusiastically partici-pates; Toby's body-art performance videos have gone viral with more than half a million views. Dick's erect-brick artwork is broken by a wild dance party in the studio. It has lost its rectitude as well as its verticality, and the artists of Marfa are moving in new ways to new places. It will likely not be a linear journey. It is surely a fantasy, but maybe, via feminist community,

4.8. Chris taping her letters in Marfa. *I Love Dick* (Joey Soloway, 2016–17).

4.9. Women inspired by Chris's letters. *I Love Dick* (Joey Soloway, 2016–17).

we could make it real. The open secret of Chris's letters to Dick is that they were not, in the end, received by Dick. They were received by the women of Marfa (and even Sylvère). Was Dick the intended recipient? Or was he just the occasion?²² Either way, once the letters were circulated in public, the collective cringe performed its feminist magic.

The Feminist Address

Unchallenged, mainstream film coded the erotic into the language of the dominant patriarchal order.... [We must dare] to break with normal pleasurable expectations in order to conceive a new language of desire.

Laura Mulvey (1975, 8)

As we have seen, one place *I Love Dick* situates desire is in the writing and reading of letters. Chris's letters to Dick are *about* her body and its desires, her unruly approaching-middle-age body, and her shameful, sometimes seeming like not very feminist, desires. "Dear Dick, I am obsessed by you. Tell me I'm a bad girl, Dick!" The letters are addressed to Dick, but do not really communicate with him: he misinterprets, intentionally doesn't understand, can't read the signs. He is obtuse to the physical signs of Chris's body, as evidenced by the wetness debacle. Her letters, which baffle and then embarrass Dick, become vehicles for the opening and speaking of desire for several other women.

I read *I Love Dick* as *itself* a love letter, but one that is addressed not only to Dick. At least not only to the man named Dick. It may sometimes include "dick" as such, but also, as events unfold, several women and some men in the series (and in the audience?) include themselves as readers, and maybe potential writers, of Chris's letters and their own. This shifting of the address (ostensibly to Dick but moving outward to other women) begins with the cringe and the irruption of laughter. It intensifies and moves in the direction of freedom aided by yet another series of love letters. *I Love Dick* is not only a love letter to women, but also a love letter to feminist film, feminist filmmaking, and more broadly to female creativity and the ongoing work of feminist interpretation.[23]

Little love letters to feminist film and media, dating between 1964 to 2012, are secreted within the series like cinematic Russian dolls testifying to a genealogy of women's creative freedom. Each feminist filmmaker and video artist featured in the series is attempting to do what Laura Mulvey (1975, 8) says we must dare: "conceive a new language of desire."[24] Recall that one of Mulvey's important early critiques was that cameras produce erotic ways of looking that reproduce male subjectivity. Whether we can change this dynamic depends on creative camerawork that also includes use of sound, play with genre, innovative editing (or in Akerman's case, use of duration), as well as how audiences and critics read and interpret and feel in response to what we see, hear, and sense.

Completely unexplained, wholly surprising, always extremely odd, and generously sprinkled throughout the series, these clips (for me) make *I Love Dick* a rightful iteration and continuation of the work of Chantal Akerman. Writer and director Logan Kibens worked with Soloway to choose them: "I was responding to the scripts as they were coming in," Kibens said. "It was like a really hard crossword puzzle. Every piece had to relate to one of the main characters and what she was going through while keeping in mind the theme of the show. Taken together, the clips offer a short history of women in film" (quoted in Frank 2017). Of Akerman specifically, Kibens says, "Chantal Akerman was someone I initially thought of. She was deeply important to me. I admire how much she pushed against her critical response. She would get negative pushback because her work was difficult to understand, but she really stayed true to her voice. That struggle and stubbornness and purity of vision was an interesting parallel to Chris's journey. Chris is this woman who was really beaten up by outside perspective, who needs to find herself from the inside. She's trying to get past the [white?!] noise" (quoted in Frank 2017).

These confusing short clips from the history of feminist media appear at beginnings of episodes or break into the story. They range from cinema to performance art, dance, and video, but they all feature people (sometimes with animals) engaging in strange or outrageous behavior, often including weird-looking sex. They arrive as high-powered energetic jolts, arousing curiosity, bewilderment, or, for some, annoyance, or a cringe—certainly discomfort. Whatever our response, these are cuts that make us feel.[25]

To explore these feelings and what they might do further, let's lean back into the cringe. *New Yorker* critic Emily Nussbaum assessed *I Love Dick* as a "narcissistic spectacle framed as a liberating vision quest" (2017). Does the explicit expression of women's sexual desire merely highlight one (usually white) woman's sexual journey, or does it open the possibility for new iterations of love, family, the erotic, and even the political? To lean *especially* hard into the cringe, I return to Beauvoir's 1959 essay on Brigitte Bardot, and in particular to Bardot's character, Juliette, in Roger Vadim's film *And God Created Woman* (1956). Beauvoir makes the surprising claim that the male gaze is not disrupted specifically by camerawork or by viewer identification or sympathy with Bardot's point of view. Beauvoir says it is Bardot's body moving onscreen, positioned as a woman's desiring body, that is the significant disruptive force:

> Her body rarely settles into a state of immobility: she walks, she dances, she moves about. . . . [H]er eroticism is not magical but ag-

gressive. . . . [T]he male is an object to her, just as she is to him. . . . Bardot's face has the forthright presence of reality. It is a stumbling block to lewd fantasies and ethereal dreams alike. Most Frenchmen like to indulge in mystic flights as a change from ribaldry, and vice versa. With BB (bébé) they get nowhere. She corners them and forces them to be honest with themselves. They are obliged to recognize the crudity of their desire, the object of which is very precise—that body, those thighs, that bottom, those breasts. ([1959] 2015, 119–20)

Bardot is like a striptease artist who "offers herself directly to every spectator" ([1959] 2015, 22). Is this just another kind of voyeurism? Beauvoir casts "bébé" as the "woman-child," the literal baby-woman, or nymphet, a new erotic object. But she insists that this move is not automatically synonymous with disempowerment and might indicate something else. Writing sixty or so years after Beauvoir, and in the wake of queer scholarship and politics that often position public sex as progressive, media scholar Damon R. Young reads *And God Created Woman* to ask about the possibilities and problems of Bardot's body in Vadim's film. Young's primary query, "Public sex might be erotically thrilling, but is it politically subversive or radical?" (172), is put to films that position the appearance of women's bodies and queer sexualities onscreen as figures of political contestation, aspiration, and allegory that are central to imagining sexuality, individual freedom, and social responsibility. He concludes that sometimes women's and queer sexuality can be integrated into civic existence; at other times it is marked as undermining it, corrosive to society's fabric. Breaking with Beauvoir's reading of Bardot, Young regards Bardot's Juliette merely as a liberal sexual subject who displays autonomy. But, though Bardot fails to move us toward a "queer" world, Young admits she does interrupt the social contract of marriage, patriarchy, and the family.[26]

Beauvoir never used the language of queerness or queer politics, but she insists that public displays of women's sexual desire can radically disrupt bourgeois assumptions and values, depending on how the feminist address circulates and where it lands.[27] Beauvoir reads Bardot in *And God Created Woman* as a (shameless? cringy?) spectacle, but maintains that Juliette is not easily assimilated as an object for the male gaze. She says the sexual offer to the viewer is "deceptive, for as viewers watch her, they are fully aware that this beautiful young woman is famous, rich, adulated, and completely inaccessible" ([1959] 2015, 122). She dances; she shows off; she obeys her instincts. She is oblivious to the patriarchal demand to be a proper mother or wife. In figure 4.10, we see Juliette dancing in a circle of Caribbean men,

4.10. Juliette dancing. *And God Created Woman* (Roger Vadim, 1956).

displaying her desire as orgasmic, autoerotic, outside the control of the white men who want to rein her in. Evoking the cringe of today's readers, Beauvoir fails to mention the racialized context of this scene. But we must consider the men who circle Juliette, clapping and encouraging her. How does their onscreen presence make viewers feel?

Noticing Beauvoir's inattention to how Blackness is represented in this film, we might conclude that Juliette's dancing is a form of appropriation, and that Beauvoir intensifies this appropriation by failing to talk about it. The eroticization of femininity via Blackness in this scene is cringy, and Beauvoir's silence regarding it makes it worse.[28] However, something else might be possible. We can try to think *with but beyond* Beauvoir when she says, "The debunking of love and eroticism is an undertaking that has wider implications than one might think. As soon as a single myth is touched, all myths are in danger" ([1959] 2015, 124). Do the men in this circle simply prop up Juliette's desire, or can our attention to our uncomfortable feelings around them do more? Pressing on Beauvoir's reading of Bardot, we might say the Black bodies are themselves positioned as objects of *viewer* desire, and our cringe alerts us to it.[29] As we feel our cringe, we are invited to examine our own racialized desire for sexualized Black bodies, its political meanings, and possible reverberations.[30]

Several women in the cinema of experience go on journeys to express sexuality, creativity, and the movement of their bodies freely, not for the male gaze and not as an inner quest, but *in relationship* and response to others, and as an invitation to viewers. As witnessed in images collected from the examples of cinema of experience discussed in this book (figs. 4.11–4.17), the fluidity of desire (and fluidity of identity) is not an expression of inner truth, an impulse against repression, or just a longing for better sex. These images of movement, often represented by dancing, are more complicated than that. Their complexity provokes several forms of viewer discomfort that can be productive for feminist consciousness and conversation. When we think of desire in this way, new vistas appear, ones that we tracked earlier in the cinema of experience. There is one image that does not seem to fit: Akerman as the unnamed young woman in *Blow Up My Town*, dancing in her kitchen before taking her life. I include it here as acknowledgment that we never know what any of Akerman's inscrutable characters are thinking, as we have no access to their interiority. But the dancing of Akerman's young woman, Akerman herself at the young age of eighteen, is an homage to movement and to freedom.

In the case of Bardot's Juliette, by taking female desire out of domestic space and into public, doing exactly as she pleases, she is acting like Chris and like Marie, showing desire as fluid, constructed, contested. But we can notice, too, that in *And God Created Woman*, Juliette's dancing creates even more disruption by bringing to our attention differences between white and nonwhite men. When Bardot jumps on the table and starts to dance, the Caribbean Black men surround and join her, but the white men don't know what to do. They are in another circle, behind the nonwhite men. This circle does not join, intending, instead, to exert their power to constrain Juliette, to domesticate her. Juliette's husband yells at her to stop (he yells several times, and then he begs), but she ignores him. As she continues to dance freely in the inner circle, the frustrated husband gets a gun out of his pocket and points it at her. An older man, a father figure but also a man who wants to fuck her, jumps in and takes the bullet. They all survive, and Juliette is ordered home. Beauvoir says, however, that viewers don't really buy it. "BB" is not meant for home and hearth. Chris puts it this way: "Dear Dick, is this the dumb cunt exegesis you were expecting? I am on a mission to obliterate the walls around my desire. I will not be muzzled!"

There is a striking scene in the fourth episode of *I Love Dick* that directly echoes Juliette's public dancing in *And God Created Woman*. After being dismissed by Dick as "uninteresting," a visibly agitated Chris orders Sylvère to go home as she follows some of the fellows and locals to the packed Lost Horse Saloon. Inside the bar, a Chicano band (the Tracks, with front man Venacio Bermudez, bassist Felipe Contreras, drummer Jimmy Conde, and guitarist Johnny Santana) croons a cover of "Oh, Lonesome Me." Chris lets loose, downing shots and dancing wildly (see fig. 4.17). Dick, sitting at the

4.11. Toby dancing, inspired by Chris's letters. *I Love Dick* (Joey Soloway, 2016–17).

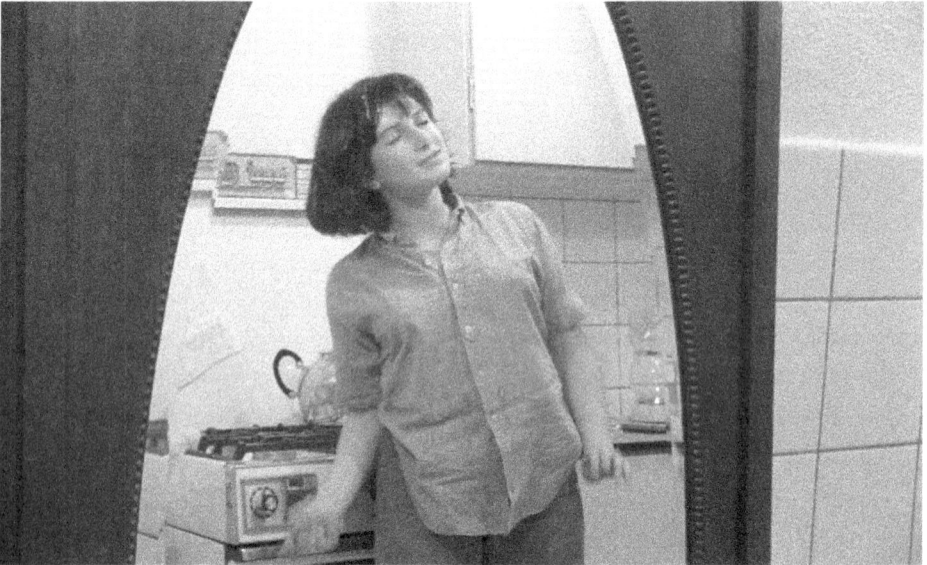

4.12. Akerman, playing unnamed woman, dancing. *Blow Up My Town* (Chantal Akerman, 1968).

4.13. Ada and Souleiman/Issa dancing. *Atlantics* (Mati Diop, 2019).

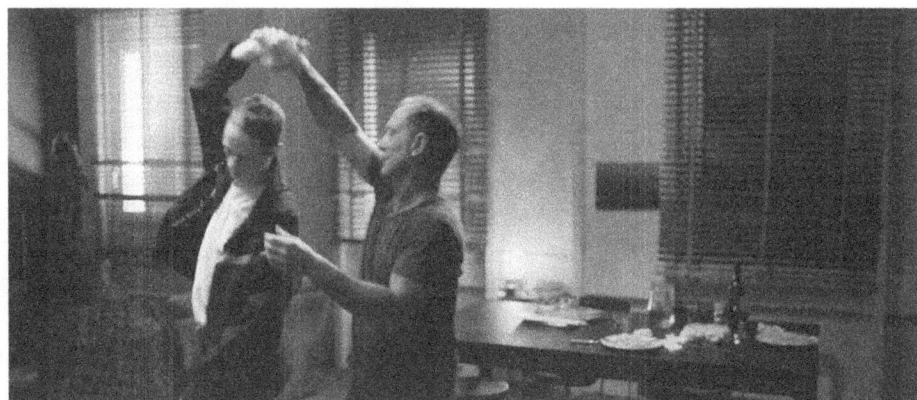

4.14. Alexia and Vincent dancing. *Titane* (Julia Ducournau, 2021).

4.15. Anne dancing. *Happening* (Audrey Diwan, 2022).

bar, looks at Chris disapprovingly. "DEAR DICK, DID YOU THINK THIS WAS GOING TO BE PRETTY?" appears on the screen as Sylvère, having disobeyed Chris's orders, enters the bar. A visibly angry Sylvère grabs Chris's arm, forcefully pulling her from the dance floor, but she successfully resists. Exasperated, Sylvère sees Dick seeing Chris, and Sylvère follows Dick to the bathroom where the two have a chat about the "problem" of Chris's behavior (fig. 4.18). "My wife, she's, uh, not acclimating here, very well, in Marfa," Sylvère says to Dick. "I see that," says Dick. "Kinda losing it, going a little crazy," Sylvère adds, and then, "Dick, I'm gonna make this go away." "Well, that's ok with me," Dick says and walks out. Sylvère orders Chris home, and she goes, following behind him on the streets of Marfa. But viewers know better than to assume Chris is suddenly domesticated. Like "BB," Chris is not meant for home and hearth!

In spite of this conversation in the men's room with Dick, Sylvère knows better, too. By the end of the series, we see that Sylvère was only momentarily contaminated by Dick's embarrassment, partially and briefly convinced by

4.16. Arabella and Terry dancing. *I May Destroy You* (Michaela Coel, 2020).

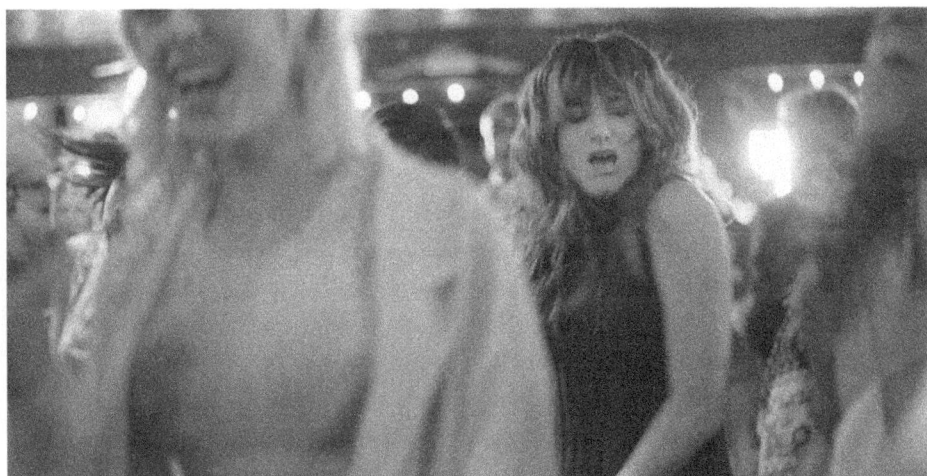

4.17. Chris dancing. *I Love Dick* (Joey Soloway, 2016–17).

Dick's assessment that Chris is a "distraction" from his work. Once home, Chris reminds him of how their work has always been connected, that they are each the other's best reader and critic, and that they share a life. Viewers have seen evidence of these connections between the two throughout the series. The couple explores all kinds of new expressions of desire through sex and other forms of connection once Chris begins her project of writing letters to Dick. Their dry spell is over because of the letters! In one notable conversation, Chris shares her vision of queer desire with Sylvère: "In like a hundred years, it's like none of this will matter anyway because we'll just be like formless, genderless balls of just pure light just floating around constantly fucking each other." Sylvère responds, "sounds amazing." And by the last episode of the series, Sylvère is writing his own letter to Dick and dancing in Devon's Beauty Dance (see fig. C.7, in the "Coda"). Chris's desire has transformed him, too, and it has permeated everything and everyone.

Enter French writer Hélène Cixous, who famously says in her 1976 essay "Laugh of the Medusa" that there is no universal female subject, no female sexuality "uniform, homogeneous, classifiable into codes" (876). "Woman's imaginary is inexhaustible, like music, painting, writing," she writes; "my desires have invented new desires" (876). Cixous recommends a kind of writing from the body: "A woman without a body, dumb, blind, can't possibly be a good fighter"; "censor the body and you censor breath and speech at the same time" (880). Cixous encourages us explicitly to "desire the other for the other, whole and entire" (891). "In one another we will never be lacking" (893).

This somatic feminism might help us feel. It is certainly one that acknowledges that the comportment, sensations, projections, fluids, and psycho/mind articulations of the body, and of bodies encountering other bodies, are the source of all relationships, all politics. As Beauvoir comprehensively documents, male fears of the body, of contingency, of filth, of mortality, of nature, and of nothingness fuel men's anxiety, their horror, their ugly refusal of, and hence desire to control, women's bodies and their powers and potential. Women's bodies terrify men and make them cringe. Beauvoir gives examples of the "spontaneous embarrassment," the "spontaneous repulsion" at the "pregnant woman's stomach," the "swollen breasts of the wet nurse" ([1949] 2011, 164–65). We cannot forget Dick's visible cringe when he sees his fingers covered with Chris's menstrual blood. In *Romance*, Paul asks Marie whether she likes his penis. She says she likes its smell. His reply? "You're disgusting!" Audience members walked out of the theater during the childbirth scene when Breillat's camera showed the baby's head and whole

4.18. Dick and Sylvère at the urinals discussing the "problem" of Chris. *I Love Dick* (Joey Soloway, 2016–17).

body emerging from Marie's vagina. Woman-identified viewers might also cringe in these moments, just as young Paula cringed when she saw the string hanging from her previously adored mother's vagina. How could we not cringe, trained as we are (all *too* well trained) to absorb the fantasies, myths, desires, and "tastes" of patriarchy?

The denial of the body, the pinning of all bodily contingency and meaning onto women is, for Beauvoir, the source of a tragic and misguided politics that also denies ambiguity—the encounter of self and other within one's self, the simultaneous existence of object and subject, our two-ness. We know from Irigaray that women cannot deny it, have not denied it, and women's fantasies acknowledge it. Cixous finds it to be a source of power. Beauvoir insists that men, *too*, are a sex "which is not one," but men work really hard at denying that fact. White men use *their* power in an impotent quest to outrun death (as we saw in the motherwork chapter) and control women and nonwhite people (as we saw in the sound and genre chapters). Is it possible that women's multiple and contaminated desire can be a start for rejecting the kind of deluded thinking that any of us might be *the* sex (*the* race, *the* age, *the* category) that is *one*? Is this where discomforting feeling becomes most subversive?

Exemplary of feminism's love letters, and echoing several of the examples of the cinema of experience I discussed in previous chapters, *And God*

Created Woman, Romance, and *I Love Dick* appeal to women via the look of female desire—captured, as it inevitably is, between men's and women's fantasy worlds, racialized politics, everyday refusal, stubborn persistence, but escaping in this case via comedic (existentialist, absurdist, hilarious) effects and bodily affects (the irruption of laughter and the cringe). The mother's body, her work and her aging, women's sexuality expressed in dancing, wetness, the bursting of bubbles, the writing of letters: all are on view, they are not confined to invisibility or the place of lack. These images create space for our feelings of ambivalence, stasis, horror, cringe (and next, in the "Coda," plasticity) to be aired and shared, for us to affirm and challenge each other, for us to begin to feel like feminists. Addressing each other, letters of love, circulating desire, making us feel uncomfortable, cringe, weep, laugh, and maybe even dance. Is this the refusal of prefabricated romance? Could it be the death of patriarchy?

CODA IN PINK:
PLASTICITY

pink: as pigment, intermediate between red and white; as descriptive, exquisite, fashionable, or smart; as associated with femininity, girlhood, charm, and romance

plasticity: the quality of being easily shaped or molded; the adaptability of an organism to changes in its environment or differences between its various habits; or, according to painter Mark Rothko, the willingness to take a journey

CULTURAL OBJECTS — like Barbie the doll and *Barbie* the film—do not themselves need to express feelings, evidence of interiority, or any particular political perspective to elicit these responses from audiences and critics, and to invite intense and disturbing feelings all around. The *New York Times Magazine* story that announced the backstory, themes, intentions, and intensities of Greta Gerwig's *Barbie* (2023) called it "a 113-minute love letter" to the doll (Paskin 2023). In chapter 4, we saw how controversial love letters can be; we witnessed what the disruptive feelings they release and circulate can do. Feeling this disturbing love, and maybe feeling this kind of love was inappropriate or misdirected, *Barbie* was very controversially received.

Before *Barbie* the movie, Barbie the doll, a plastic object for projection by mothers, daughters, and everyone else, also invited diverse, complex, and difficult feelings. Some mothers worry about the effects that Barbie's impossible physical attributes may have on the self-esteem of their daughters. They might reject Barbie's over-the-top and normative femininity and thus disallow play with Barbie. That wasn't my mother's position. A home economics teacher at our local South Dakota high school, my mom encouraged my love of Barbie and my longing to *be* Barbie by sewing clothes on her Singer sewing machine for both me *and* Barbie. I combed through displays of Butterick and Simplicity patterns and chose the best ones. The pencil-drawn cover models donning chic outfits fed my dreams of the popularity that would surely soon arrive, but when I tried on the finished products, my hopes were always dashed. This disappointment was mitigated (a little) by the fact that Mom's handiwork always suited Barbie perfectly: a swing-skirted, striped dress; bright orange bell-bottomed pants and crop top; and boldly purple faux fur coat, all slipped effortlessly onto Barbie's lovely figure. I saved these precious ensembles for my daughter's Barbies, but her Barbies turned out to be what Gerwig's film calls "weird," damaged when "played with too hard." My daughter's Barbies became moldy from long sessions in the bathtub, clothes always wet, haircuts always crazy. But they led much more adventurous lives than my own childhood versions. They traveled to imaginary lands, fought off Nazis, and returned home triumphant. Before my daughter came of age to play with Barbies, my son played with the Barbies he inherited from my stepdaughter. His Barbies lived in the basement, but they visited the bathtub, too. In all locations, Barbie was always available to be a girlfriend for the "guys" (never Ken, but Batman, Spiderman, and other plastic Marvel and DC heroes).

Barbie (Greta Gerwig, 2023)

Just as Barbie the doll, accompanied by her fabulous Dream House, inspires multiple fantasies and feelings, Gerwig's film attracts all the feelings, too—in part because it is a live-action blockbuster about a simultaneously beloved and hated doll, and Mattel, Barbie's maker, is now busy signing up directors to create films about its entire toybox (Barasch 2023). Some feminist critics love *Barbie* for its biting humor, while others lament its lack of substance, compromised messages, and corporate packaging. Right-wing figures decried its "wokeness," and Barbie dolls were burned in protest, incidentally and accidentally creating "weird" Barbies. Gerwig's response to these intense feelings (and actions) in response to the film was to say, "Certainly, there's a lot of passion. My hope for the movie is that it's an invitation for everybody to be part of the party and let go of the things that aren't necessarily serving us as either women or men. I hope that in all of that passion, if they see it or engage with it, it can give them some of the relief that it gave other people" (Buchanan 2023).

Barbie the plastic doll may be burned, but Barbie, as an idea, a collection of feelings, cannot be destroyed, only made into something weirder. The *New Yorker*'s Anthony Lane (2023) is dismissive of Barbie's intense affects and effects, calling the film "a plug for a chunk of plastic," and complained that "watching the first half hour of this movie is like being waterboarded with Pepto-Bismol." And yet, in midsummer 2023, millions of women viewers embraced and rocked this "Pepto-Bismol" vibe, showing up at cineplexes wearing Barbie pink, calling themselves and their friends "Barbie," and shouting their fandom on social media.

I think that the hot-pink address of Gerwig's *Barbie* calls to and intensifies viewer experiences of plasticity—molded by the demands of femininity, women-identified viewers are practiced in adapting and crafting themselves in response to the white male gaze reflected in normative consumer and aesthetic desire. At the same time, Gerwig's use of saturated color and a camp aesthetic in her story of the plastic doll creates space for feelings of plasticity more in tune with the kind of existential reckoning that abstract painter Mark Rothko hoped to achieve with his brilliant hues and formal style.[1] For Rothko, feelings of plasticity evoke existential angst while simultaneously opening the possibility of journey and transformation. Maybe *Barbie*, like my daughter's Barbies, can inspire us to fight Nazis and change the world? The double evocation of plasticity in *Barbie*—plasticity as already determined script to which we must conform, *as well as* the possibility for movement, change, journey, and transformation, reinforces the (at least) two registers on which the film delivers its punch. It is banal and existential, simple and profound, threatening and empowering, all at once.

While feelings in response to *Barbie* run hot, in Barbie Land there are no feelings at all . . . at first. Barbie Land's mythic origins are loudly announced

C.1. Barbie changes the world. *Barbie* (Greta Gerwig, 2023).

in the first frame with reference to Stanley Kubrick's *2001: A Space Odyssey* (1968). Swimsuit Barbie (a portrayal of the doll's 1959 debut version) appears from the sky to land within a group of glum little girls who are mechanically ironing clothing, doing the dishes, and playing at being "mommy" with their baby dolls (fig. C.1). Encountering glorious Swimsuit Barbie (Margot Robbie flashes her enchanting smile, lowers her sunglasses, and winks) causes the girls to violently hurl their baby dolls against the rocks. Why play at being a mother when you can stand still and run with *Barbie*? Helen Mirren's triumphant voice-over announces the Good News: "Barbie changed everything. . . . Because Barbie can be anything, women can be anything."

This (tongue-in-cheek, too confident) dispatch sets viewers up for the neoliberal fantasy of progress that explodes in the next scenes. *Barbie* is highly stylized and couldn't be more artificial. Barbie Land itself is a vision of bright colors, clichéd gestures, and shallow, surface emotions. The threat that Barbie—and *Barbie*—poses to patriarchy, its presentation of a new (promising or disappointing) feminist future that is happening just alongside, in the same time frame, as the "Real World," is administered in the key of camp. Perhaps it is the inside joke of it all, or the wink and nod to viewers that there are other worlds possible inside our own, that makes men's rights activists (and those identifying with men's rights lite) so furious.

In Barbie Land, though, all is not utopia. Girl power, inclusion, diversity, and happiness are all on display, but only on the surface. Dazzling panorama song-and-dance numbers feature Barbies and Kens of all ethnicities, races, body shapes, sizes, and abilities. Black Barbie (Issa Rae) is the president! Ken's "buddy" Allan (Michael Cera) is also included in the fun. Allan is unique in having no multiples and emitting a queer vibe in a world that we later come to understand lacks all sexual desire and where sexual parts are made of plastic—both situations (asexuality and plastic parts) themselves queer. Allan gravitates toward the Barbies as easily as the Kens, and by the end of the film, he has traded his striped shirt for all pink.

In a 2017 issue of *Film Quarterly*, Kristen Warner called this kind of fantasy of progress "plastic representation." As an example, Warner noted the appearance of "collectible Barbie doll" Ava DuVernay, "complete with the mise-en-scène of a director's chair to establish that all little black girls need to see DuVernay's image in tandem with a chair to believe they could work in film." Warner further described what "plastic representation" looks and feels like, and how it operates:

> Plastic representation uses the wonder that comes from seeing characters on screen who serve as visual identifiers for specific demographics in order to flatten the expectation to desire anything more. In this instance, then, progress is merely the increase of black actors on screen in both leading and supporting roles. . . . Plastic representation operates as a system that reifies blackness into an empirical system of "box checking." It is a mode of representation that offers the feel of progress but that actually cedes more ground than it gains for audiences of color. (35)

Using Warner's definition, *Barbie*'s representational politics in Barbie Land are plastic, but *self-consciously so*. The diversity on display is a hollowed-out pageantry. It's enjoyable and witty, and it can feel exuberant to feminist viewers who are in on the jokes. But at its core, this feminist utopia is empty. It draws attention to itself as spectacle, not substance. And even as spectacle, there are gaps and absences underlining the point that diverse representation is not only never enough, it is also always just out of reach. There are no aging characters, and we notice explicit unease with the only pregnant character, Midge (Emerald Fennell, director of *Promising Young Woman*). We learn that Midge was discontinued by Mattel shortly after her launch.

Apparently, a plastic replica of a pregnant body is too cringy for Mattel and its consumers, too evocative of the relationship to life and death that, as we observed in chapter 1, Beauvoir says pregnant bellies and mothers remind us of too readily.

In an interview about cinematic influences on *Barbie*, Gerwig leans into the "chunk of plastic" insult, lovingly calling its aesthetic an "authentic artificiality" (Vicino 2023). She cites the intense color palette of Jacques Demy's *Les parapluies de Cherbourg* (*The Umbrellas of Cherbourg*; 1964), but she might just as well have called our attention to Akerman's *Window Shopping* (1986; released outside the United States as *Golden Eighties*). Akerman's 1970s films (*Jeanne Dielman* and *Je tu il elle*, as examples) mostly complied with Laura Mulvey's 1975 insight that breaking the male gaze in film requires feminist filmmakers to produce avant-garde work that remaps and even destroys visual and narrative pleasure. As we have seen, Akerman's static camera, long takes, and durational gaze mandate that viewers "feel time passing" and are the opposite of entertaining and distracting, forcing viewers to instead sit with uncomfortable feelings. But *Window Shopping* is a bit different. A Barbie who always refused a box (we will remember that Akerman did not like the labels "feminist" or "queer" as descriptors of her films, even though they were often both), the highly stylized *Window Shopping* plays with feelings of exuberance and joy elicited by the musical. Akerman's typical focus on framing and everyday gesture remains, but *Window Shopping* is awash in the colors and visual pleasure that Technicolor MGM musicals of the 1940s and 1950s exude.

Window Shopping tracks overlapping love triangles and the frustrations of bad timing and unrequited love in a Brussels shopping mall. As film theorist Steven Shaviro notes, "Even as the film gratifies the viewer's cravings for color and movement, music and dance, it also converts the feelings of being in love into a series of postures or poses. . . . Subjectivity is fragmented, or analyzed into a number of isolated moments" (2007, 13). It moves between four self-contained bright and uniform little worlds of appearance and representation: dress shop, beauty salon, cinema, and snack bar (a place not only to hang out, but to be seen). In its opening scene, we see no bodies or faces, just high-heeled shoes hurrying to and fro, clickety-clack. Just like in Gerwig's *Barbie*, Akerman's lookalike, exchangeable characters are free of ambiguity and depth as they burst into song and dance. In the beauty salon, the shopgirls counsel each other against getting hung up on the main heartthrob's attention, steeling themselves and their feelings against love's ups and downs: "Don't lose your sleep, he's not your scene!" (fig. C.2). Pre-

C.2. The hair salon; "Don't lose your sleep, he's not your scene!" *Window Shopping* (Chantal Akerman, 1986).

sented as generic, even "stereotypical," with sanitized feelings, viewers eventually discover, however, that the main character, Jeanne (Delphine Seyrig), is a survivor of Nazi concentration camps and is haunted by worries about safety and economic security. She does not want to do anything that might change her settled world, including experiencing any real emotion.

There are complex feelings just under the surface of Barbie Land's visual extravaganza as well. To her (and our) surprise, Barbie brings a Barbie Land "blowout party with . . . planned choreography" to a silent and shocked halt when, midnumber, hands poised to clap, she pauses to say, "Do you guys ever think about dying?" The next day, Barbie is further assaulted and disoriented by bad breath, spoiled milk, burnt toast, and the inability to float. These events also call to mind Akerman's *Jeanne Dielman*.[2] Disturbing feelings for viewers (and a lack thereof onscreen) haunt this story of a housewife/widow/middle-class prostitute, even though nothing is given away by her face (recall that Jeanne is played by Delphine Seyrig—the same character name, same actress as *Window Shopping*, but eleven years earlier). The Holocaust sits just in the background in *Jeanne Dielman*, with some critics saying that it is evidenced by Jeanne's desire for control and rigidity (fig. C.3). There could be other or different reasons; as is true for every Ak-

C.3. Jeanne Dielman, anxious and alone in her living room. *Jeanne Dielman, 23, quai du Commerce, 1080 Bruxelles* (Chantal Akerman, 1975).

erman film, viewers are not privy to a back-story for any characters, and we only can know what we observe in the film. But the change in orientation experienced by Barbie, and witnessed by viewers, in the aftermath of her onslaught of uncomfortable feelings about death, echo the footsteps laid by *Jeanne Dielman*. We might say, though, that Jeanne is both more fortunate than Barbie (at least she has an orgasm) and less (not having any other Jeannes to talk to).[3]

Passing and surpassing the Bechdel test, Barbie can share her feelings with other Barbies, and they together surmise that her thoughts of death are linked to other horrifying bodily transformations (fig. C.4). Her feet are flat! She is developing cellulite! Barbie is told by her Barbie comrades that she must consult Weird Barbie (Kate McKinnon, with smeared makeup, short hair, and legs often splayed in the splits), from whom Barbie learns that the only way to soothe her discomforting feelings and restore her body to normal is to travel to the Real World to find the girl whose sadness has permeated the membrane between the two worlds. Feeling has been introduced and must be eradicated! In 1975, the anxiety of Akerman's Jeanne led to murder; in 1986 the Jeanne of *Window Shopping* rejects passion to remain safely with her merchant husband in the mall; in 2023, Gerwig will

C.4.   Barbie sharing her anxieties with her comrade Barbies. *Barbie* (Greta Gerwig, 2023).

take Barbie and *Barbie* somewhere else. But we remember the violence of the little girls smashing the heads of their baby dolls against the rocks in *Barbie*'s opening, and we may wonder or worry what feeling can do.

More distressing feelings arise for both Barbie and Ken (Ryan Gosling) as they come into contact with Real World patriarchy. Barbie finds her girl, Sasha (Ariana Greenblatt), but instead of being greeted with gratitude and hugs as she had expected, she is told that Barbies make girls feel bad about themselves and is called a "professional bimbo" and a "fascist." Likewise, Barbie feels shock and disappointment after discovering that Mattel, the "mothership," does not necessarily have her best interests at heart. Playing Mattel's CEO, Will Ferrell leads an all-male board of directors and claims to manufacture and sell Barbies to "empower girls," but then yells at a freedom-seeking Barbie, "Get in the box, you Jezebel!"[4]

Meanwhile, Ken feels enchanted by recognition as "*the* man," "*a* man," *any* man. Attracted to powerful-looking policemen on horses, Ken likens horses to "man extenders" and vows to bring horses *and* patriarchy back to Barbie Land. Too late to stop Ken's coup that changes Barbie Land into Kendom, Barbie arrives back in Barbie Land with Sasha, and Sasha's mom, Gloria (America Ferrera), in tow, the latter who turns out to be the actual feeling culprit whose depression has ruined Barbie Land. Gloria, struggling to accept Sasha's burgeoning independence and rebellion, is an employee at Mattel who has been sketching "weird, dark, and crazy," pictures of "Irrepressible Thoughts of Death Barbie," and "Cellulite Barbie." These Barbie versions surely can't be "good" for anyone, right? The fantasy of being Barbie is flawless *un*feeling, of drinking milk that isn't sour but also isn't there (it's just air); she floats, but she doesn't fly.

The questions surrounding whether or not Barbie and *Barbie* are good or bad for women, or whether the diversity of Barbie Land appropriately represents all of womanhood, all miss the point. Moreover, when critics obsess over whether Gerwig had creative control over the film's content, which (feminist) message(s) she hopes to transmit to viewers, and how those messages will be received, the film's preoccupation with how cultural objects reflect our anxieties and exceed their makers is lost. "You're the creator, don't you control me?" Barbie asks in her encounter with Ruth Handler (Rhea Perlman), creator of Barbie, in the last moments of the film. "I can't control you any more than I can control my daughter," Handler replies. Maybe the fact that Gerwig's artificial worlds foreground our lack of control over our daughters, our cultural products, and our feelings is what makes Barbie so dangerous—to some feminists and antifeminists alike.

In a sense, Will Ferrell might be right to want to put Barbie and her feelings back in her box. They have unleashed chaos! Barbie's feelings, initiated by Gloria's feelings (which permeated the border between the two worlds), have dangerously catapulted Barbie out of her feminist dream utopia (of sorts) and into patriarchy. Having accompanied Barbie to the Real World, Ken's new feelings of pride and hubris have prompted him to introduce patriarchy and co-opt Barbie Land. Besotted by the patriarchy, Ken betrays Barbie by stealing her house, brainwashing her friends, and converting the government to one "of the Kens, by the Kens, and for the Kens." Not even a sweet Mojo Dojo Casa House can squelch Ken's "feelings" hurricane. He sings his worries: "Am I not hot when I'm in my feelings?" The secret is that Ken has had feelings all along, earlier threatening to "beach off" a fellow Ken and throwing himself into a set of plastic waves just to get Barbie's attention and approval. Desperately trying to push away these confusing emotions, which never seem to leave him but just shift contexts, Kendom's anthem becomes the Matchbox Twenty song refrain "I want to push you around, and I will, and I will!"[5]

Barbie has her own feelings anthem, "Closer to Fine" from the Indigo Girls. The lyrics hint at Barbie's willingness to explore her feelings even in a plastic world: "There's more than one answer to these questions, pointing me in a crooked line."[6] Ken cannot accept the "crookedness" of his own, or Barbie's, feelings and flips the binary instead. When Ken announces the change from every night being "Girl's Night," to every night being "Boy's Night," he aggressively confronts Barbie to ask, "How's that feel? It's not fun, is it?" Despondent, in turn, Barbie confronts Gloria: "Why did you wish me into your world using your complicated thoughts and feelings?"

When Kendom is challenged by the Barbies, Ken tries to fight but he starts to cry and admits to Barbie, "It was hard running stuff, I didn't love it." "I don't know who I am without you," he goes on to Barbie. "I was created to be in the warmth of your gaze.... I'm just another blonde guy who can't do flips." Barbie urges Ken to just figure it out, and Ken's response is to try to kiss her, mimicking an old-fashioned romantic dance move. "This isn't the answer!" Barbie admonishes him. Does Ken have actual feelings for Barbie? Or is this performance of heterosexual romance what it looks like when Ken goes on autopilot, playing the part, rather than exploring what it looks like—and feels like—when he decides he is, on his own, "Kenough"? Some have noted that Ken acts like an incel ("involuntary celibate") in the film, taking out his aggression on Barbie after she rejects his advances (Nicholas 2023). In this interpretation, when Barbie apologizes to Ken for hurting his feelings about every night being Girl's Night, she is apologizing to her abuser.

But maybe there is hope for Ken and the Kens, and a different future, after all. A super-stylized dance number, a "dream ballet," is arguably the most beautiful moment of the film. Gerwig says this ballet recalls *Singin' in the Rain* (1952): "There are so many great things in *Singin' in the Rain*, but the dream ballet inside of the dream ballet is one of the most incredible, beautiful, completely unhinged things" (Vicino 2023). This "dream ballet" features all the Kens on a soundstage dressed in black against a turquoise wall and pink striped floor. "The main thing," choreographer Jennifer White says of this number, "was to have the Kens feel like they were allowed to break free of their masculine limitations" (Kourlas 2023). I note here that Gerwig might have also referenced Devon's "Beauty Dance," in Joey Soloway's *I Love Dick*, both in its fantastical, and then its real, iteration, where Devon, inspired by the letters of Chris, teaches the men of Marfa how to reject the rigid plastic of gender norms, and go on a journey toward moving and acting differently (see figures C.5, C.6, and C.7).

In *Sight and Sound*, Hannah McGill argues that the feelings most at the forefront of *Barbie* are "feminist angst": "Not the straightforward kind that is induced by, say, being commanded to smile for a stranger on the street, or apprised of some of the entry-level basics of one's job by a less qualified man—but the gnarly stuff, where the fundamental inequities addressed by

C.5. Kens in the Kendom dance. *Barbie* (Greta Gerwig, 2023).

C.6. *Nowhere* (Dimitris Papaioannou, 2009), which inspires Devon's "Beauty Dance" in *I Love Dick* (Joey Soloway, 2016–17).

C.7. Devon leading the men of Marfa in the "Beauty Dance." *I Love Dick* (Joey Soloway, 2016–17).

the second-wave feminism of the 1960s and 70s jam up against the inter-sectional, sex-positive, consumerist adaptations of the third wave" (2023, 30). Feminist angst is certainly one of a complex mix of feelings invited by the film. Discomfort, dread, ambivalence, cringe, and joy are there, too, and maybe for some the film invites the desire to join with others on a journey to undo the plastic artifice of hierarchy and the violent destruction of dif-ference that have been built up by habit and repetition over time.

The articulation of all these feelings would be a philosophical mouth-ful; although some characters' feelings are expressed in song, none of them announce *this* precise mix of feelings and the ambiguity and contradictions they express. There is one moment in the film, however, when difficult feelings are expressed as speech, and that is when real-world mom Gloria speaks her "truth" about the feelings projected *onto women* by those try-ing to control them (children, men, other women, patriarchy). Doing so, she gives voice to the cognitive dissonance experienced by women in re-sponse to the several roles women are expected to fill and the impossible standards women are expected to meet ("You have to never get old, never be rude, never show off, never be selfish, never fall down, never fail, never show fear, never get out of line"). Several viewers say this speech made them feel *seen*. In the film, hearing the burdens and expectations around being a woman spoken loud and clear wakes Barbies up to the detrimental changes of Kendom, and the Barbies are deprogrammed. But, much like the staging of diversity in Barbie Land as the solution to gender inequality, the consciousness-raising revolution initiated by Gloria to save Barbie Land indulges a liberal fantasy of a "click moment" and promises an easy fix. The idea that women might come to consciousness in one glorious moment and take back Barbie Land *feels good*. These progressive and feel-good fantasies built into the film compete with its campy vibe, artificiality, excessiveness, and the more difficult feelings of plasticity it invites.

One of the moments when difficult feelings are invited occurs near the end of the film when Barbie admits to Handler, "I don't feel like Barbie any-more." Handler warns her that "humans have only one ending" and that they "make things up, like patriarchy, like Barbie, to deal with how uncomfortable it all is, and then we die." Barbie accepts this fate and, holding hands with Handler, is gently coaxed in her transformation: "Close your eyes. Now *feel*." Viewers witness Barbie's feelings as a beautiful video-reel montage of women and girls. The change in aesthetic signals the change in Barbie from plastic to something else. Like the love letters to feminist creativity spliced into *I Love Dick*, this interruption of Barbie's aesthetic by video-reel, home-movie-looking footage is a love letter to women's lives that stages a different kind of intervention, and lingers more hauntingly, than the "click moment" of Gloria's speech. The women and girls in the video reel appear in all kinds of situations and locations, connected in a world whose architecture is shaped by inequalities in gender, race, class, age, ability, nation, and more. The images invite viewer feelings that make us long for connection despite all we know about the antagonisms and discomfort of feminist politics.

Another ambiguous scene unfolds as the film's ending. Driven by Gloria, Sasha, and Sasha's dad to downtown Santa Monica (they park near the landmark statue of Saint Monica, patron saint of mothers, wives, widows, and abuse victims), Barbie gets out of a car and walks into an office wearing not high heels but pink Birkenstocks. The receptionist asks her name—"Handler comma Barbara," she replies—and Barbie then crows, "I'm here to see my gynecologist!" The film ends here, with Barbie's sunny smile, our presumed laughter. Many audience members may have smiled, too, feeling that visiting the gynecologist is just as thrilling as landing a new job, moving to a new city, or (vagina in tow) directing the highest-earning blockbuster film of the summer of 2023! This would be the feel-good interpretation.

But what kind of ending is this? It left me with questions and, frankly, feelings, too. It feels terrifying to have a uterus in today's political climate where women are forced into Midge's "Pregnant Barbie" condition, whether they choose it or not, and transgender folks are targets in culture wars. What will Barbie encounter in the examining room, and why is she there? Barbie is in California, so if she is there to ask that a vagina be created out of her plastic parts, she may well be accommodated. Does she have health insurance? She may be refused, and perhaps reported, in Texas, Florida, South Dakota, and more than half the states in the United States. It is a reminder of our times in which going to a gynecologist can be a gothic experience with many patients surely wondering: will they help me or inform on me?

Barbie leaves us pondering Beauvoir's unanswered query from *The Second Sex*: "What is a woman? '*Tota mulier in utero*: she is a womb,' some say. Yet speaking of certain women, the experts proclaim, 'They are not women,' even though they have a uterus like the others" ([1949] 2011, 3). Beauvoir argues that "it is hard to know any longer if women still exist, if they will always exist, if there should be women at all, what place they hold in this world, what place they should hold" (3). To my mind, Gerwig's film, like Beauvoir's text, refuses to answer the question "what is a woman?" by linking the artificiality of representation to the artifice of gender binaries to the artificiality of prefabricated feeling.

The real hope, the film seems to suggest, is to move beyond both "plastic representation" and the "intimate publics" of female complaint lamented by Lauren Berlant (2008). The former is displayed in Barbie Land's display of diversity, and the latter—a form of "women's culture" of sincerity—circulates via Pepto-Bismol pink girl power, Gloria's speech, and Barbie's happy smiles at the desk of the gynecologist. These feel-good moments and feelings are dangerous. They are forms of feminism easily and readily co-opted by whiteness, capitalism, and neoliberal diversity. But I have suggested there is more to *Barbie* than that, and for these reasons it can be included in a cinema of experience. *Barbie*'s bold artificiality, intense color palette, and camp aesthetics unsettle and remain long after the film ends. Can the discomforting feelings of plasticity invited by *Barbie* move us to seek the kind of existential freedom that only a reckoning with inequality, relationality, and difference can promise? Are we brave enough, willing enough, to feel our feelings, accompany Barbie on this journey, and refuse a plastic destiny?

Postscript: Invitation(s)

invitation: an appeal or request—verbal, written, or aesthetic—to do something, go somewhere, or participate in something, to entertain a change of heart or mind, to join others in a common cause

"Coda in Pink: Plasticity" on Greta Gerwig's *Barbie* (2023), treats the film as a "feminist address," a love letter to feminism, not because of its diverse "plastic representation" of women (Barbie dolls are now diverse and multiple, as well as highly accomplished, as witnessed in the film), its feminist "messaging" (Barbie Land turns patriarchy upside-down, pulses with girl power, and circulates the female complaint), or its ability to meet or exceed the Bechdel rule (the Barbies are always talking to each other, even about revolutionary plans such as overturning Kendom). The most important and potentially transformative feminist element of the film, I suggest, is Gerwig's depiction of plasticity invoked by its camp aesthetic, heightened artificiality, use of color, and Barbie's journey. The plasticity, exchangeability, stereotypicality, and commodity status of Barbie the doll, and *Barbie* the film, not only inspires Weird Barbies, but also weird feelings about Barbie and *Barbie*.

Barbie is the most recent example of a growing archive that I have named a cinema of experience. My examples of feminist film and television depict experiences of ambivalence, stasis, horror, cringe, and plasticity that, in turn, invite and hold the discomforting feelings of viewers. This archive, itself a feminist address, is not just one thing but many: a call that dares to invite feelings and desires heretofore too private, too upsetting, or too inexpressible to say; a holding space where discomforting feelings can be acknowledged; a collection of aesthetic objects around and wherein viewers who learn to feel like feminists can commune and imagine a different world not in the future but inside our own. As I have theorized it here, the cinema of experience might utilize cinematic mechanisms that shift the gaze, create a new aesthetic language, and more fully represent the diversity of people's lives and experiences. But what is distinct and most important for me is that the cinema of experience reorients affective and relational pathways and assemblages (in our heads and in the world) by stirring up unfamiliar and often unwelcome forms of feeling, feelings so buried by habitual gesture and ways of thinking, moving, and reproducing, that they do not rise to the level of consciousness. Attending to feelings lodged beyond discursive knowledge, stylistic and thematic techniques in the cinema of experience push viewers to question our comfort, or acknowledge our discomfort, with familiar and familial attachments, habits, and situations. Though films and television in the cinema of experience initially might make women-identified viewers (and, as we learned from *Barbie*, male-identified viewers, too) feel uncomfortable, they can also make us feel less crazy and certainly less alone.

Audre Lorde's faith in the transformational possibilities of feelings has been a lodestar for me as I have written this book.

> Within living structures defined by profit, by linear power, by institutional dehumanization, our feelings were not meant to survive. Kept around as unavoidable adjuncts or pleasant pastimes, feelings were expected to kneel to thought as women were expected to kneel to men. But women have survived. As poets. And there are no new pains. We have felt them all already. We have hidden that fact in the same place where we have hidden our power. They surface in our dreams, and it is our dreams that point the way to freedom. These dreams are made realizable through our poems that give us the strength and courage to see, to feel, to speak, and to dare. ([1984] 2007, 39)

These dreams are made realizable not only in poetry but also in cinema, a language of dreams and the unconscious. My poet dreamers are Chantal Akerman and Simone de Beauvoir. For me, Akerman's cinematic style and Beauvoir's mode of address are particularly resonant for eliciting and processing the experiences and feelings that help us feel like feminists. How to bring the experience of the marginalized to our (visible, auditory, sensational) attention, and what happens politically when we try to do so, continues to be debated in cinema studies. The cinema of experience is not a way to more fully account for the dizzying varieties of experiences of women-identified subjects or the ways experiences are structured by political and social inequality, although the latter becomes more legible as we reckon with the feelings that the cinema of experience invites.[1] I think of the cinema of experience not as building an archive of better and more accurate representation of women's diverse experiences, but rather as an interpretive and creative method to restore sentience and feeling for viewers whose senses have been dulled by the white noise of patriarchy.[2] It is exemplified by the cinema of Akerman and some contemporary iterations of her lexicon that I have named, and it follows a path indicated by Beauvoir's feminist phenomenological method for exploring and soliciting experiences in *The Second Sex*.

Recall that in 1949, Beauvoir asked "What is a woman?" and she replied in two volumes. The first volume offered responses from male writers, scientists, and thinkers, and the second volume gathered many voices from a vast archive of diaries, gossip, films, plays, poems, novels, and the memoirs of girls and women. While the men offered definitive answers to the question, the experiences of women and girls collectively dismantled the possibility of providing an answer. Readers of volume 2 are invited to listen, see, touch, and taste the worlds of girls and women; to themselves compare, identify, amend, challenge, or refuse. Instead of providing an answer to "What is a woman?," Beauvoir creates a space to feel and think with multiple others in an author/reader community. *The Second Sex* provides neither an answer to what is a woman nor a feminist road map to change the world. What it does offer is a space where experiences and the feelings they elicit are invited, held, and processed. As feminist writer Vivian Gornick so aptly puts it, the publication of *The Second Sex* initiated "an epistolary love affair between Beauvoir and her readers that ended only with her death in 1986" (2020). I have tried to show that this love affair extends far beyond Beauvoir's death and that it takes on new forms in media spaces. For me, Beauvoir's appeal to her readers, her writings on the power of images, her own lifelong love of cinema, and her changing relationship to cinema over many years emerged in new relief as I read her in the company of Akerman's distinctive use of camera, sound, image, and the timing or the extended duration of the cut.

We might say that Akerman's films complement, intensify, and vivify the archive of experiences Beauvoir catalogs, but I also have shown that Akerman's cinematic lexicon is distinctive for the way her films create holding spaces for a different way to experience time, in effect *creating time* to feel like feminists.[3] Akerman's techniques vitalize by making what is familiar seem strange, waking us up to the reality around us. Rather than lull us to sleep with familiar narratives, framing, and pace, they trigger our feelings, demand our active engagement, and spur thinking. They leave us unsatisfied and confused. Experiencing space and time differently—facilitated by duration of scene, fixed camera, silence or disorienting sound, the invitation to boredom, the envelopment of atmosphere and mood, or a surprising explosion of color and song—opens a holding space for us to notice and attend to feelings that we are all too practiced in pushing away.[4] Her techniques alter our mood and our senses, serving to prompt the kinds of conversations and confrontations that help us name, explore, and compare meanings and varieties of experience encountered by woman-identified subjects.

Beauvoir's and Akerman's distinct literary and aesthetic strategies for bringing women's experiences to life have been further enlivened in these pages by the contemporary feminist directors whose art I have also featured. There could have been several more and different choices to include in my cinema of experience! Works of art are multivalent and elicit diverse feelings. My choices reflect my own proclivities and my particular viewing habits, not only my deliberate but also my coincidental encounters with films and the ways certain of them stuck with me. Some of my examples may appear to diverge from what I have identified as Akerman's key techniques. *I May Destroy You*, for example, features a clear narrative structure and story arc that plays out over its twelve episodes, and we are privy to Arabella's consciousness. *I Love Dick* is famous not for durational shots, but for its short interspliced (and unexplained) cuts of feminist media artists within the narrative. *Titane* is the opposite of slow cinema, featuring a pace that sets viewers' pulses racing. Each film or series I have included, however, is theorized as an iteration of Akerman's cinematic lexicon by the use of aesthetic choices that feature the experiences of women and girls in ways that discomfort, prompting the invitation to feel like feminists.

Focusing on camerawork (chapter 1), sound (chapter 2), genre (chapter 3), montage (chapter 4), color and music (the coda), and critical interpretation (throughout), I have explored cinematic tools in an Akerman-inspired feminist film toolbox that frees viewers to feel like feminists. I want to emphasize again that feeling like a feminist does not mean always agreeing, having the same reactions, or sharing the same experiences or historical moment. But it does promise new companions and might beckon new friends and allies, even in surprising times and places. As we learned from *Barbie*, the creator never controls her creations or what viewers might feel in response to them. The feminist filmmaker Lizzie Borden, most famous for her film *Born in Flames* (1983), has talked about how she has found new company by letting go of her films after they are complete. They become something else and are re-created by the people who watch them, taking on a life of their own. Laura Nelson (2023) reports that "Borden describes how she doesn't 'see the film as "mine," but as an "entity" I follow around and observe.' Through this dispossession of her films, she allows audiences to find in them the themes and questions that resonate." Borden adds that although the film doesn't change, "it feels like it changes because [these] new audiences have different feelings, perspectives on it, and so in some ways they possess it" (Nelson 2023).

These holding spaces and this company can reorient our senses such that we might together feel our way to an alternative present tense, to explore and imagine better futures within our current moment. Dedicating her book to "Simone de Beauvoir, who endured," Shulamith Firestone describes the process of finding new comrades with whom to do this work on the first page of *The Dialectic of Sex*: "The first women are fleeing the massacre, and, shaking and tottering, are beginning to find each other. Their first move is careful joint observation, to resensitize a fractured consciousness" ([1970] 2015, 3).[5] Bonnie Honig brings this aspect of Shulamith Firestone's method to the twenty-first century in her collection of essays on "feminist criticism after Trump," called *Shell-Shocked*. Reading George Cukor's *Gaslight* (1944) with the first season of the television series *Stranger Things*, and Toni Morrison's *Home*, Honig says we learn "the importance of fixing on what we know and working from there in concert with others to resensitize senses deadened by domination or disaster" (2021d, 26). While Honig orients us to the details of what we know, I turn our attention to the feelings that we would rather not know.[6]

Near the end of chapter 3, I summed up a few "rules" of feminist film-making—the Bechdel rule, the realism rule, and the diversity rule—that work to dismantle the male gaze and to shift our perspective and our imagination, often in profound ways. The Bechdel rule mandates that there be (at least) two women in a film that speak to each other about something other than men; the realism rule debunks what Beauvoir called the myth of the "eternal feminine" to show the world from the perspective of actual women's (diverse) experiences; and the diversity rule emphasizes the different situations of women to insist that what matters most in feminist film is that marginalized and diverse perspectives be adequately showcased. The Bechdel rule situates the terms and participants of conversation; the diversity rule attends to more aspects of representation to add differently situated and differently embodied interlocutors to the scene; and the realism rule shifts our view from the male gaze to the experience of those who are feminized.

Many of the films and television shows that I collect in this book meet (or exceed) these rules, although there are some exceptions.[7] I have interpreted the realism rule most expansively to ground my contribution about discomforting feelings being the best way to move toward feeling like feminists. Following the path set out by Akerman's motherwork camerawork, discussed in chapter 1, the ways that Akerman utilizes sound in her films to alert us to the white noise of patriarchy, the focus of chapter 2, I expanded and built on the realism rule in chapters 3 and 4 to name "feminist realism" as moving our bodies through horror and cringe to feel our way away from the male sensorium to new vistas, soundscapes, and ways of touching and feeling. The experiences I refer to as feminist realism, we should not forget, are absorbed through senses that are *themselves* the product of a dominant male sensorium. But in the cinema of experience, our interpretation of the evidence gathered by these senses is *transformed by* discomforting feeling held by motherwork camerawork and the sharing of these feelings with others.

Conversations about discomforting feelings might (or might not) happen onscreen but certainly will arrive for viewers over time (if viewers can let them in). They linger, collect, and return to body and mind. Viewers are often surprised to notice the feelings prompted by a cinema of experience, and sometimes they are not ready for them. My students often say that feelings that previously felt individual, pathological (they say "crazy"), or too uncomfortable to acknowledge and must be tucked away, are *made tolerable and even transformed* by feeling with others, even when those "others" are not real-life people, but instead are onscreen characters. Whatever the form those "others" might take, a cinema of experience recognizes that *we need others* to decipher the significance of our own experience, to even know that we had an experience. We need others to notice that experiences exist and that we have feelings about them. Feeling like a feminist is to feel, move, argue, and imagine in a collective.

Looking for resistance, community, for new forms of care, family, and love, my book has put stock in the confusion and discomfort elicited by difficult and unacknowledged feelings in response to experiences evoked by the literary and cinematic techniques I have highlighted here. Further rumination, conversation, and encounter with other readers and viewers—reading the opinions of critics, talking with students in classes, emailing with friends, connecting with strangers on blogs and in chat rooms—can help viewers unpack and work through the feelings that onscreen experiences invite, notice how they compare with our own, and discuss the possibilities they contain. What sometimes happens in my classroom is that students are able to express their feelings of vulnerability, their raw emotions and reactions, so that we can together ponder, reframe, and imagine. At their best, these conversations affirm and nurture our otherwise buried feelings and bring them into a space for conversation. When these miraculous moments unfold in the holding space of my classroom, I feel changes afoot. This is what holding spaces created by text or art, and then nurtured in a conversation, can do.

With my film readings, my intention has been to extend ongoing invitation(s) to the feminist address, an address that is itself a love letter to Akerman and Beauvoir, to their readers and viewers, and to my readers. Selby Wynn Schwartz, the author of the novel *After Sappho*, describes the magic that can occur when an invitation is issued, a response is offered, and new things are said and known. What might spring up from such encounters?

> We arrived in unknown cities, in the port of southern islands, at the houses of anyone appearing to be a sister. We shuddered and threw off our names. We began to find each other, slowly at first because we were so new. You would see someone in the street, someone like X, and wonder and know at the same time. Or there would be a glance like R's, wondering and knowing, rising to meet you on the balcony where you were standing because it was the farthest limit of your father's house. Then we would write our first uncertain letters to each other, hesitant to ask, to tell, with what word, stretched over silences; we took a little false courage in seeing our lines torn and gasping on the page like Sappho's: *to pray for a share/ . . . towards/ . . . out of the unexpected.* Afterwards we sat very still waiting for a response, hoping for a correspondence of fragments. (2022, 44)

Following these leads, eager to answer, and willing to ask, I have tried to open a space where we can together explore what it might feel like to feel like feminists. At the very least, films in a cinema of experience keep us company when we are lonely. The cinema of experience is a feminist address to keep handy. These are places we can go when we need solace, care, inspiration, courage, a space to think and feel with others. But these films also do more! If we let ourselves notice, they also show us ways to *find* others with whom to take the risk of seeing, hearing, and feeling in different ways. Following the feminist address, located within a cinema of experience, we can together gather and move in new configurations these films only now imagine.

Notes

Epigraph source: Definitions are my own, in some cases adapted from the *Oxford English Dictionary*.

I thank Marie-Anne Lescourret, who served as translator and editor for an earlier portion of this introduction published in the essay "Simone de Beauvoir et la rencontre cinématographique," *Cités* 90 (2022): 131–44.

1   Feminist and cultural theorist Sara Ahmed (2010) names these disturbances as feeling like an "affect alien." She says the feminist is blamed for killing the joy of others (as they celebrate family, children, heterosexual romance, and the like), hence her affirmation of the figure of the "feminist killjoy."

2   Marking the dedication in her 1970 book, *The Dialectic of Sex*, "for Simone de Beauvoir, who endured," Shulamith Firestone puts this quite vividly when she says, "The first women are fleeing the massacre, and, shaking and tottering, are beginning to find each other. Their first move is careful joint observation, to resensitize a fractured consciousness. This is painful: no matter how many levels of consciousness one reaches, the problem always goes deeper. It is everywhere" ([1970] 2015, 3).

3   Audre Lorde speaks powerfully about how difficult it is to acknowledge differences between people ("we have all been programmed to respond

to human differences between us with fear and loathing and to handle that difference in one of three ways: ignore it, and if that is not possible, copy it if we think it is dominant, or destroy it if we think it is subordinate") ([1984] 2007, 115). More significant for this context, she also speaks powerfully about how these differences and the way we respond to them have crippled feminism when it becomes apparent that differences between women are relational (and hierarchical): "I speak out of direct and particular anger at an academic conference, and a white woman says, 'Tell me how you feel but don't say it too harshly or I cannot hear you.' But is it my manner that keeps her from hearing, or the threat of a message that her life may change?" (125).

4   See my entry "Feminism" (Marso 2015) in *Encyclopedia of Political Thought*.

5   I struggle a bit here to assign a name to the subjects and viewers who interest me. I say "woman-identified" while also acknowledging that to identify with women may require at least a protofeminist consciousness, a discomfort with cultural norms, or an awareness of the threat of losing bodily autonomy. Complicating things further, were I to say that I am interested in feminist-identified subjects and viewers, I could dispense with "woman-identified," but feminist-identified subjects and viewers assumes an even stronger political commitment. To be feminist-identified, one must be already in solidarity with woman-identified and feminized persons.

6   See my essay (Marso 2010) and other essays in *Perspectives on Politics* 8, no. 1.

7   Feeling often gets conflated with affect, but when distinguished, the latter is categorized as involuntary, preconscious, outside of language. Both affect and feeling are embodied, and I insist that both are also social and political. Ann Cvetkovich's *An Archive of Feelings* (2003) and Victoria Hesford's *Feeling Women's Liberation* (2013) each deal with feelings in the way I am theorizing here, although they focus their attention on different sites. Cvetkovich explores everyday trauma to develop a queer approach that reads oral histories from lesbian activists, writers, and scholars. Hesford focuses on rhetorical strategies of the second wave, by feminists and in the media to argue that the "feminist-as-lesbian" was a persistent "image-memory" of women's liberation. Hesford says this memory has obscured the complexity of the movement, which she discovers by exploring feelings about feminism in films and media texts.

8   In *Feminism in Coalition: Thinking with US Women of Color Feminism* (2022), Liza Taylor shows how very difficult it can be to form feminist coalitions, but argues that Women of Color feminist thought can lead the way. Women of Color feminism is, for Taylor, a theoretical and po-

litical orientation, rather than a race or class designation, although she says it is also important to notice the latter.

9 Feelings of collective joy and shared laughter are explored in my readings of Joey Soloway's *I Love Dick* (2016–17) and Greta Gerwig's *Barbie* (2023). See chapter 4 and the coda.

10 Some have suggested to me that *Legally Blonde* might be positioned as a precursor to *Barbie*. Playing Barbie, Margot Robbie is also often dressed in pink from head to toe, and in the summer the film was released, fans wore pink to the cinema, snapped selfies, and posted them on social media. In the coda, I suggest that a more appropriate precursor to *Barbie* is Chantal Akerman's *Window Shopping* (1986). Staging what Gerwig calls an "authentic artificiality" (Vicino 2023), *Barbie*, like *Window Shopping*, uses color, music, and humor, but still invites uncomfortable feelings for viewers and critics.

11 In *Uncomfortable Television* (2023), Hunter Hargraves uses the modifiers "uncomfortable" and "discomforting" to describe television of the first decade of the twenty-first century. Arguing that "television thus began to normalize discomfort during this time as a strategy of governmentality" (1), he notices that television started to employ discomforting affects at the very moment that neoliberal structures of governance were beginning to dominate in the economic sphere. Hargraves observes that "audiences learned to transform feelings of discomfort to feelings of pleasure," thus attuning capitalist subjects to the discomforting structures of economic precarity characterizing late capitalism (1). I am attracted to the way Hargraves links innovations in television to economic changes in the capitalist economy. Asking what feminist film can do to resist capitalism and patriarchy was a key question for feminist filmmakers and thinkers beginning in the 1970s. Noting that film is most often an ideological apparatus for patriarchy and capitalism sparked conversation about whether and how feminist film might be or become an art form that resists the dominant forces that Hargraves charts in his book. But Hargraves's "uncomfortable television" is not a force for resistance. He characterizes it as exemplified by "unlikeable protagonists, widespread profanity, depictions of graphic violence and explicit sex, and the exploitation of cultural minorities" (2). In my work, I pay less attention to theme, narrative, and character (although these can be important) and more to formal innovations such as "motherwork camerawork," breaking of narrative, jarring use of sound, innovation with genre, and so on to find that stylistic discomfort can be subversive. Akerman's way of creating holding spaces in her films and Beauvoir's attention to the lived existence of woman-identified subjects both, I contend, show us ways to think and act otherwise, and do not turn discomfort with patriarchy

and capitalism into pleasure, *even though*, as Beauvoir always reminds us, there are distinct and specific forms of pleasure (affective and material) to be gained for women who conform to patriarchal norms.

12 Eugenie Brinkema's *The Forms of the Affects* (2014) shows how affects are invited by innovations in form and produced through formal mechanisms. Her interest in affect shows an interest in bodies and feelings and does not explicitly reject phenomenology as a method for reading film, although it is not her method. In Brinkema's later book, *Life-Destroying Diagrams* (2022), however, she explicitly rejects phenomenological interest in embodiment of any sort and is exclusively concerned with the formal features of film. In a recent interview, she says, "Of course I have wept at movies, I have shuddered, and have had embodied reactions; I just don't think these reactions are that interesting. I don't actually think they're speculatively generative; I would be intellectually mortified to produce a kind of diaristic account because I just can't imagine that anyone else would be that interested in what my body does. And I think it's a very strange thing to keep calling certain intellectual positions to account for producing such a record." See also Anger and Jirsa (2019). I engage Brinkema's work in chapters 3 and 4 on the sources of affective impacts of feminist horror and on what counts as cinematic and ontological evidence of women's desire.

13 It is important to notice that Beauvoir's phenomenological method begins not from a "universal" body or consciousness, but from the embodied position of the "other." Turning to Beauvoir to ground my own phenomenological thinking about film supports my position that bodies should not be theorized as universal nor general but always situated. Bodies are always situated through and in relationship to dominant aesthetic and political conceptions of the (white, male, able) body's limits, look, and capacities. In an important critique of the limits of phenomenology *tout court*, Rizvana Bradley argues that phenomenology is unable to "think the black aesthesis which emerges in the *absence* of a body." She writes that "black people have never *had* (which is to say, never had the capacity *to lay claim to*) bodies in the sense presumed by phenomenology" (2021, 37). For Bradley, this is an aesthetic problem, in addition to being a philosophical and political problem, precisely because "it is by means of aesthetic fabrication that [freedom] is sustained as an idea, as an attachment, as a right to be defended" (20).

14 I reacted with joy when I read this news, even though I understand how unfair and arbitrary (at best) and soul-killing, oppressive, and destructive acts of canon formation and rankings of these sorts can be. For the most vivid articulation of the problems of lists, see "Against Lists," by film theorist Elena Gorfinkel (2019). In that essay, she states, "Claiming

aesthetic supremacy begins with the list. Would that we had other ways to create spheres of value altogether, and along with them the capricious and impoverished arbitration of what counts as cinematic art, art worth watching and worth fighting for. The list consolidates as if self-evidence, reasserting in all that it doesn't list, all that its lister failed to learn, to see, to know. Lists are for laundry, not for film. If we wash out our eyes and ears and minds, we will find that what clings to us, after the suds clear, are the tendrils of another cinematic world, of images, spaces, voices, passages, struggles, and time: time recovered from its theft by narcissistic cinephilia's allegiance with capital."

15   Following the release of *Je tu il elle* (1975), Akerman is quoted as saying, "Each time I was asked to present my film in a gay festival, I would say no. I don't want to take part in gay or women's festivals. I don't want to take part in Jewish festivals. I just want to take part in regular festivals." See Cardamenis (2016), in an article announcing a major retrospective of Akerman's films at the Brooklyn Academy of Music following her 2015 death. Cardamenis writes that Akerman's films exceed any category and that *Jeanne Dielman* cannot represent them all. The article contains a great summary of Akerman's major films and concludes this way: "What Chantal Akerman deserves—what any director of a high caliber deserves—is not to be reduced to the films that exemplify a particular tendency, but to receive equal or greater consideration for the works that diverge from, complicate or even reject her most identifiable characteristics. Akerman's films reveal a belief that looking, really *looking*, at something in its entirety—rare is the close-up or insert in a Chantal Akerman film—is a springboard for recognition and understanding. The least we can do is open our eyes to her work as widely as she opened hers to the world."

16   See Fuery (2020). Kelli Fuery defines "empty time" in film as a form of traumatic duration for viewers. This is a "formal aesthetic specific to potential audience emotional experience to time" (209), wherein slow tracking or panning shots, static moments, or lengthier shots create an "in-between time for both the character and the audience" (210).

17   Catherine Fowler (2021) discusses how unfamiliar Delphine Seyrig was with these kinds of tasks, and as a participant in feminist movements, she did not identify with a housewife's work. Yet Seyrig felt "an empathy for Jeanne and the urgency for the protagonist's depiction on screen" (44). Seyrig, Fowler notes, had to be coached through all these tasks. In a television interview she admitted to never having made coffee from scratch. Fowler says, "The lengthy scene on day two in which Jeanne grinds the beans, boils the water and then filters the coffee grounds carefully, so as to refresh her spoilt morning cup, would have required much instruction

and rehearsal for Seyrig" (44). One brilliant example of Seyrig's radical feminism is evident in an essay from 2022 by Ros Murray in *Another Screen*. Writing about Seyrig's collective feminist media work, Murray says the following:

> An extraordinary example of video's capacity to disrupt and reinvent the hegemonic, bland, and watered-down politics of feminism as it was shown on television screens in 1975, *Maso et Miso vont en bateau* concludes by displaying the informal signatures of four women ("Carole," "Delphine," "Ioana," and "Nadja") intent on proving that only video provides the emancipatory tools their politics require. In this video, Carole Roussopoulos, Delphine Seyrig, Ioana Wieder, and Nadja Ringart, collectively known as *Les Muses s'amusent* ("Muses amuse themselves"), take up their proverbial scalpels, using editing as a political tool to cut up men. They edit and rework an existing television program from the same year, inserting images, comments and exasperated interjections. As Seyrig argued, "everyone dreams of responding to the television": this is what they did.

18   Ivone Margulies wrote the first important, brilliant book on Akerman's films and her distinctive style in *Nothing Happens: Chantal Akerman's Hyperrealist Everyday* (1996). I hope my own book will add to a growing body of Akerman scholarship. The work of Marion Schmid, Sandy Flitterman-Lewis, Carol Mavor, Griselda Pollock, Janet Bergstrom, Juliana Bruno, Cyril Béghin, Gwendolyn Foster, Caroline Fowler, Alice Blackhurst, Kate Rennebohm, Joanna Hogg, and Adam Roberts, among several others, has taught me so much, including how to be a sensitive and thinking/feeling viewer of Akerman's films and installations. In addition, many special journal issues and journal articles on Akerman are consulted and cited within my chapters and are listed in the references. I have also enjoyed listening to and learning from Kate Rennebohm and Simon Howell's excellent podcast *The Akerman Year* (2021–23), where they and several guests discuss Akerman's films. I have also found Ara Osterweil's discussion of fleshy bodies in films that otherwise seem cold and distant very relevant for thinking about Akerman's cinema, even though she does not discuss Akerman's films. See Osterweil (2014).

19   Akerman seems to disavow the quest to "know" by making her characters unknowable. Kate Rennebohm (2021) characterizes this as an exploration of skepticism in Akerman's work. In a chapter discussing Akerman's *La captive* (*The Captive*; 2000) in conversation with the philosophy of Stanley Cavell, and in particular his emphasis on skepticism, Rennebohm notices that "[Akerman's] formal depictions of bodies as impassable sites, housing interiorities that can neither be dismissed nor accessed; her narrative depictions of characters struggling to overcome

isolation or their own inexplicabilities; and her regular confrontation of spectators with extended, frontal close-up shots of opaque characters, through which she challenges those spectators to accept or abandon these figures in their unknowability, all speak to her investigations into and expressions of this philosophical problematic [skepticism]" (255). My own reading of *La captive* emphasizes Simon's desire to know and possess Ariane, a trait he shares with Almayer's wanting to control his daughter in Akerman's 2011 *La folie Almayer*, an adaptation of Joseph Conrad's novel *Almayer's Folly* (1895). I conclude in a short *Los Angeles Review of Books* essay on *La captive* (2024b) that, "in Akerman's films, we witness the pathologies of colonial, patriarchal, and racialized ways of knowing as possession, the forms of captivity they create and repro-duce, and how we can do more to transform these with others than we can do alone. Most important, though, and important not to miss, is that her films feature women inhabiting forms and scripts (motherhood, art, music, love, sex, friendship, colonialism, captivity) in new ways."

20 In an essay called "Phenomenology in the Kitchen" (2024c), I read *Jeanne Dielman* with Audrey Diwan's *Happening* (2021) and Lizzie Borden's *Born in Flames* (1983) to explore feeling time like a feminist in these three iconic feminist films.

21 I think here of Akerman's insistence (2004) that she wanted viewers to "feel time passing" as they watch her films: "You know, when most peo-ple go to the movies, the ultimate compliment—for them—is to say, 'We didn't notice the time pass!' With me, you see the time pass. And feel it pass. You also sense that this is the time that leads toward death. There's some of that, I think. And that's why there's so much resistance. I took two hours of someone's life."

22 I return to why and how the detail matters in chapter 1, as I read three of Akerman's films with Roland Barthes's focus on the *punctum*. In a recent book, *Deconstruction, Feminism, Film* (2018), film theorist Sarah Dillon engages the work of Jacques Derrida on the detail to mine his work for a method for reading feminist film. Dillon says close attention to detail is what Derrida calls "metonymic reading" (138). Derrida recommends this particular kind of reading when confronted with a text (visual, written, or otherwise) that does not conform to the logic of narrative to which we are accustomed. The way to do a metonymic reading, according to this explanation, is to focus on the seemingly inconsequential detail in a slow and in-depth way while also moving with "sustained speed across the text" (139). The relationship between the part and the whole, between slow attention and quick understanding, is complex and vexed. How can we resist conjuring the "whole" when putting all the details together? Or, as Derrida would say, how can we avoid spectral logic that compels

that the specter will remain even in the magnification of the detail? I reviewed Dillon's book in Marso (2021).

23   Hunt-Ehrlich spoke at a session of "Combahee Experimental: Black Women's Experimental Flimmaking," a series curated by Tina Campt and Simone Leigh at Princeton University. On October 22, 2020, she and Nuotama Bodomo were the guest interlocutors. See Bodomo et al. 2020.

24   I am not aware of any work to date that situates Akerman's films in explicit conversations about the pedagogical political work of film, nor do I know of work on Akerman that is in conversation with feminist political thought. As a political theorist, I am always in conversation with the literatures of political and feminist theory, and in this book especially, I engage with the work of Lauren Berlant on intimacy and comedy; Saidiya Hartman on fabulation; Bonnie Honig on refusal and feminist criticism; Christina Sharpe and Shawn Michelle Smith on Barthes and the *punctum*; Patricia Hill Collins on Black feminist thought and mothers; Jacqueline Rose on mothers and motherwork; Tina Campt on acoustics in photography; Cressida Heyes on experience at the edge; and Audre Lorde, Victoria Hesford, Sara Ahmed, and Ann Cvetkovich on feeling. I also engage the work of film and media scholars such as Laura Mulvey on the male gaze; Jenny Chamarette, Kelli Fuery, and Vivian Sobchack on phenomenology; bell hooks on the oppositional gaze; Maggie Hennefeld on laughter; Kara Keeling on the image of the Black femme; Rosalind Galt on global cinema; Carol Clover, Linda Williams, Joan Hawkins, Adam Lowenstein, and Alison Pierse on horror/gender/genre; Eugenie Brinkema on form/affect/horror; Rizvana Bradley on attunement and "Black aesthesis"; and Michael Gillespie on "cinematic blackness."

25   Several recent books bring Beauvoir into the study of cinema, and with this book, I am delighted to be in their company. An edited volume by Jean-Pierre Boulé and Ursula Tidd, *Existentialism and Contemporary Cinema* (2012), offers several Beauvoir-inflected film readings. Kate Ince's *The Body and the Screen* (2017) attends to how female subjectivity onscreen exemplifies women's embodiment in writings of Beauvoir, Luce Irigaray, and Christine Battersby. Kelli Fuery's *Ambiguous Cinema: From Simone de Beauvoir to Feminist Film Phenomenology* (2022) highlights the discomforting feeling of ambiguity that arises from formal and narrative choices in exemplary feminist films. Fuery's engagement with Beauvoir's writings and her use of Beauvoir's phenomenological method to study film is closest to my own. She says, "The emotional turbulence that results from ambiguity holds specific significance for a phenomenology of film experience" (2022, 219).

26   I began my entry on *The Second Sex* (Marso 2016b), this way:

Since its publication in 1949, reception of *The Second Sex* has been ambivalent and fraught with emotion. Listen to how Beauvoir describes early response to the book in her 1963 autobiography, *Force of Circumstance*: "Unsatisfied, frigid, priapic, nymphomaniac, lesbian, a hundred times aborted, I was everything, even an unmarried mother. People offered to cure me of my frigidity or to temper my labial appetites; I was promised revelations, in the coarsest terms but in the name of the true, the good and the beautiful, in the name of health and even of poetry, all unworthily trampled underfoot by me." . . . Beauvoir goes on for several pages documenting violent and aggressive reactions to her book.

In an opposing stance, also emotional and deeply ambivalent, Beauvoir was cast as the "mother" of feminism, a label she disavowed in a 1974 interview remarking that "mother-daughter relations are generally catastrophic" . . . and "people don't tend to listen to what their mothers are telling them." . . . Her text has also been called "the feminist bible" even though Beauvoir herself was an atheist. . . . Over half a decade later, the text still solicits powerful reactions. Reviewing the new 2010 translation in the *New York Times*, Francine du Plessix Gray says: "Beauvoir's truly paranoid hostility toward the institutions of marriage and motherhood—another characteristic of early feminism—is so extreme as to be occasionally hilarious." She goes on to say that "pessimism runs through the text like a poisonous river" while reassuring us that Beauvoir did not hate men.

27   It is especially frustrating for readers, I think, that Beauvoir does not name one source, origin, or cause of patriarchal oppression (that can be fixed or opposed) and instead details how patriarchy creates a sensorium that surrounds and permeates everything and everyone. On this point, Davide Panagia (2024) cites my work in which I characterize Beauvoir's account of patriarchy as "a complex assemblage of affects keeping us emotionally, psychically, materially, and bodily captive to the falsely created hierarchy of sexual difference" (118, citing Marso 2017, 24). Panagia calls this a "dispositional power" such that "manner, decorum, and style" are able to "shape personhood by disposing bodies and arranging their movements" (117).

28   In *The Second Sex*, Beauvoir mostly discusses the negative power of images, although as we will see, her view on what cinema's images can do is a touchstone for me as I theorize how they appeal to the viewer's freedom. For a fascinating account of what cinematic images, and in particular the "reconciliation image" can do to redress the violence that is inflicted on difference, see Schoolman (2020). Reading with Adorno and Whitman, Schoolman offers an account of aesthetic education via cinematic images.

29 As Jane Bennett pointed out to me in conversation, the word is apt, as it names a particularly subtle, insidious, and indirect form of causality. Today Laurence would be Yaya (Charlbi Dean) in Ruben Östlund's film *Triangle of Sadness*, which won the 2022 Palme d'Or at Cannes: a beautiful, partially complicit, woman who sells her face and body, and selfies of her staged activities, to generate profit and goodies. One of these goodies is to travel (and work) on a high-end cruise where she has to reckon with the ugliness of wealth in all its gross excesses and absurd inequalities. In Östlund's story, this world is revealed as made literally of shit and vomit. Beauvoir's story is not quite as obvious (or as hard-hitting, or at all bitingly humorous like Östlund's) but they share the same critique of our shared world rife with inequality, alienation, and oppression.

30 Jonathan Kaplan was here reviewing a film that Akerman made on the "making" of *Golden Eighties* that premiered at the New York Film Festival in 1983. See Kruger (1983).

31 Relatedly, Michael Shapiro says Bergman's close-ups signify a collective potential inviting "possible confrontations, expectations, creations" and allowing the viewer to "feel the world differently." See Shapiro (2021, 5).

32 In *Politics with Beauvoir* (2017), I utilized Beauvoir's writings as I analyzed several films, but, like scholars who also engage Beauvoir on film, I did not at that time theorize how Beauvoir's writings themselves are cinematic. What I did notice was that Beauvoir solicits the feelings of readers in the second volume of *The Second Sex*. I have since come to understand Beauvoir's solicitation of feeling via cinematic writing and the unique qualities of film as helping to realize the political potential of feminist film as the invitation of discomforting feelings.

33 Another thing to note about volume 2 of *The Second Sex* is that Beauvoir collects a multitude of experiences of young girls, adolescents, and women as they move through life at every stage, titling the chapters *as if* the experiences are collective even though these experiences happen to each woman as her own. The chapter titles are "Childhood," "The Girl," "Sexual Initiation," "The Lesbian," "The Married Woman," "The Mother," "Social Life," "Prostitutes and Hetaeras," "From Maturity to Old Age," "Woman's Situation and Character," "The Narcissist," "The Mystic," "The Woman in Love," and "The Independent Woman."

34 Beauvoir also emphasizes that women's individual choices and women's collective ability to effect change within the present and for the future are always situated within and influenced by conditions of oppression and the accumulated weight of the past. Beauvoir shows that the time and timing of women's work is often invisible, undervalued, and repetitive; women's freedom is always at risk of being stolen if/as we move toward

female destinies; and a future for feminism can be fought for and won, but it is never easy, predictable, or certain.

35 Women themselves get invested in femininity and take it up by habits and, seemingly, by choice. For an especially compelling and clear examination of why and how women get pleasure from submission across Beauvoir's oeuvre, see Garcia (2021).

36 In Sarah Polley's mesmerizing film *Women Talking* (2022), the women of an isolated religious community explore these options, and viewers come to understand how difficult it is to enact any of these strategies, even though several of the women and their female children have been subjected to sexual abuse for years.

37 Feminist literary scholar Meryl Altman draws our attention to arguments in Beauvoir's work that seem outdated, wrong, or politically incorrect. Altman digs into Beauvoir's recounting of experiences of bad sex, lesbians, and race and class, which makes students cringe. See Altman (2020) and Marso (2023).

38 I am also thinking here of how Fred Moten and Stefano Harvey theorize feeling as moving in community, "a way of feeling through others." What they call "hapticality" is born in the hold of transatlantic slave ships as "a feel for feeling others feeling you." See Moten and Harney (2013, 98). "When Black Shadow sings 'are you feelin' the feelin'?' he is . . . asking about a way of feeling through others, a feel for feeling others feeling you. This is modernity's insurgent feel, its inherited caress, its skin talk, tongue touch, breath speech, hand laugh" (2013, 105). For an excellent overview of Moten's political theory, see Shulman (2020).

39 I appreciate the way Angela Davis (1985) talks about art and politics when she says "progressive art can assist people to learn not only about the objective forces at work in the society in which they live, but also about the intensely social character of their interior lives. Ultimately, it can propel people toward social emancipation." The way I am theorizing the relationship between art and politics, however, does not draw such a straight line of causality.

40 I note here that Laura Mulvey moved from worrying about the positioned passivity of female viewers in 1975 to a more complexly and richly evocative theorization of the role of gender and spectatorship as she discusses technical and social changes in film production and ways of viewing. See Mulvey (1975, 2006).

41 In case it is not already clear, I emphasize again here that there is no "ground" to these experiences, nor any claim that "the personal is political" means that personal experience is a "correct" picture of the world. To claim a space for "experience," as Beauvoir and Akerman do, and as

I do in this book by collecting an archive of cinema that opens these spaces, is to invite multiple and contradictory interpretations and claims.

42   In *Feeling Women's Liberation* (2013), Victoria Hesford keeps her focus on the image of "feminist as lesbian" precisely because of the figure's ability to remain strange. She says the following:

> By reincorporating her [Kate Millet as "feminist as lesbian"] into the ongoing, expansive, and diverse elaboration of a feminist symbolic space, the figure of the feminist-as-lesbian becomes a sign of the possibilities—unrealized as well as realized—of women's liberation. . . . She becomes a sign, for example, of the movement's complex challenge to heterosexuality as a sociocultural institution, a sign of that movement's resistance to the claims of the normal, the mainstream, and the legitimate. . . . She becomes a sign of how, in the early years of the women's liberation movement, a significant collectivity of women became consciously, actively, and visibly strange in relation to the sociocultural norms of their particular moment. (248)

43   Quoted in Smith (1998). Akerman is famous for her "long takes" and slow filmmaking. Mike Shapiro discusses the "'long take style,'" as the Russian film director Andrei Tarkovsky describes it, which "gives the viewer 'an opportunity to live through what is on screen as if it were his own life, to take over the experience imprinted in time on the screen.'" Shapiro adds that "what also happens with long takes is the viewer's ability to 'feel the camera,' as the Italian film director Pier Paolo Pasolini points out" (2021, 4). Beauvoir singles out Pasolini as a filmmaker who "tr[ies] to communicate their vision of the world to me; and mine is enriched if they succeed in doing so" ([1972] 1993, 180). She says:

> This was the case with Pasolini's *Medea*. He answered a question that had worried me—how was it that some civilizations were able to reconcile a high degree of culture with the barbarous rites of human sacrifice? In *Medea* Pasolini brings forward no new evidence. But by means of a great deal of work and by the choice of astonishing landscapes and of [Maria] Callas—an extraordinary actress in this film—he succeeds in re-creating the world of the Sacred. A superb young man is put to death, cut to pieces and devoured before our eyes: the sight is so gravely beautiful that we are not in the least horrified. As she hurries away towards the sea, Medea cuts off her brother's head and throws his quivering flesh behind her chariot; yet the act does not take away from the nobility of her face. Later, when she is set down in rationalistic Greece, Medea loses her magical powers: this second part seemed to me much less successful. (180–81)

I note here, too, that Alice Diop features sections of Pasolini's *Medea* in her *Saint Omer*, discussed in chapter 1.

44 Challenging the early Mulvey and reading Julie Dash's *Daughters of the Dust* (1991) and *Illusions* (1982), bell hooks says Black women take pleasure in film by reading images oppositionally. See hooks (1992), 116. We also might think with Stuart Hall in regard to encoding and decoding. Hall identifies three positions for a reader of the encoded-message media texts: agreement, opposition, and negotiation. The "negotiated" position has the advantage of avoiding the binary of either agreeing or opposing, but it is my understanding of bell hooks that she, too, sees a third way within her oppositional gaze. See Hall (1980).

45 The challenges to "perfect," or even adequate, representation, aesthetic and political, are many. In *Cinema Pessimism* (2019), Joshua Foa Dienstag explores how and why the representative project is so vexed. See his chapter 5 on the *Up* series for an especially fascinating take on how difficult it is to truly represent individuals who themselves are moving, changing, and may not even understand themselves, even over a long period of time. I share Dienstag's pessimism about representation, but his primary worries are about the individual. My worries about representation acknowledge the impossibility of capturing the diversity of women's lives as we recognize how this "diversity" is itself produced through patriarchal, capitalist, extractive, and racist power configurations.

46 Meryl Altman leans into the cringiest responses to Beauvoir's writings from today's perspective in her *Beauvoir in Time* (2020). I reviewed the book for *Simone de Beauvoir Studies*, characterizing it this way: "Altman digs into three recurring aspects of Simone de Beauvoir's thought—bad sex, lesbians, and 'race and class'—which have in recent years been considered embarrassingly 'of her era,' and which remain underdiscussed despite the current renaissance of serious scholarship on Beauvoir. . . . We all know these passages: the ones that make our students say 'we (feminists? women? scholars?) wouldn't (shouldn't?) say that now!,' the ones on which critics focus, the ones that can cause Beauvoir scholars to blush, cringe, or get defensive" (Marso 2022d, 177).

Chapter 1. Motherwork Camerawork: Ambivalence

Epigraph source: Definitions are my own, in some cases adapted from the Oxford English Dictionary.

I thank Cristina Beltrán and Libby Anker for shepherding an earlier iteration of this chapter to publication as "Camerawork as Motherwork," in *theory&event* 24, no. 3 (July 2021): 730–57.

1   Black women's labor—gestational and otherwise—was/is central to ra-
     cialized slavery's logic. Having to constantly confront and navigate state
     and structural violence against their children, Black feminist thinkers
     have long explored forms of violence that use Black bodies for profit and
     the reproduction of slavery, separate mothers from children, and police
     categories such as mother and human to deny the humanity of Black
     women. See Hartman (2008a, 2008b, 2016, 2019), Sharpe (2016), Nash
     (2009), and Collins (1994, 2006).

2   In the patriarchal model, work and family are split by gendered norms,
     and mothers struggle for autonomy in domestic space. But as Patricia
     Hill Collins (1994) notices, this perspective distorts the experience of
     nonwhite women and women in alternative family structures. I distin-
     guish motherwork as defined by Collins, which helps us see specifically
     what Black women do, from care work as defined by Joan Tronto, which
     expands beyond motherwork to how we maintain ourselves as a species.
     Tronto defines care as "a species activity that includes everything we do
     to maintain, continue, and repair our world so that we may live in it as
     well as possible. That world includes our bodies, our selves, and our envi-
     ronment, all of which we seek to interweave in a complex, life-sustaining
     web" (2015, 3). Akerman's motherwork camerawork emphasizes creativ-
     ity and transformation beyond motherwork or carework. It holds our
     discomfort about our captivity to mothers and the labor mothers do,
     makes room for us to feel relational freedom within remarkably unfree
     situations, and gestures to the possibility of transformations in how we
     structure the idea of mothering, who is a "mother," what care looks like,
     and how and toward whom we practice activities of care.

3   I link the words *motherwork* and *camerawork*—ordered both ways, "cam-
     erawork motherwork" and "motherwork camerawork"—to explore the
     method of filming, its effects, and the feelings of ambivalence invited
     by the films I feature in this chapter. Motherwork camerawork creates
     a distancing effect, making us question what we think we know about
     cameras, mothers, and the normative ways of viewing mothers that re-
     sembles and repeats distorted views of mothers. The films make us ask
     whether, how, and if cameras can capture truth; if we know, or can know,
     the truths of our mothers and ourselves. The films also play with space
     and time to see the distortions we reproduce by viewing mothers from
     positions too far and too close to mothers. Supposedly familial and fa-
     miliar, mothers in these films are positioned as distant and strange. The
     idea of the strange at the heart of the idea and experience of mothers
     is also taken up in historical terms by Saidiya Hartman (2008a), who
     reports that the most universal definition of a slave is a stranger, that
     the enslaved and their descendants are cast in a space where *mothers*

are strangers, where the past is figured as traumatic loss. Asking how we might revisit the scene of subjection without replicating the grammar of violence, Hartman "imagines what could have been" and "envisions a free state" that might have emerged from the "infelicitous speech, obscene utterances, and perilous commands" that gave birth to the characters we find in the archive (2008b 6–7).

4   Jennifer Nash notes that "Alice Walker's now-canonical *In Search of Our Mothers' Garden* is a call for 'daughters' to reclaim their mothers' histories of creativity and artistic production." Nash characterizes the book as "a plea for radical Black feminist historiography that sees theory-making and resistance in the quotidian, including quilting, gardening, cooking, and other ordinary practices of survival. . . . For Walker, it is this recovering of 'our mothers'' histories that enables us to connect more fully and deeply with ourselves, to practice the 'womanist' politics the book advocates, one rooted in love, spirituality, and self-regard" (2009, 559). My intervention is less focused on the quotidian, though I note that Akerman *films the quotidian*, most famously in *Jeanne Dielman*, and again in *No Home Movie*.

5   Medea's unmotherly act of murder happens after helping Jason steal the Golden Fleece from her father's kingdom of Colchis, and her escape with Jason and the Argonauts to Corinth. Once there, Jason deserts Medea to marry the daughter of the king, and in response, Medea kills their children. Medea is the ultimate bad mother (no surprise that she is also an immigrant, branded as a barbarian and sorceress). Why Medea kills her children is the interpretive question at the heart of the myth. The mix of feelings stirred by encountering her—awe, sympathy, disgust, condemnation—show the deep well of ambivalence evoked by a mother who departs from the vision of self-sacrifice, care, and unwavering love that is demanded from mothers.

6   Saying this, Rose connects the psychological/existential with the historical/structural. See Beauvoir ([1949] 2011) and Rose (2018). See also Marso (2019).

7   See for example, how Tina Campt discusses the technical, political/social, and subjective conditions that can determine how a photograph is received. In *Listening to Images* (2017), Campt explores what she calls the "lower frequencies" of the quotidian by "listening" to photographs. She recommends what Ariella Azoulay calls "watching" instead of the term "looking," but goes even further by alerting us to sound (which is what Fred Moten does, too, in "Black Mo'nin'" [2003], and which I will turn to in chapter 2). Attending to a range of photos of Black diasporic subjects (including passport photos), Campt asks us to be attentive to how "quiet" registers as a "lower range of intensity" in photos that appear to be mute. See also Azoulay (2008).

8	See Shawn Michelle Smith's chapter, "Race and Reproduction in *Camera Lucida*," in *At the Edge of Sight* (2013). Reviewing Barthes's comments on the James VanDerZee portrait of an African American family from 1926, Smith says, "Barthes's explanation of the studium is laden with a paternal racism that readers are asked to ignore in pursuit of that which really interests him, the punctum. He calls upon the studium as if it is apparent, transparent, as if this lovely formal portrait could not be read in any other way, as if all readers would share his bemused reaction to the image and its subjects" (24). I say more about this in conversation with Akerman's work later in this chapter. Christina Sharpe has taken up Smith's work on Barthes, too, in her *Ordinary Notes* (2023). In a long middle section of this fascinating book of "notes," Sharpe attends to several photos of her own mother and grandmother, points out the *punctum* in each, and criticizes the way Barthes fails to understand how *studium* works (as a "gaze," with "all the ordering structures of white supremacy") and thus "misnames and mis-sees" the *punctum* in the 1926 family photograph of the Osterhouts taken by James VanDerZee (183–84n123).

9	See Mulvey (1975). In the last several decades, there have been diverse and multiple efforts by feminist filmmakers to break this repetition, including Mulvey's own avant-garde films. For a reading of Mulvey's 1977 film, *Riddles of the Sphinx*, a film about motherhood that explores "maternal" camerawork to counter the phallic male gaze, see Liss (2009), 17–21.

10	Of course, technophilia can also be a feminist proclivity. Recall Shulamith Firestone's 1970 utopian wish that technology might save us from biological determinism ([1970] 2015). In spite of Firestone's revolutionary ideas about how to reorganize families and rethink kin beyond patriarchy, her belief in technology as a "fix" failed to fully grapple with the power of patriarchy to harness it, too.

11	As Mateus Araujo (2016, 34) describes, "The mother's answer is spread out, also in voice-over, across five passages of the film, in segments one or two minutes long and at less and less regular intervals, ranging from one to 23 minutes long. These segments of her answer, in turn, are heard over the images of the filmmaker getting closer to the grandmothers, or even going inside their houses, so as to suggest the personal motivation of her quest and to color her meetings with the other women. Everything happens as if her mother's experience functioned as a backdrop for her research about the memories of others."

12	Importantly, this is a shot of Akerman with her back to a baby rather than bent over a baby, such as those examined by Adrianna Cavarero in *Inclinations* (2016). For a reading of this posture (inclination) and its relationship to freedom, see Marso (2018).

13   In *Gendered Frames, Embodied Cameras* (2014), Cybelle H. McFadden explores a subset of French female filmmakers, including Akerman, to argue that they show both their cameras and their bodies onscreen to make their situated ways of seeing explicitly visible. For McFadden, it is especially important that these women filmmakers turn attention to *themselves*, their own bodies, to make a link between their creative vision and their distinctly gendered embodied persons—aging, depressed, working, and so forth.

14   See Haraway ([1984] 1990).

15   Ivone Margulies's *Nothing Happens* (1996) was published prior to the release of *From the Other Side* and *No Home Movie*.

16   In the BFI Film Classics series title on *Jeanne Dielman, 23, quai du Commerce, 1080 Bruxelles* (2021), Catherine Fowler includes illuminating chapters on the collaborative process that went into the making of the film, and on what Delphine Seyrig brought to the process not only with her acting, but also with her feminist political commitments.

17   Steven Jacobs writes, "Only rarely do Akerman's characters feel at home in the household spaces that her camera so extensively and meticulously records.... Benjamin's thesis that the nineteenth century interior, like a cocoon or womb, offers a sense of security, is one that Akerman only rarely seems to illustrate" (2012, 82).

18   Cyril Béghin (2016, 49) elucidates Akerman's techniques:

> Akerman liked to end her films with...long...takes. There is the reverse tracking shot in New York Harbor at the end of *News from Home* (1977), or the one on the road in *Sud* (*South*, 1999); there is Delphine Seyrig tetanized in the living room in *Jeanne Dielman, 23, quai du Commerce, 1080 Bruxelles* (*Jeanne Dielman, 23 Commerce Quay, 1080 Brussels*, 1975) or Stanislas Merhar similarly dazed at the end of *La folie Almayer* (*Almayer's Folly*, 2011). The minimal action gives the viewer time to remember the preceding scenes; the films are recapitulated and condensed at the same time that the fatigue of the projection itself weighs upon the viewer's gaze: the final long take has the duration of a last extended thought in which the blend of fascination and distance, or clarity of consciousness, is at its most intense and inextricable. When a body or a face is the image that is seen, this psychology of the reception of the film is recognized in part as the psychology of the character, and there one reaches the most consistent and mysterious place in Akerman's work, where the aesthetic emotion seems in accord, or in syntony, with a fictional state.

19   This idea is developed in a compelling way in Flitterman-Lewis (2003).

20 See Morgan (2016) for a reading of camera movements that debunks what he calls the "epistemological fantasies" of point of view, that is, a perspective in which as viewers we feel we are moving with a character in a film as the camera moves.

21 For a fascinating discussion of this and other Akerman installations regarding the role of light to project "relational desire" in "imaginative aesthetic atmospheres," see Bruno (2022), chap. 8.

22 Noted in Charlesworth (2017).

23 The truth, of course, is always complicated. The opening lines of Akerman's "autobiography," *My Mother Laughs*, are these: "I wrote all of this and now I no longer like what I've written. It was before, before the broken shoulder, before the heart operation, before the pulmonary embolism, before my sister or my brother-in-law calls so I may say goodbye to her (forever). Before she returns home to Brussels forever. Before she laughs. Before I understand that I might have misunderstood everything. Before I understand that I had only a truncated and imaginary vision. And that I was capable of only that. Not the truth, not of anything even resembling my truth" (2013, 30). Writing about this work, Marion Schmid says, "For Akerman, being truthful is perhaps first of all finding a language away from the beaten track of conventional forms that is supple enough to convey emotion" (2016, 1138).

24 Hartman resorts to this strategy because, as we will see with Barthes, she cannot find the photographs she hopes to find. Originally, she says she "searched for photographs exemplary of the beauty and possibility cultivated in the lives of ordinary Black girls and young women and that stoked dreams of what might be possible if you could escape the house of bondage" (2019, 17).

25 "By advancing a series of speculative arguments and exploiting the capacities of the subjunctive (a grammatical mood that expresses doubts, wishes, and possibilities), in fashioning a narrative, which is based upon archival research, and by that I mean a critical reading of the archive that mimes the figurative dimensions of history, I intended both to tell an impossible story and to amplify the impossibility of its telling" (Hartman 2008b, 11).

26 Bonnie Honig also echoes Hartman in calling fabulation a method of refusal. Honig notes that fabulation refuses the "authority" of the archive by "draw[ing] on empirical examples, texts, or archives that are then elaborated in the service of world-transformations that can only be imagined" (2021b, chap. 3).

27 Trying to put together a life out of observed small details for another "minor figure," Hartman studies a photo of a young Black girl reclining

on an arabesque sofa, staring out at us with dead eyes: "Looking at the photograph, it is easy to mistake her for some other Negress, lump her with all the delinquent girls working Lombard Street and Middle Alley, lose sight of her among the surplus colored women in the city, condemn and pity the child whore. Everyone has a different story to share. Fragments of her life are woven with the stories of girls resembling her and girls nothing like her, stories held together by longing, betrayal, lies, and disappointment. The newspaper article confuses her with another girl, gets her name wrong" (2019, 13).

28   Surrounded by all white men and one white woman, a white border agent says,

> Father we come before you today with pain and sorrow. Our human nature asks you why. I know the answer to that question may never be revealed to us, but we pray for strength, and comfort, Father. I lift up Agent [?]'s family to you. Help them Father with this great loss. I pray also, Father, for all the men and women who protect our borders and interiors in this country. I pray that you will continue to give them strength, wisdom, and fortitude as we step up to the frontlines of this daily war. How long, oh Lord? Will you forget me forever? How long will you hide your face from me? How long must I wrestle with my thoughts and every day have sorrow in my heart? How long will my enemy triumph over me? Look on me and answer oh Lord, my God. Give light to my eyes or I will sleep in death. My enemy will say I have overcome him, and my foes will rejoice when I fall. My heart rejoices in your salvation. I will sing to the Lord for He has been good to me.

29   Of her mother's death in April 2014, a little over a year before the premiere of *No Home Movie*, Akerman says, "Even if I have a home in Paris and sometimes in New York, whenever I was saying I have to go home, it was going to my mother . . . and there is 'no home' anymore, because she isn't there, and when I came the last time, the home was empty" (quoted in Rapold 2015). Drew Daniel (2016) cautions against reading Akerman's suicide backward into her work, to view the body of work solely through the lens of tragedy. He says, "Fraught with this new fact, the knotted cords of her life and work risked taking on the seemingly inevitable lineaments of tragedy, a genre quite at odds with her astringent, sometimes comic vision." I hear this warning, but at the same time I reject the idea, as any good feminist should, that we should treat Akerman's films as having no reference to the life and death to which they are tied.

30   As Max Nelson (2018) notes in a *New York Review of Books* piece that discusses several of Akerman's films,

The daughters in her movies worry about their mothers. ("I've often wanted to kill myself," she wrote matter-of-factly in *Ma mère rit*. "But I told myself I could not do that to my mother. Afterwards, when she's not there anymore.") They steel themselves against pressures to start families and waver about what they owe themselves. In *Tomorrow We Move*, a chain-smoking writer of erotic fiction named Charlotte sets up house with her mother—a Holocaust survivor—in an immense Paris apartment through which several troubled, eccentric secondary characters pass. In an old piece of furniture she finds a diary written in Polish by her maternal grandmother. The words with which it begins—"I am a woman! Therefore I can't express all my feelings, my sorrows, and my thoughts"—come directly from the diary Akerman's own grandmother kept from when she was a teenager until her deportation to Auschwitz.

31   I thank Bonnie Honig for this insight.

32   In an interview with Ivone Margulies (2019), Akerman's film editor, Claire Atherton, with whom Akerman worked closely for thirty years, says that the origin story of *No Home Movie* is "particular": "In April 2014," she says, "we were supposed to work together on an installation based on images she had shot in the desert. And that was when Chantal's mother died" (16). A few weeks later, Akerman mentioned to Atherton that she had been filming her mother for the past two years. From this conversation, the two started to think about whether and how the footage of Akerman's mother could become a film or become part of the current installation on which they were working. And so it happened. Like *From the Other Side*, the first iteration of *No Home Movie* was an installation, this time titled *From the Mother to the Desert*, shown in Jerusalem in 2014. I note here that 2014 was another moment of Intifadah and brutal suppression, and that in June 2014 four Palestinian children (Ismayil Bahar, nine; Aed Bahar, ten; Zacharia Bahar, ten; and Muhammed Bahar, eleven) were killed by an Israeli drone strike on a beach in Gaza, in broad daylight, presumably mistaken for Hamas militants. The crosshairs again, and the violence of naming and acting on what we think we know: "After killing the first boy, the drone operators told investigators, they had sought clarification from their superiors as to how far along the beach, used by civilians, they could pursue the fleeing survivors. Less than a minute later, as the boys ran for their lives, the drone operators decided to launch a second missile, killing three more children, despite never getting an answer to their question" ("Report: Four Boys on Gaza Beach in 2014 Killed by Drone," August 12, 2018, https://imemc.org/article/report-four-boys-on-gaza-beach-in-2014-killed-by-drone/).

33   In her reading of *No Home Movie*, Margulies sees Akerman's embrace of the "directness of the home movie form" as a template for understanding and mapping anew "the intricate relationship of symbiosis and distance" between daughters and their mothers (2016, 63). In this way *No Home Movie*'s aesthetic of "gauzy imperfection" also makes steps toward overcoming what Jacqueline Rose has termed the "deadly template" of the mother's "absolute devotion," the cultural expectation that mothers dedicate themselves completely to their children. See the review of Jacqueline Rose, *Mothers*, in *London Review of Books* 36, no. 12 (June 19, 2014): 17–22.

34   In conversation, Davide Panagia suggested to me that not reproducing the Winter Garden photograph of his mother could be Barthes's way of saving her from becoming an object for others. This is possible. Another way to see this choice is offered by Fred Moten. Moten (2003, 69) reflects on Barthes's unwillingness to show the Winter Garden photograph as compared with Emmett Till's mother's (Ms. Bradley in Moten's text) showing of the photograph of the body of her tortured and murdered son. Moten says,

> So what's the difference between the son's inability to reproduce the photograph of his dead mother and the mother's insistence on the reproduction of the photograph of her dead son? The difference has to do with distinguishable stances toward universality, with what the discovery of a performance or a photograph has to do with universality, with the meaningful and illusory difference and relation between Performance and Performativity, the Photograph and Photography. If "the Winter Garden Photograph was indeed essential, it achieved for [Barthes], utopically, the impossible science of the unique being." This impossible science, the unique and universal word or logos, is achieved only in a kind of solipsism, only in the memory that activates the unique photograph's capacity to wound. Meanwhile, Ms. Bradley sidesteps (by way of an insistent publicity wherein is carried the echo of whistling and mo'nin', in the interest of getting to some other—which is to say real—place) the utopic intersection of hermeneutics, phenomenology, and ontology that mark the origin and limit of Barthes's desire. For Barthes the inability and/ or unwillingness to discover a photograph is driven by the positing of a universality and singularity that can only be mourned; for Ms. Bradley the discovery of a photograph in the fullness of its multiple sensuality moves in the drive for a universality to come, one called by what is in and around the photograph—black mo'nin'.

35   This was the case for me, as I saw the film for the first time at the 2015 New York Film Festival days after her suicide. After the screening of the

film, the audience sat in silence in front of a black screen for what felt like forever but was likely around ten minutes.

36 Joanna Hogg's *Eternal Daughter* (2022) captures this ambivalence via the uncanny. Playing both roles in the film, Tilda Swinton as the filmmaker and daughter desperately tries to capture the memories of Tilda Swinton as mother. The film's setting and mood is gothic horror, and seeing Swinton mirrored in both roles, mother and daughter, each trying to reach the other, makes it all deeply weird and unsettling.

37 While the two primary objects in *No Home Movie* are the camera and the mother, we can notice that domestic objects populate Akerman's films throughout her oeuvre. And here what is important is the laptop, which enables the Skype screen. Akerman's objects typically defy and fulfill our will, thwart and manage desires, and mediate and make possible what we can do and with whom. And they are almost always domesticated, or put to domestic use (like the laptop in these scenes). Indeed, the film itself can be thought of as that *most domestic of objects*, the love letter. It is a conduit for our desire: it circulates, energizes, destabilizes, and produces change, even out of traumatic circumstances.

38 In a review of the film, *Hollywood Reporter* writer Lovia Gyarkye (2022) begins by saying, "The details of the case are grim. On a chilly November day in 2013, Fabienne Kanou surrendered her fifteen-month-old daughter, Adélaïde, to the sea. She chose the shores of Berck-sur-Mer because of its linguistic proximity to impurity: 'Berck' sounded like 'Beurk,' the French word for 'yuck.' Later, when asked by police for her motive, Kanou replied cryptically: 'It was simpler that way.' During her trial in 2016, she attributed her actions to malevolent forces. Nothing in her story made sense, she said. 'Even a stupid person would not do what I did.'"

39 By naming Akerman's films and other feminist films aesthetic objects that can do feminist political work, however, I want to be careful to not undermine their aesthetic integrity or reduce cinematic language and style in the films and television that I treat to their political functions. As mentioned in the introduction, Akerman deliberately chose not to identify as a feminist or queer filmmaker, even though her filmmaking is inarguably feminist, queer, anticolonialist, and often directly engaged with racialized patriarchy and the remains of colonial conquest, the history of chattel slavery, enduring and repetitive trauma experienced by Holocaust survivors and their children and grandchildren, and institutionalized racism. Akerman's feminist and queer commitments are woven through all her films; we will see that again and again in this book. We also see how Akerman's political commitments inform her documentation of the frightful intersections of racism, capitalism, and patriarchy in her filming of the US-Mexico border in *From the Other Side*, for example. We also

see these political commitments at the thematic forefront of two films I do not discuss in this book: *South* (1999), where Akerman's elegiac camerawork achieves its most emotionally disruptive effects via a prolonged tracking shot of the road where James Byrd's body was dragged behind a moving truck in 1998 in Jasper, Texas; and *Almayer's Folly* (2012), her adaptation of the 1895 Joseph Conrad book, which Akerman places in an unnamed, previously colonized, South Asian country, and centers around Nina, the mixed-race daughter of the alienated, impotent, and frustrated Almayer. I discuss *Almayer's Folly* briefly in Marso (2024b) in relationship to *La captive* (2000), Akerman's adaptation of Marcel Proust's *The Captive* (1923), the fifth volume of *In Search of Lost Time*.

40   "I'm also an absolute fan of the films of Frederick Wiseman. The first film of his that I saw when I was a student was *Public Housing*, and I knew that I had to become a documentarian. When I was casting my actresses, I showed them a scene from *Welfare*, the story of Valerie Johnson. It's a long, 40-minute scene showing a Black woman trying to get her documents for housing assistance. I showed this shot to my actresses for the truth in the face of this woman" (quoted in Girish 2022).

41   Wiseman, ninety-two years old, screened his new film, *A Couple*, at the sixtieth annual New York Film Festival in 2022 (where Alice Diop also screened *Saint Omer*) and participated in a New York Film Festival conversation with Diop about the making of documentaries. Relevant to note here is that Wiseman's *A Couple* is scripted from the diaries of Sophia Tolstoy, one of the sources to which Beauvoir returns again and again in the second volume of *The Second Sex*. In *A Couple*, as in *The Second Sex*, a completely different perspective opens up on the characterization of individual genius, the situation and frustrations of housewives and mothers, the naming and sources of what constitutes creative work, the act of creation, and more.

42   In her interview with Yasmina Price (2023), Diop also says,

> What is worse than not being represented is not having a belief that your story is even worth telling. My parents told me little about the lives they left behind because it was, in a way, a story of defeat, and this absence conditioned me and made me enter the world with an enormous fragility. You're left feeling as though what you can tell of yourself, what you can say and who can be, is not legitimate, does not merit being told. And so the films I make repair the way I entered into the world with this false idea that was transmitted by my parents but had been imposed on them through the violence of this colonial system which relegated their own histories to something that was not even deserving of being shared. So finally becoming a filmmaker, centering these stories, narratives, bodies—inventing cine-

matic forms to express everything that hadn't been told for me—is also a psychoanalytic form of repair.

43 As Diop said in her interview with Devika Girish (2022), "It's not entirely my story, but it's not that far from my story either."

44 In an interview with Nicole Brenez (2012), Akerman says the following about how Duras reacted to *Jeanne Dielman*:

> At Cannes, after the screening, the first one up was Marguerite Duras. Right away she tried to dismiss the film. She said that she wouldn't have filmed the murder, she would have made a "chronicle." I don't think she understood anything. She said, "that woman's crazy," so she could relate the character to her own world. I was furious. For me that woman was like all the women I'd known as a child. Were they crazy or was it a way to fight against craziness, anxiety? Marguerite built up airs around herself that she would promote and flaunt nonstop. With Agnès [Varda], we were sometimes competitive, but Agnès is capable of moments of great generosity toward women, where Marguerite was only capable of generosity to men; she loved them madly. It would have been better if I hadn't met her. We spent three months together, since *Jeanne Dielman* and *India Song* came out at the same time and were shown side-by-side at all the festivals. Marguerite was often on the bad side, first during the war, then with the Communist Party . . . but there are these flashes in her work; I went to see *Eden Cinema* (1977) on stage, and it was magnificent. And, deep down, I nevertheless liked her.

45 Claire Mathon is *Saint Omer*'s cinematographer, an artist whose camera-work is also featured in Mati Diop's (no relation to Alice Diop) *Atlantics* (2019), discussed in chapter 2.

46 We might think here, again, with Sandy Flitterman-Lewis's article (2003) aptly titled "What's Behind Her Smile?"

Chapter 2. White Noise: Stasis

Epigraph source: Definitions are my own, in some cases adapted from the *Oxford English Dictionary*.

I thank Jennifer McWeeney and my anonymous reviewers for comments on a version of this chapter published as "White Noise: Promising Young Women and the Noise of Patriarchy," in *Simone de Beauvoir Studies* 34, no. 1 (2022): 39–58.

1 My definition of stasis is influenced by the work of Tina Campt in *Listening to Images* (2017). Campt studies the "affects" of Black women's "stilled

faces and stunning profiles" across an archive of the Black diaspora, locating a "stillness that might suggest thoughtfulness and interiority" (50), but she instead finds stasis. She defines stasis as "tensions produced by holding a complex set of forces in tension" and "unvisible motion held in tense suspension or temporary equilibrium; e.g., vibration" (51).

2   Because Akerman is so attentive to sound in this short (as in all her films) and uses it so deliberately and so strangely, I started to pay attention to sound as a *distinct* sense that affects our experience as viewers and might alert us to the white noise of patriarchy constantly humming in the background. We will see that *Promising Young Woman* and *I May Destroy You* use sound in a more conventional way than does Akerman, and were we not paying attention, the way sound is deployed in these films might go unremarked (although not unfelt). But once our ears are trained by Akerman, we can hear *Promising Young Woman* and *I May Destroy You* differently. I position Akerman's short film in this chapter as alerting us to cues and clues, and sounds and feelings, in more familiar (more narrative) kinds of feminist films where technical interventions might otherwise go unnoticed.

3   For Beauvoir's source, see Balzac ([1829] 1932), 55.

4   For the source of the quote, see Guyot ([1859] 1931). I have always read this sentence as "woman is a *man* stringed instrument," but it is actually "woman is a *many* stringed instrument." I title this section with my misreading, as it better captures how Beauvoir thinks about women's bodies, men's "playing," and "playing with" them.

5   In the first chapter of *The Souls of Black Folk*, "Of Our Spiritual Strivings," W. E. B. Du Bois describes the moment when he first realizes he is seen by others as Black, trapped by what was perceived by white folk as a different and inferior body. For Du Bois, this realization occurs when he was a schoolboy and a young white girl refuses to accept his visiting card. "The exchange was merry, until one girl, a tall newcomer, refused my card,—refused it peremptorily, with a glance. Then it dawned upon me with a certain suddenness that I was different than the others; or like, mayhap, in heart and life and longing, but shut out from their world by a vast veil" ([1903] 2014, 4).

6   As noted in my introduction, Davide Panagia calls Beauvoir's articulation of patriarchy a "dispositional power of domination." For him, it is an account of "domination without sovereignty" that "disposes the right order of things." Panagia includes Beauvoir's way of theorizing patriarchy as an example of the political thinking of sentimental empiricism. Panagia's way of seeing what Beauvoir is doing dovetails with my account of Beauvoir's political thinking, and I find his way of describing

it, as well as rooting it in the tradition of sentimental empiricism, very compelling. See Panagia (2024, 116–17).

7   This short was filmed in Chantal Akerman's own tiny Brussels kitchen. See Bergstrom (2019, 31).

8   Paul Hegarty warns us against speculation about the meaning of this young woman's actions: "We need to exercise caution in thinking about the film as culminating in a suicide that comes about because of alienation.... Signs of this are few and far between, as what we do see and hear are actions of resistance, an undoing of the domestic space" (2017, 157).

9   Marion Schmid, however, deftly reminds us of context: the year is 1968 and the place is Brussels, just a short distance from France where "during a few weeks of utopian euphoria, the dream of a more egalitarian society where men and women, of all social classes, First and Third World, enjoy the same rights and freedoms, seems to have become a genuine possibility" (2010, 17).

10   Akerman's camera does not move with her subjects from their subjective visual perspective. Instead, through intentional manipulation of time and space by camera and sound, she introduces her characters from a physical and emotional distance, and sometimes positions them as only one of many objects in a frame. Holding the frame for a discomforting period of time brings objects that we may not have otherwise noticed into our view, and helps us hear what we otherwise might not.

11   I thank Çiğdem Çıdam for pointing this out to me, as this was her experience of wondering what happened to the sound on her computer.

12   In a private conversation, Morton Schoolman offered a different interpretation from my own, using the language of "harmonics" to characterize the conflicting presence of both white noise and alternative soundscapes in Akerman's short film:

> In music, recall, there is the phenomenon of "harmonics," which may actually serve as a template further illuminating certain multiple shadowy dimensions of the sort you thrust into the light. When the strings of a violin or viola or cello, say, are bowed or plucked in a certain way, the dominant (or dominating) note/tone played (let's call it the fundamental tone) also produces other tones—overtones— which, importantly, are actually independent of one another even though the human ear does not hear the tones in that distinguishable way, but rather hears them together with the fundamental tone as part of a single tonal effect. In the context of your discussion, it seemed to me there may be a tonal effect that included a number of overtones produced by a fundamental tone. The fundamental tone

would be what you described as "white noise"; the overtones, each taken by itself, could then be imagined as responses to the white noise/fundamental tone, which the latter drowns out so that they are not sensible. Hence early on in this section you note the sounds of the train and of construction noise—perhaps a fundamental tone—drowning out other sounds being made by Akerman in her apt. Here, then, harmonically understood, we have at least four layers of sound—(1) a dominating white noise that makes it impossible to perceive other sounds/overtones it produces in response: Akerman barely perceptible as an overtone by the viewer/listener who strains to hear Akerman over the white noise that drowns her out; (2) alienation, the first overtone introduced as Akerman engages in exaggerated housework in a maniacal way; (3) resistance to the white noise as Akerman strains to be heard, her voice taking multiple forms with increasing volume; (4) the explosion, an act of freedom. One thus need not decide among the interpretive possibilities you elaborate, as they are all present as indistinguishable overtones which the film helps us to first become aware of and to then more or less precisely distinguish or differentiate in the evolutionary way you describe. And the argument you make about sound not being synced with the image is right—for the fundamental white noise tone of sound is out of sync with the images of Akerman in her apt. But, from what you have argued, is it also possible that the harmonic overtones produced by the fundamental tone (e.g., situation) gradually and steadily become (re-)synced with the image so that harmonic sounds (overtones) and image illuminate each other (2–4 above)? A re-syncing of sound and image and for disentangling both sound and image from the narrative governed by white noise.

Schoolman's compelling insights here in regard to my reading of Akerman's film echo and build on his work on the reconciliation image in his latest book, *A Democratic Enlightenment: The Reconciliation Image, Aesthetic Education, Possible Politics* (2020).

13   Are we to imagine the hot dog as a penis? In the off-Broadway musical *Teeth*, which played at the Playwrights Horizon Theater in New York City in the spring of 2024, playwrights Michael R. Jackson and Anna J. Jacobs imagine their "promise keeper" young heroine, Dawn O' Keefe, as having teeth inside her vagina. When she is fondled by her stepbrother at the age of seven, when her boyfriend date rapes her, when she gets assaulted by a gynecologist, and when she is unknowingly filmed having sex by a boy whom she thought was a friend, her vaginal teeth activate and bite off the fingers or penis of the offender.

14   For commentary on this film as pedagogy, see Honig (2021c).

15   Watching this film in the summer of 2021, it is impossible not to think about Britney Spears, another promising young woman whose freedom and promise were stolen for years. See Farrow and Tolentino (2021).

16   Cressida J. Heyes reminds us that sexual assaults while unconscious or drugged "reinforce a victim's lack of agency and expose her body in ways that make it especially difficult for her to reconstitute herself as a subject" (2020, 56). Arabella's reconstitution is also well characterized by Honig's description of feminist criticism in concert with others: following details, piecing together, weaving a *new* cloth, which, as Honig (2021d) notices, is much like what Penelope does.

17   This ending is beautiful; however, from another view it is unsatisfying because the racial dynamics (a Black woman raped by a white man) seem to recede in favor of a solution of individualist process of working-through, in this case made possible because of Black sociality and networks of friendship.

18   Jennifer McWeeney noticed that this dedication echoes that of Beauvoir to her dear friend (known as Zaza) in *Inseparable*: "If I have tears in my eyes tonight, is it because you have died, or rather because I'm the one who is still alive? I should dedicate this story to you: but I know that you are nowhere now, and that I am speaking to you through literary artfulness" (Beauvoir 2021, dedication "To Zaza").

19   Here I think of Lida Maxwell's "Queer/Love/Bird Extinction" (2017). Maxwell reads the letters between Rachel Carson and Dorothy Freeman in which they depict their love as a multispecies achievement enabled by their love of birds.

20   Hartman tells us that while there was a mix of white and Black girls, the Black girls were "more likely to be punished and to be punished more harshly" (2019, 265).

21   In a wonderful afterword to his book *The Democratic Sublime*, Jason Frank reads the photographs of Glenn Lignon, a contemporary artist working in the Black radical tradition, alongside the work of Jacques Rancière and Saidiya Hartman as an occasion for "listening more attentively to the 'politics of the lower frequencies'" (2021, 195).

22   Brown reminds us that Bergson "uses the metaphor of music to explain the nature of consciousness and time, matter, and memory" (2021, 9), quoting his observation: "In this way twenty different broadcasting stations throw out simultaneously twenty different concerts which coexist without any of them intermingling its sounds with the music of another, each one being heard, complete and alone, in the apparatus which has chosen for its reception the wave-length of that particular station" (Bergson ([1934] 2007, 62).

Chapter 3. Genre Trouble: Horror

Epigraph source: Definitions are my own, in some cases adapted from the Oxford English Dictionary.

Portions of this chapter originally appeared in "Feeling Like a Feminist with Audrey Diwan's 'Happening,'" *Los Angeles Review of Books*, June 30, 2022, https://lareviewofbooks.org/article/feeling-like-a-feminist-with-audrey-diwans-happening/; and "How Do You Solve a Problem Like 'Titane'?," *Los Angeles Review of Books*, February 18, 2022, https://lareviewofbooks.org/article/how-do-you-solve-a-problem-like-titane/.

1   Linda Williams names pornography, horror, and melodrama as "body genres" that are known for "seemingly gratuitous excess" mostly because the body feelings and reactions of viewers mimic what is happening on-screen. See Williams (1991). This mimicking is not necessarily the case for Diop's *Atlantics* or Ducournau's *Titane*, but it is often the case in Diwan's *Happening*.

2   Ducournau is only the second woman to win this honor, with Jane Campion being the first, with *The Piano* in 1993.

3   In my overview of Coppola's oeuvre in the *Los Angeles Review of Books*, I appreciate her ability to create gorgeous images and her attention to gender dynamics, for example, in *Priscilla* (2023). I notice how Elvis's masculine aesthetic completely envelops and traps Priscilla's, thus turning her "dream come true" into a nightmare. I worry, however, that Coppola's girly aesthetic gets trapped by "nostalgia for a dead and deadening white life ... promising beauty and (false) power." See Marso (2024a).

4   Given the accusations that Greta Gerwig's *Barbie* (2023) is a mere vehicle for product placement, I note that these acclaimed directors take part in this series, also clearly organized around product placement.

5   See the discussion by Neyat Yohannes on the Mubi website: https://mubi.com/notebook/posts/isolation-cinema-s-latest-addition-close-up-on-mati-diop-s-in-my-room, and view the film here: https://www.youtube.com/watch?v=q2Bd77yfvNM.

6   *Bande de filles* (*Girlhood*; 2014), directed by Céline Sciamma, and *Mignonnes* (*Cuties*; 2020), directed by Maïmouna Doucouré, are exceptions to this trend of focusing on male characters. Young immigrant women are featured in *Girlhood*, and young immigrant girls in *Cuties*, but the location is France, not Senegal. Each film is about girls/young women in the *banlieue*, finding other girls/young women with whom to connect and explore; each features remarkable, even luminous, moments of collective girlhood joy expressed through bodily moments (sports

and dance). Both films, however, have attracted intense criticism, for different reasons. Sciamma has recently said of *Girlhood* that she would have made different choices were she making the film today: "For me, it's really simple. If people you consider political allies are telling you, 'This is not helping the revolution. This is even slowing the revolution,' then they're right. That's it." Although well received by mainstream critics, the film was disappointing to Black feminist critics due to its stereotypes—abusive brother, absent father, silent mother, and Mariame, the central character, becomes a drug runner. Sciamma goes so far as to say her first three films were collaborating with cinema and with patriarchy, but now she does things differently. See Batuman (2022). *Cuties*, in contrast, attracted criticism for sexualizing the young girls depicted in the film (Fathia Youssouf, the main actress playing a French Senegalese Muslim girl, was fourteen when the film was made, but her character was eleven), who are encouraged by social media to act in hypersexualized ways. Doucouré has defended the film in print and in interviews, arguing that she wanted to start a conversation about the sexualization of young girls. See Doucouré (2020).

7 See Galt's 2022 essay about *Atlantics* for "reflections on what anticolonial aesthetics could look like today, for the generation of Black diasporic filmmakers who have inherited both the histories of Third Cinema in Africa and assimilationism and its refusal in Europe." In her earlier (and related) study of the significance of the appearance of a female vampire, or the "pontianak," in Malay cinema, Galt says the pontianak makes apparent "a space of lively contestation in postcolonial culture," in which "injustices both past and present are animated in horrifying form." The young women of *Atlantics*, possessed by the wronged young men, signify the "painful inheritances of a familial and national history" (Galt 2021, 1, 12).

8 We could think with Bonnie Honig and see their actions as refusal. Challenging conventional readings of the *Bacchae* in *A Feminist Theory of Refusal* (2021b), Honig shows us that the bacchants' collective refusal to work and reproduce the patriarchal hierarchies of Pentheus's Thebes is less the doing of Dionysus and can instead be read as an unknowing collective remaking by women who refuse.

9 The question of the "real" (what is real, and to whom? what makes experience verifiable and believable under conditions of racialized patriarchy?) is explored in my discussion of the use of fabulation in Akerman's Mexico-US border film, *From the Other Side* (chapter 1) and, from another perspective, in Catherine Breillat's film *Romance* where the "fantastical" experience of women is documented (chapter 4).

10 Diop (2019), at minute 48.

11 Diop (2019), at minute 49.

12 Mathon (2019). Mathon also shot Céline Sciamma's gorgeous *Portrait de la jeune fille en feu* (*Portrait of a Lady on Fire*; 2019).

13 For an interesting essay on how the music enhances and sets the different moods of *Atlantics*, see Spielberg (2024). He says, for example: "Al Qadiri's use of the Guitaret and its pervasive timbre establishes the unusual, impossible-to-emulate mood of *Atlantics*: both organic and electronic, brightened tones and darkened moods. It's a little otherworldly. 'I didn't want to make a folk score,' she explains. 'Even though I was born in Dakar, I didn't feel like a Senegalese folk score was right for me to make, you know?' Fittingly, Al Qadiri uses virtual instruments, so the sound that eventually makes it into *Atlantics* is a digital recreation of an electronic version of the folk instrument."

14 Tracing an arc of refusal in Euripides's *Bacchae*, Bonnie Honig insists that the bacchants complete the arc by returning to the city to fundamentally change it. See Honig 2021b.

15 In *Shimmering Images: Trans Cinema, Embodiment, and the Aesthetics of Change* (2019), Eliza Steinbock follows Barthes's writing on the shimmer to trace a shimmering affectivity that denotes something that is emergent, affective, and processual. Steinbock often calls the shimmer "twinkling," and although in *Shimmering Images* the focus is on trans-cinema, I think the emphasis on shimmer is appropriate for the transformations occurring in several images of *Atlantics*, for example when Issa morphs to Souleiman and the two blend with Ada. I call the image of the ocean "shimmering" here, too, as it defies any ontology as just one thing. Diop's work with color and camera and music to affect a kind of shimmering seems, to me, to complement the "transsexual logic of cinematic embodiment" explored by Steinbock.

16 See Sandy Flitterman-Lewis's excellent chapter on *Vagabond* (1990: 285–315). In addition to charting how the film restructures relations of desire "both *in* the text (desire of its characters) and *for* the text (desire of its viewers)" (285), Flitterman-Lewis also brings our attention to Varda's genre-bending form that blends "fictional construct with documentary research in a unique articulation which defies traditional categorization" (286).

17 While viewing this film at New York City's IFC Center, an older man behind me breathed heavily and uncomfortably in an otherwise utterly quiet theater, his gasps and breaths mixing with Anne's.

18 See Galt and van der Zaag (2022) for a wonderful reading of *Raw* that addresses the racializing logic of white feminism that they detect in the film.

19 Of *Trouble Every Day*'s heroine, Sophie Monks Kaufman says this: "Coré is a caged beast made spectacular by the full bloom of her savage desire."

"She is governed by the supernova intensity of each passing moment. She is out of range of moral teachings, but still connected to her conscience. To me, she is extremity itself; a symbol for our most antisocial sexual tendencies, whatever they may be. . . . Coré is irretrievably lost in the present; more vivid than anyone else, and more dangerous" (Baughan 2022).

20 In *All Said and Done*, Beauvoir admits, "I rarely take pleasure in watching documentaries. They batter me with pieces of knowledge, quite divorced from any context, at times when I have no wish to absorb them" ([1972] 1993, 190).

21 Joey Soloway, who directed *I Love Dick*, has changed their name, but the other directors of the film and television I interpret in this book all identify as women.

22 Brinkema on this question: "The root of radical is radix, it means the root, the same that Martin Hägglund talks about in relation to radical atheism; so what is the root of formal thinking? What kind of roots could it offer for speculative questions?" (Anger and Jirsa 2019, 73).

23 I find Brinkema's attention to close reading, and to form in particular, inspirational as I attend to formal aspects in my film readings, in this chapter specifically in regard to how these films experiment with the genre of horror. But Brinkema's disinterest in reception is, to my mind, not well suited to feminism. Brinkema would certainly agree. She would not want to close down her readings by political imperatives. I also worry that her insistence on form can become an insistence on expertise for film study. I am also interested in form, narrative, and cinematic technique as I notice how each invites discomforting feelings that appeal to the feminist feelings of viewers. Whether woman-identified or not, my films invite audiences on a journey of becoming with the possibility that many more will be feminist-identified upon the close of the film. And for these reasons, Clover's attention to the complications of affect and of gender in traditional horror has been especially instructive for me. Although she doesn't frame her contribution this way, I would argue that Clover is also interested in how and who might be cinematically invited to feel like a feminist. The older man who sat behind me at a screening of *Happening* (see note 17 above) and breathed along with Anne during the intense abortion scene in (what I assume was) empathy for her pain and situation reminds me of Clover's adolescent boys who cheer on the "final girl" in slasher films.

Chapter 4. Epistolary Archive: Cringe

Epigraph source: Definitions are my own, in some cases adapted from the *Oxford English Dictionary*.

I thank Mary Caputi at *Politics and Gender*, where a much earlier version of this chapter was published. See "Feminist Cringe Comedy: Dear Dick, the Joke Is on You," *Politics and Gender* 15, no. 1(2019): 107–29.

1   Both *Romance* and *I Love Dick* stage body politics. They challenge our too-easy, too-comfortable assumptions about female sexual desire, whether from the perspective that it should be celebrated (sex-positive) or hidden (protected, saved from violation). The two examples ask, instead, what happens when we see women's sexual desire onscreen in ways that veer from norms that dictate women's desire must be tastefully, correctly, nonpornographically staged, and how it makes us feel when we see, hear, and experience desire expressed from the perspective of feminist realism.

2   Interested in the politics of women's joy, cinema scholar Maggie Hennefeld explores how women's laughter was depicted as dangerous and even deadly in obituaries published between 1870 and 1920. The invention of cinema, however, made it possible for women to laugh in public. In an article titled "Death from Laughter, Female Hysteria, and Early Cinema" (2016), Hennefeld says that symptoms of the laughing hysterical woman were calmed by the hysterical laughter invited by early cinema's technologically enhanced shape-shifting images of bodies doing incredible things. Hennefeld says the "rise of motion pictures—an entertainment form, a social institution, and a technological apparatus devoted to the visual representation of physical automatisms—[is] a salve to the gendered crosscurrents between female hysteria and hysterical laughter" (70).

3   See Ahmed (2010) and Mehra (2017).

4   Lauren Berlant and Sianne Ngai suggest that "comedy helps us test or figure out what it means to say 'us'" (2017, 235). Linda Mizejewski's *Pretty/ Funny* demonstrates that women's comedy has become a primary site where "feminism speaks, talks back, and is contested" (2014, 6). She notes, "In the historic binary of 'pretty' versus 'funny,' women comics, no matter what they look like, have been located in opposition to 'pretty,' enabling them to engage in a transgressive comedy grounded in the female body—its looks, its race and sexuality, and its relationships to ideal versions of femininity" (2014, 5). Today's female comedians, such as Phoebe Waller-Bridge, Janelle James, and Diona Reasonover—like their predecessors Sarah Silverman, Tina Fey, Ali Wong, Jessica Wil-

liams, and Lena Dunham, to name only a few—unabashedly employ the "subversive force of feminist humor" (Willet and Willet 2013, 16) to make "disruptive spectacle(s)" of themselves (Karlyn 1995, 31). They eagerly abandon constraints for modeling positive behavior and they refuse to buttress and perpetuate erotic attraction to toned, white, slender bodies on the part of viewers. Feminist visual culture that departs from "positive" representation by refusing the use of inspiring role models and predictably progressive narratives is sometimes controversially received by feminist (and other) critics, even though pitched as an appeal to woman-identified viewers, and even as it has recently gained a more enthusiastic audience with innovative shows such as *Fleabag*. Podcasts and comedic television series with central female roles achieve comedic impact through the use of both irony and candor as they model body diversity and explore sexual shame. They share humiliating (and what some would deem politically incorrect, inappropriate, or tawdry) stories and situations with the audience and each other. Ali Wong was an innovator of this genre when she paraded her very pregnant body on stage in her Netflix special *Baby Cobra* in 2016. Undermining public goals of feminism and evoking sexist stereotypes simultaneously, she proudly announced that she tricked her boyfriend into marrying her so that she won't have to work. She doesn't want to "lean in," she says; she wants to "lie down!" Some in the audience cringe (even as they laugh) due to Wong's wordplay with racial and gender stereotypes, her scatological body humor, and her deliberate political incorrectness. Feminists in particular cringe because we wonder whether we *should* be laughing. What is the effect of Wong's performance on female audiences, and the political upshot for feminism? While feminists may well criticize the corporate capitalist advice to "lean in" (Sandberg 2013), Ali Wong says women should be housewives so they can shit in their own toilets. All the while, Ali Wong is standing up, visibly pregnant, and *working*.

5   Letters can play an important role in constituting communities, mediating their desires and aspirations, and imagining new ways of being. See Kathy Ferguson's *Letterpress Revolution: The Politics of Anarchist Print Culture* (2023), in particular the chapter "Epistolarity," for a fascinating account of the role of letters in turn-of-the-century American anarchist visions and politics.

6   Arguing against a "realist aesthetics that casts racial blackness in over-ridingly 'positive' terms," Phillip Brian Harper (2015, 2) stakes a claim against realism and for abstractionist aesthetics in African American art. But I argue that an antirepresentational aesthetics can still be considered a form of realism and, in this case, one of feminism's realisms. Expanding the definition of realism as I do in this chapter (and in chapter 3 on hor-

ror) by introducing a conception of "feminist realism" can expand our sense of what realism is and what it can do in cinema or television. Feminist cringe comedies that are a form of feminist realism do not privilege a representational aesthetics, that is, that all women must be represented or accounted for (race, class, ability, age, sexuality), and that women must be represented as role models. Their "feminist realism" stems from their dismissal of male fantasies about sex in favor of a willingness to show female struggle, masochism, degradation, and other bad and ugly feelings and situations in a humorous way. Eschewing representation that seeks to perpetuate "positive" models, cringe comedies are never ethical or preachy (we know how to feel when we see this kind of film or series, and any discomfort is quickly assuaged). A key component of the feminist cringe comedy is that it never takes itself too seriously, and does not present its characters in a positive light.

7   Much like the "women's weepy," or the female melodrama, cultural products that are marketed specifically to female audiences are frequently belittled. One prominent case is Anthony Lane's review (2008) of the first *Sex and the City* movie in the *New Yorker*, which was accompanied by a degrading and overwrought caricature of the four actresses in the film with wide ugly mouths. The caption reads: "Superannuated fantasy posing as a slice of modern life." Lane's review drips with misogyny disguised as sarcasm. He concludes that "all the film lacks is a subtitle: 'The Lying, the Bitch, and the Wardrobe.'" This review shows that the legitimacy or veracity (the realism) of female fantasies and the credibility of woman-identified viewers is undermined by critics who do not see the sex as real, who deem it narcissistic or politically incorrect, or who are ashamed or undone by their own (and other's) laughter. How should we account for this kind of resistance to these filmic texts? I concur with the idea that we should encourage more politics and less narcissism in the realm of feminist aesthetics. But labeling the products of women artists and auteurs as extreme, fantastical, narcissist, or individualist is, in most cases, a way to dismiss their work too easily. Never changing his tune, Lane also dismissed Greta Gerwig's *Barbie* with the comments, "Watching the first half hour of this movie is like being waterboarded with Pepto-Bismol," and "What we have here in short, under layers of stylization, is a standard-issue journey of discovery" (2023). I suspect these kinds of critiques are themselves symptoms to analyze. Are such criticisms linked to the cultural invisibility of female desire and an unwillingness to see women's desires (and feminist cinema) as attractive, smart, legitimate, or real?

8   What a female or feminist fantasy looks like is itself a loaded question, often mired in debates between sex-positive and sex-negative feminisms.

See Lorna Bracewell's *Why We Lost the Sex Wars* (2021) for a comprehensive and corrective account of the feminist sex wars that occurred primarily in the United States, but more broadly in Anglo countries, from the mid-1970s to the early 1990s. Bracewell notes that these wars were also known as "the lesbian sex wars, the feminist sexuality debates, and most reductively, the porn wars" (5). One thing her book does is expertly debunk what she calls the "catfight narrative" (5) between anti-porn and sex-radical sides, restoring not only the ambiguity and reach of each perspective but also the radicalism. She demonstrates how both were appropriated by liberal discourse and laments that, even though each side was far more revolutionary than we seem to remember, neither adequately or fully addressed the criticisms and perspectives of women of color and Third World feminist counterparts. I reviewed Bracewell's book in *Perspectives on Politics* (Marso 2022a) and participated in an exchange initiated by the book in *Contemporary Political Theory* (Marso 2022b). As I talk about sex in *Romance* and *I Love Dick*, I am less interested in the history of feminist perspectives on whether we can locate and name female desire, and more interested in what a visual representation of female fantasies, whether explicitly or controversially feminist or not, makes possible in regard to the feelings of woman-identified viewers.

9   See Marso (2017), chap. 2, "(Re)Encountering *The Second Sex*," for a reading of volume 1 that explores how male fantasies and anxieties shape the "scientific" field of biology, as well as history, literature, art, and religion.

10   At the Edinburgh Film Festival, it is reported by Peter Bradshaw (1999) of the *Guardian*, "At one stage, Breillat suggested censorship was basically a male urge and that the X certificate was related in some subconscious cultural way to the female chromosome. 'Fuck off!' shouted one man, and walked out."

11   See MacKinnon (1989). "A theory of sexuality becomes feminist to the extent it treats sexuality as a social construct of male power: defined by men, forced on women, and constitutive in the meaning of gender. Such an approach centers feminism on the perspective of the subordination of women to men as it identifies sex—that is, the sexuality of dominance and submission—as crucial, as a fundamental, as on some level definitive, in that process" (316).

12   In her review of Breillat's most recent film, *L'Été dernier* (*Last Summer*; 2023), Ela Bittencourt (2024) explores Breillat's relationship to feminism:

> "Feminists do not love me. My own position is that a woman must be a militant feminist in life, but when she is making a work of art, things are different," Catherine Breillat told Ginette Vincendeau in *Monthly Film Bulletin* back in 1989, promoting her early film *36 Fillette*, known in the UK as *Virgin*. "Real life is confused. As a feminist

artist, it is difficult to take responsibility for feelings such as unease, confusion, shame, self-destruction, sado-masochism—all these are human feelings you can claim as an individual, but as a feminist they are obviously not the ones you can easily highlight."

13   But film theorist Liz Constable notices that in *Romance*, Breillat "embeds her cinematic representations of women's sexual subjectivity in a network of other representations of women as sexual subjects seen and interpreted by male directors: Jean-Luc Godard's *Le Mepris* (1963) [*Contempt*], Nagisa Oshima's *Ai No Corrida* (1976) [*In the Realm of the Senses*], and Pedro Almodovar's *Matador* (1985)" (2004, 684). On Breillat and New French Extremism, see also Wilson (2002), Ince (2006), Gorton (2007), Wheatley (2010), Angelo (2010), Young (2018), McGillvray (2020), and Baughan (2022).

14   Jane Bennett disrupts our expectations of *knowing* where things might land by invoking the words of Walt Whitman on "landing": "the press of my foot to the earth springs a hundred affections" (2020, 112).

15   Soloway's television series is inspired by, and loosely based on, the feminist classic *I Love Dick*, written by Chris Kraus and published in 1997 by Semiotext(e), the publishing house founded by French literary theorist and cultural critic Sylvère Lotringer. Kraus and Lotringer's relationship, chronicled in the book, is the model for Soloway's television version.

16   This scene reminds me of the *Saturday Night Live* opening skit from September 13, 2008, when Tina Fey played Sarah Palin and Amy Poehler played Hillary Clinton. One especially funny line is Palin (Fey) saying that anyone can be president; all you have to do is "want it." Clinton (Poehler) says, "Yeah, Sarah, looking back, if I could change one thing, I probably should have wanted it more."

17   Chris's economic and social situation is that of an approaching-middle-age white woman who finds her aesthetic, sexual, and romantic ambitions at a dead end. Her sudden and surprising lust for Dick inspires her to try to live a more satisfying sexual and artistic life.

18   Brinkema remarks on "Breillat's distinctive honour of having been the first to bring an erect male penis to mainstream cinema with *Romance*" (2006, 149).

19   Recall Brinkema's characterization of *Romance*'s Marie: "Marie is a wild explosive droplet of scarlet, like a menstrual stain, just waiting to erupt all over the purified space that she inhabits" (2006, 150).

20   In Ali Wong's second Netflix special, *Hard Knock Wife* (2018), she is pregnant again, but ironically does not mention it in a routine filled with talk of female bodies and their desires. At one point she speaks about a hookup she had to interrupt to admit that she had her period.

Her partner, she reports, said "Oh! Well, then let's make a fuckin' mess, Ali!" "To this day, that was the most romantic thing anybody has ever said to me!" she exclaims.

21 I note that Dick, Sylvère, and Paul are not stereotypical patriarchs. These men are not Donald Trump, they are not Harvey Weinstein: they would not make openly sexist comments to women, tweet about women's bodies, or deny them promotions when their desires are refused. The sexier, softer, new age cowboy, academic, and metrosexual patriarchal style of these men turns out to be oh-so-constrictive nonetheless. A better future cannot be forged just by making men better lovers or more benevolent patriarchs. Instead, each woman has to "tell the story of the *economy of her libido*" (Irigaray [1974] 1985, 43). Noticing how the women characters tell the story of the economy of their libido is not the same, however, as documenting the "ontological realism of the image" (Brinkema 2006, 152). I insist that the look of wet female desire is as untrustworthy as the money shot. There is no truth to the body, just as there is no truth in the image. Feminist realism draws our attention to how images are constructed, drawing us to see the lies, not the truth, of the so-called real. And yet I advocate a return to the body and to women's desires.

22 This is a great version of Derrida's purloined letter, as J. Hillis Miller discusses it in "Derrida's *Destinerrance*" (2006). As Miller explains, "for [Derrida], a letter may always fail to reach its destination. This means that it never really reaches its destination. Here is Derrida's careful formulation of the letter's destiny to wander and to err: 'La divisibilité de la lettre [. . .] est ce qui hasarde et egare sans retour garanti la restance de quoi que ce soit: une lettre n'arrive *pas toujours* à destination et, dès lors que cela appartient à sa structure, on peut dire qu'elle n'y arrive jamais vraiment, que quand elle arrive, son pouvoir-ne-pas-arriver la tourmente d'une derive interne' (Derrida, *La Carte postale* 517)" (Miller 2006, 897).

23 Not coincidentally, *I Love Dick* had an all-women writers' room.

24 In a recent *New Yorker* article about the filmmaker Céline Sciamma, Elif Batuman (2022) reports, "It was revelatory, Sciamma explained, to learn that her own grandmother had first been 'struck by female desire—by her own desire,' not just in a movie theatre but 'in front of a film made by a woman.' Carla had been a 'woman really connected to her own desire,' and there was no doubt in Sciamma's mind that this early encounter at the cinema had been formative: 'the female gaze saved that little girl.'"

25 Discussing Domietta Torlasco's video essay "Philosophy in the Kitchen," Olivia Landry and Christinia Landry (2019) read Torlasco's essay, and video essays more generally, with their use of interwoven and contrapuntal editing, in a way that I would characterize as "love letters" to viewers. Landry and Landry quote Eve Kosofsky Sedgwick as "formulat[ing] the

beside as a spatial positionality that embraces a wide range of relations: 'desiring, identifying, representing, repelling, paralleling, differentiating, rivaling, leaning, twisting, mimicking, withdrawing, attracting, aggressing, warping' (Sedgwick 2003, 8)" (461, emphasis added).

26   This doesn't mean that Bardot's liberated sexuality won't lead to a queer world, but it is not a sure bet, and there is nothing itself radical about exposé or publicity of sex.

27   Remembering what Jane Bennett says about the unpredictability of where things might land and when, I think also of a personal anecdote within one of Meryl Altman's chapters in *Beauvoir in Time* (2020), "Simone de Beauvoir and Lesbian Lived Experience." She says that in 1981 she was coming out, and when first reading *The Second Sex*, she "totally hated it." The parts she hated the most were about lesbian sex and in particular the chapter "The Lesbian" (85). But she returns to this text, and others where Beauvoir explores lesbian sex, such as *She Came to Stay*, as the same person at a different time and the work lands differently: "This may be a good time to look again. Beauvoir's view that lesbian lives may be lived in many ways, that gender 'inversion' and object choice are not necessarily related but sometimes may be, does not look so retrograde in this age of 'queer,' of the revaluation of bisexuality, of new transgender possibilities and subjectivities" (86). Let's remember, too, that Chris's desire "lands" in the space of Devon's and Toby's queer desire. And though their desire is sexual, it is more than that, too; it is marshaled as a creative energy that changes everything.

28   See Altman's chapter in *Beauvoir in Time* (2020), "Beauvoir and Blackness," where Altman situates Beauvoir between Richard Wright and Frantz Fanon, and the United States and Europe, weaving a path through surrealism via the influence of surrealist poet Michel Leiris. French Surrealists have a complex relationship to Blackness as they address themes that touch on anti-Black racism, anticolonial politics, "Negrophilia," fetishism, aestheticism, and representation. Altman deftly presents the international dynamics of intellectual, artistic, and political encounters between the French Left, surrealism, the French colonies, and Jim Crow America, highlighting criticisms of Beauvoir as too willing to exoticize or culturally appropriate Blackness.

29   We might think about Beauvoir's inability to see race in this scene with the way Mark Reinhardt (2017) says the optical unconscious of photography and film often captures things we do not see in everyday life.

30   Young (2018) reads the racialized bodies in this scene similarly by concluding that the scene makes the specter of French colonialism visible and "betrays the racial (racist) structure that subtends that imaginary" (33).

Coda in Pink: Plasticity

Epigraph source: Definitions are my own, in some cases adapted from the Oxford English Dictionary.

Portions of this chapter originally appeared in "Feeling Like a Barbie: On Greta Gerwig and Chantal Akerman," *Los Angeles Review of Books*, August 18, 2023, https://lareviewofbooks.org/article/feeling-like-a-barbie-on-greta-gerwig-and-chantal-akerman/.

1   In a review of Rothko's *The Artist's Reality* (written in 1940-41, published in 2006), Maria Popova (2015) quotes Rothko on plasticity:

> In painting, plasticity is achieved by a sensation of movement both into the canvas and out from the space anterior to the surface of the canvas. Actually, the artist invites the spectator to take a journey within the realm of the canvas. The spectator must move with the artist's shapes in and out, under and above, diagonally and horizontally; he must curve around spheres, pass through tunnels, glide down inclines, at times perform an aerial feat of flying from point to point, attracted by some irresistible magnet across space, entering into mysterious recesses—and, if the painting is felicitous, do so at varying and related intervals. This journey is the skeleton, the framework of the idea. In itself it must be sufficiently interesting, robust, and invigorating. That the artist will have the spectator pause at certain points and will regale him with especial seductions at others is an additional factor helping to maintain interest. In fact, the journey might not be undertaken at all were it not for the promise of these especial favors.... It is these movements that constitute the special essentialness of the plastic experience. Without taking the journey, the spectator has really missed the essential experience of the picture.

2   I discuss *Jeanne Dielman* in the introduction and in chapter 1.

3   In my "Perverse Protests," building on the work of Sianne Ngai (2007), I read Jeanne's feelings as "ugly," arising out of situations where agency is blocked. Putting Ngai in conversation with Beauvoir, I noted that "women's frequent experiences of melancholy, narcissism, anxiety, shame, resentment, paranoia, and jealousy enhance patriarchal structures and ideologies and substantially contribute to the obstruction of women's individual and collective political agency.... Nevertheless, these same behaviors and bodily pathologies also potentially signal dissent, or at the very least discomfort, with the way things are.... Rather than deny or demean negative emotions, their somatic expressions, and women's assigned structural location and tasks, Beauvoir studies them carefully to think about the ways they might be read as, and harnessed for, pro-

test and disruption" (Marso 2016a, 880–81). One problem for Jeanne is her inability to compare her feelings to others, and to learn about the meanings, significance, and political importance of her experiences in shared spaces. For me, in this book, those shared spaces can be found in film. They elicit our discomfort, and can trigger our distress, but also open a shared space for comparison, processing, and politics.

4   Writing in the September 2023 issue of *Sight and Sound*, Hannah McGill remarks, "It seems a slightly nervous move on the filmmakers' part to have enlisted the American comic Will Ferrell to play the boss of Mattell.... Ferrell's shtick from *Elf* (2003) to *Anchorman* (2004) to *The Lego Movie* (2014) is investing male archetypes with disarming, dorky energy; his practiced lovability declaws whatever critique *Barbie* may have for its parent company." But if we remember the "good guy" played by Bo Burnham in Emerald Fennell's *Promising Young Woman*, we view "good guys" like Will Ferrell with skepticism.

5   Lyrics from "Push," released on Matchbox Twenty's album *Yourself or Someone Like You* (1996).

6   Lyrics from "Closer to Fine," released on the album *Indigo Girls* (1989).

Postscript: Invitation(s)

Epigraph source: Definitions are my own, in some cases adapted from the *Oxford English Dictionary*.

1   Women actors show emotion in mainstream film and television, and woman-identified viewers might also respond to these actors and films with emotion. The feelings depicted and invited, however, have most often accorded with the narrow range available to women who have been lulled to sleep by the white noise of racialized patriarchy. I happily admit that the enervating effects of media are changing, and changing quite quickly with the addition of many, many new feminist directors of film and television. Moreover, as feminist interpreters investigate film history, new perspectives on old films arrive, and sometimes old films show themselves to be more subversive than we knew. In a review of "Cinema's First Nasty Women," a four-disc Kino Lorber box with short comic films made from 1898 to 1926 (released in 2022 and compiled by Maggie Hennefeld, Laura Horak, and Elif Rongen-Kaynakçi), Mahnola Dargis (2022b) notes that during this time, "women ran wild in movies.... [T]hey riotously schemed, fought and defied convention, racing and laughing their way to liberation—or something like it."

2   I appreciate how Michael Boyce Gillespie says that what he calls "cinematic blackness" is not encompassed by the requirements of the Black

director, Black cast, and Black audience. In *Film Blackness: American Cinema and the Idea of Black Film*, Gillespie specifies that "Black film does not and cannot satisfy identitarian fantasies of black ontologies" (2016, 7). Like Darby English in *How to See a Work of Art in Total Darkness* (2010), Gillespie seeks to move beyond the politics of identity and representation. Breaking "the belief in black film's indexical tie to the black lifeworld" (2), and foregoing "veracity critiques" (4), Gillespie reads Blackness not as the *truth of experience* but as creative process. I build on his work here in rejecting better representation, and more accurate portrayals, as the most important things feminist film can do.

3 Informed by Black feminist abolitionist thinkers, Jasmine Syedullah calls these kinds of spaces "congregations" and she sees such a space enacted in Julie Dash's *Daughters of the Dust*: "Beginning with 'the silence that you can't understand' requires sitting with another ontology of utterance, naming, and meaning-making, as Julie Dash's 1991 *Daughters of the Dust* reminds us, one where the past is prologue time and again" (2022, 110).

4 Carol Mavor likens the experience of time in Marcel Proust's *In Search of Lost Time* to the way time is experienced watching *Jeanne Dielman*. Mavor calls it "time told queerly . . . where days become years and years become days" (2007, 402). Yet another way to think of "time told queerly" is as a kind of Sabbath space. Judith Shulewitz (2011) writes about glimpses of a different order of time in Sabbath spaces. Shulewitz talks about Sabbath (Shabbat) as an act of creation that makes something extraordinary out of the ordinary, dramatically shifting our experience of time. This idea of time outside of time resonates very strongly with the way Akerman creates holding spaces in her films that make us experience the ordinary as strange, and that allow us the space and time to hold, confront, and ultimately to share the discomforting feelings that I argue are central to feeling like a feminist. Akerman's *Histories d'Amérique* (1988) is her most "Jewish" of films in subject matter as it is about the Jewish-American diaspora experience, shot in vacant lots in Brooklyn, but "Jewishness" is also captured in a film like *Jeanne Dielman*, which Akerman herself said was inspired by watching her mother and aunts do housework with the same rigor and precision that are required for Jewish rituals. On this point, Ivone Margulies says this: "Channeling the memory of chants heard at the synagogue into her modernist art, Akerman has said that what 'interests me in dialogue is that it rounds up with rhythm, a psalmody where the sentences don't make sense.' Infused with her fondness for rituals—domestic, Jewish—her lines accrue meaning nevertheless" (2009). And here, finally, is Akerman talking about the rituals of Shabbat (quoted in Brenez 2012):

I wanted my mother to keep the Sabbath, to light the candles; it came from the death of my father's father (my mother's father died in the camps), the man who had accepted me as a girl. At his death, I was still little; they took me out of Jewish school overnight, and it was a shock, since it broke off another connection to my grandfather. To keep the Sabbath, for me, meant reviving my ties with this man who had accepted me as a girl. It's a really beautiful ritual, powerful and even philosophical when you grasp it. The idea of the ritual has to do with the passage from animal to human. According to the dietary rules, you have to know what's a milk-product, or product of other foods, you have to think before eating. I like that idea. I don't keep kosher, but at least I know the basics. I know why you can't eat shellfish: because they never fully developed.

5   I cited this passage in Firestone's *Dialectic of Sex* in note 2 of my introduction in reference to how upsetting it can be to acquire a feminist consciousness.

6   Namwali Serpell quotes literary critic Rita Felski's relationship to aesthetic objects in *Uses of Literature* (2008) as blending "analysis and attachment, criticism and love" (Serpell 2015, 23). I identify with this description of my own relationship to the films I include in my cinema of experience.

7   Akerman's films feature only white women, and thus always fail the diversity rule, and several of my films fail or barely pass the Bechdel rule. In *Titane*, Alexia never reaches out to other women, and she unflinchingly kills a female lover. Breillat's *Romance* fails the Bechdel test, as does Akerman's *Blow Up My Town*. *Jeanne Dielman* barely passes, or maybe it fails. There is an instance where Jeanne talks to an unseen neighbor behind her barely open door about which is the best cut of meat to buy at the butcher shop, but since this woman is unseen and she is unnamed, it likely fails.

Filmography

Readings

Akerman, Chantal. 1968. *Saute ma ville (Blow Up My Town)*.
Akerman, Chantal. 1975. *Jeanne Dielman, 23, quai du Commerce, 1080 Bruxelles*.
Akerman, Chantal. 2002. *De l'autre côté (From the Other Side)*.
Akerman, Chantal. 2015. *No Home Movie*.
Breillat, Catherine. 1999. *Romance*.
Coel, Michaela. 2020. *I May Destroy You*.
Diop, Alice. 2022. *Saint Omer*.
Diop, Mati. 2019. *Atlantique (Atlantics)*.
Diwan, Audrey. 2021. *L'Événement (Happening)*.
Ducournau, Julia. 2021. *Titane*.
Fennell, Emerald. 2020. *Promising Young Woman*.
Gerwig, Greta. 2023. *Barbie*.
Soloway, Joey. 2016–17. *I Love Dick*.

Referenced

Akerman, Chantal. 1975. *Je tu il elle*.
Akerman, Chantal. 1977. *News from Home*.
Akerman, Chantal. 1980. *Dis-moi (Tell Me)*.
Akerman, Chantal. 1986. *Golden Eighties* (aka *Window Shopping*).
Akerman, Chantal. 1988. *Histoires d'Amérique: Food, Family, and Philosophy*.

Akerman, Chantal. 1999. *Sud* (*South*).

Akerman, Chantal. 2000. *La captive* (*The Captive*).

Akerman, Chantal. 2011. *La folie Almayer* (*Almayer's Folly*).

Borden, Lizzie. 1983. *Born in Flames*.

Breillat, Catherine. 1976. *Une vraie jeune fille* (*A Real Young Girl*).

Breillat, Catherine. 2023. *L'Été dernier* (*Last Summer*).

Campion, Jane. 1993. *The Piano*.

Coppola, Sofia. 1999. *The Virgin Suicides*.

Coppola, Sofia. 2023. *Priscilla*.

Dash, Julie. 1982. *Illusions*.

Dash, Julie. 1991. *Daughters of the Dust*.

Demy, Jacques. 1964. *Les parapluies de Cherbourg* (*The Umbrellas of Cherbourg*).

Denis, Claire. 2001. *Sangre caníbal* (*Trouble Every Day*).

Denis, Claire. 2008. *35 Rhums* (*35 Shots of Rum*).

Diop. Alice. 2020. *Nous* (*We*).

Diop, Mati. 2020. *In My Room*.

Doucouré, Maïmouna. 2020. *Mignonnes* (*Cuties*).

Ducournau, Julia. 2017. *Grave* (*Raw*).

Hitchcock, Alfred. 1958. *Vertigo*.

Hittman, Eliza. 2020. *Never Rarely Sometimes Always*.

Hogg, Joanna. 2022. *The Eternal Daughter*.

King, Don Roy, and others. September 13, 2008. *Saturday Night Live*.

Kelly, Gene, and Stanley Donen. 1952. *Singin' in the Rain*.

Kubrick, Stanley. 1968. *2001: A Space Odyssey*.

Lanzmann, Claude. 1985. *Shoah*.

Lichtenstein, Mitchell. 2007. *Teeth*.

Luketic, Robert. 2001. *Legally Blonde*.

Mambéty, Djibril Diop. 1973. *Touki Bouki*.

Mulvey, Laura. 1977. *Riddles of the Sphinx*.

Östlund, Ruben, 2022. *Triangle of Sadness*.

Pasolini, Paolo. 1969. *Medea*.

Polley, Sarah. 2022. *Women Talking*.

Resnais, Alain. 1956. *Nuit et brouillard* (*Night and Fog*).

Resnais, Alain. 1959. *Hiroshima, Mon Amour*.

Sciamma, Céline. 2014. *Bande de filles* (*Girlhood*).

Sciamma, Céline. 2019. *Portrait de la jeune fille en feu* (*Portrait of a Lady on Fire*).

Uman, Naomi. 1999. *Removed*.

Vadim, Roger. 1956. *Et Dieu... créa la femme* (*And God Created Woman*).

Varda, Agnès. 1976. *Daguerréotypes*.

Varda, Agnès. 1985. *Sans toit ni loi* (*Vagabond*).

Vertov, Dziga. 1929. *Man with a Movie Camera*.

Waller-Bridge, Phoebe. 2016. *Fleabag.*
Welles, Orson. 1941. *Citizen Kane.*
Wiseman, Frederick. 2022. *A Couple.*
Wong, Ali. 2016. *Baby Cobra.*
Wong, Ali. 2018. *Hard Knock Wife.*

References

Ahmed, Sara. 2010. *The Promise of Happiness*. Durham, NC: Duke University Press.

Akerman, Chantal. 1983. "Getting Ready for the Golden Eighties: A Conversation with Chantal Akerman." *Artforum*. https://www.artforum.com/print/198306/getting-ready-for-the-golden-eighties-a-conversation-with-chantal-akerman-35484.

Akerman, Chantal. 2004. "In Her Own Time: An Interview with Chantal Akerman." *Artforum*. https://www.artforum.com/print/200404/in-her-own-time-an-interview-with-chantal-akerman-6572.

Akerman, Chantal. 2013. *My Mother Laughs*. New York: Song Cave.

Altman, Meryl. 2020. *Beauvoir in Time*. Leiden: Brill.

Angelo, Adrienne. 2010. "Sexual Cartographies: Mapping Subjectivity in the Cinema of Catherine Breillat." *Journal for Cultural Research* 14, no. 1: 43–55.

Anger, Jiří, and Tomáš Jirsa. 2019. "We Never Took Deconstruction Seriously Enough (on Affects, Formalism, and Film Theory): An Interview with Eugenie Brinkema." *Iluminace* 31, no. 1: 65–85. https://www.iluminace.cz/pdfs/ilu/2019/01/06.pdf.

Araujo, Mateus. 2016. "Chantal Akerman, Between the Mother and the World." *Film Quarterly* 70, no. 1: 32–38.

Azoulay, Ariella. 2008. *The Civil Contract of Photography*. Cambridge, MA: MIT Press.

Backman Rogers, Anna. 2019. *Sofia Coppola: The Politics of Visual Pleasure*. New York: Berghahn.

Bal, Mieke. 2013. *Thinking in Film*. London: Bloomsbury.

Balzac, Honoré de. [1829] 1932. *The Physiology of Marriage*. Translated by Manuel Komroff. New York: Liveright.

Barasch, Alex. 2023. "After 'Barbie,' Mattel Is Raiding Its Entire Toybox." *New Yorker*, July 2. https://www.newyorker.com/magazine/2023/07/10/after-barbie-mattel-is-raiding-its-entire-toybox.

Barthes, Roland. 1980. *Camera Lucida*. Translated by Richard Howard. New York: Hill and Wang.

Batuman, Elif. 2022. "Céline Sciamma's Quest for a New Feminist Grammar of Cinema." *New Yorker*, January 31. https://www.newyorker.com/magazine/2022/02/07/celine-sciammas-quest-for-a-new-feminist-grammar-of-cinema.

Baughan, Nikki. 2022. "Pleasures and Pains of the Flesh: Women, Physical Autonomy and the New French Extremity." British Film Institute, May 17. https://www.bfi.org.uk/features/pleasures-pain-new-french-extremity.

Beauvoir, Simone de. [1949] 2011. *The Second Sex*. Translated by Constance Borde and Sheila Malovany-Chevallier. New York: Vintage.

Beauvoir, Simone de. [1954] 1999. *America Day by Day*. Translated by Carol Cosman. Berkeley: University of California Press.

Beauvoir, Simone de. [1959] 2015. "Brigitte Bardot and the Lolita Syndrome." In *Simone de Beauvoir: Feminist Writings*, edited by Margaret A. Simons and MaryBeth Timmermann, 114–25. Urbana: University of Illinois Press.

Beauvoir, Simone de. [1965] 2011. "What Can Literature Do?" In *Simone de Beauvoir: "The Useless Mouths" and Other Literary Writings*, edited by Margaret A. Simons and Marybeth Timmermann, 197–209. Urbana: University of Illinois Press.

Beauvoir, Simone de. [1966] 1968. *Les belles images*. Translated by Patrick O'Brian. New York: G. P. Putnam's Sons.

Beauvoir, Simone de. [1972] 1993. *All Said and Done*. Translated by Patrick O'Brian. New York: Paragon.

Beauvoir, Simone de. 1985. "Preface." In *Shoah: The Complete Text to the Acclaimed Holocaust Film* by Claude Lanzmann, iii–vi. New York: Da Capo.

Beauvoir, Simone de. 2021. *Inseparable*. Translated by Sandra Smith. New York: HarperCollins.

Bechdel, Alison. 1986. *Dykes to Watch Out For, #1*. Ithaca, NY: Firebrand Books.

Bechdel, Alison. 2008. *The Essential Dykes to Watch Out For*. Boston: Houghton Mifflin.

Béghin, Cyril. 2016. "The Long Take, Mastery." *Film Quarterly* 70, no. 1: 48–53.

Bennett, Jane. 2020. *Influx and Efflux: Writing up with Walt Whitman*. Durham, NC: Duke University Press.

Bergson, Henri. [1934] 2007. *The Creative Mind: An Introduction to Metaphysics*. Translated by Mabelle L. Andison. Mineola, NY: Dover.

Bergstrom, Janet. 2019. "With Chantal in New York in the 1970s: An Interview with Babette Mangolte." *Camera Obscura* 100, no. 34: 31–57.

Berlant, Lauren, ed. 2000. *Intimacy*. Chicago: University of Chicago Press.

Berlant, Lauren. 2008. *The Female Complaint: The Unfinished Business of Sentimentality in American Culture*. Durham, NC: Duke University Press.

Berlant, Lauren. 2011. *Cruel Optimism*. Durham, NC: Duke University Press.

Berlant, Lauren, and Sianne Ngai. 2017. "Comedy Has Issues." *Critical Inquiry* 43: 233–49.

Bittencourt, Ela. 2024. "*Last Summer*: Catherine Breillat's Most Heartbreaking Film to Date." *Sight and Sound*, April 19. https://www.bfi.org.uk/sight-and-sound /reviews/last-summer-catherine-breillats-most-heartbreaking-film-date.

Blackhurst, Alice. 2021. *Luxury, Sensation and the Moving Image*. Oxford: Legenda, Modern Humanities Research Association.

Bodomo, Nuotama, Madeleine Hunt-Ehrlich, Tina Campt, and Simone Leigh. 2020. "Combahee Experimental: Black Women's Experimental Filmmaking [October 22, 2020]." Combahee Experimental: Conversation Video Replay, Lewis Center for the Arts, Princeton University, October 26. https://arts.princeton .edu/news/2020/10/combahee-experimental-conversation-video-replay/.

Boulé, Jean-Pierre, and Ursula Tidd, eds. 2012. *Existentialism and Contemporary Cinema: A Beauvoirian Perspective*. New York: Berghahn.

Bracewell, Lorna. 2021. *Why We Lost the Sex Wars: Sexual Freedom in the #MeToo Era*. Minneapolis: University of Minnesota Press.

Bradley, Rizvana. 2021. "On Black Aesthesis." *Diacritics* 49, no. 4: 20–52.

Bradshaw, Peter. 1999. Review of *Romance*. *Guardian*, August 28. https://www .theguardian.com/film/1999/aug/28/edinburghfilmfestival.festivals.

Brenez, Nicole. 2012. "Chantal Akerman: The Pajama Interview." *LOLA*, no. 2. http://www.lolajournal.com/2/pajama.html.

Brinkema, Eugenie. 2006. "Celluoid Is Sticky: Sex, Death, Materiality, Metaphysics (in Some Films by Catherine Breillat)." *Women: A Cultural Review* 17, no. 2: 147–70.

Brinkema, Eugenie. 2014. *The Forms of the Affects*. Durham, NC: Duke University Press.

Brinkema, Eugenie. 2022. *Life-Destroying Diagrams*. Durham, NC: Duke University Press.

Brown, Jayna. 2021. *Black Utopias: Speculative Life and the Music of Other Worlds*. Durham, NC: Duke University Press.

Bruno, Juliana. 2019. "In Memory of Chantal Akerman: Passages through Time and Space." In *Chantal Akerman Afterlives*, edited by Marion Schmid and Emma Wilson, 7–12. Oxford: Legenda, Modern Humanities Research Association.

Bruno, Juliana. 2022. *Atmospheres of Projection: Environmentality in Art and Screen Media*. Chicago: University of Chicago Press.

Buchanan, Kyle. 2023. "Greta Gerwig on the BlockBuster 'Barbie' Opening (and How She Got Away with It)." *New York Times*, July 25. https://www.nytimes .com/2023/07/25/movies/greta-gerwig-barbie-movie.html.

Campt, Tina. 2017. *Listening to Images*. Durham, NC: Duke University Press.

Cardamenis, Forrest. 2016. "There Was So Much More to Chantal Akerman." *Brooklyn Magazine*, March 13. https://www.bkmag.com/2016/03/30 /chantal-akerman/.

Cavarero, Adriana. 2016. *Inclinations: A Critique of Rectitude*. Stanford, CA: Stanford University Press.

Chamarette, Jenny. 2012. *Phenomenology and the Future of Film: Rethinking Subjectivity beyond French Cinema*. New York: Palgrave Macmillan.

Charlesworth, Amy. 2017. "On Absence and Saturation in *From the Other Side*." *Oxford Art Journal* 40, no. 2. https://union.illiad.oclc.org/illiad/illiad.dll ?Action=10&Form=75&Value=143585.

Choudhury, Bedatri D. 2022. "'Not Just the Filmer Filming the Filmed': The Ethical Softness of Alice Diop's Documentaries." *Documentary Magazine*, July 11. https://www.documentary.org/online-feature/not-just-filmer -filming-filmed-ethical-softness-alice-diops-documentaries.

Cixous, Hélène. 1976. "The Laugh of the Medusa." Translated by Keith Cohen and Paula Cohen. *Signs: Journal of Women in Culture and Society* 1, no. 4: 875–93.

Clover, Carol. [1992] 2015. *Men, Women, and Chainsaws: Gender in the Modern Horror Film*. Updated edition. Princeton, NJ: Princeton University Press.

Coffin, Judith G. 2020. *Writing Simone de Beauvoir: Sex, Love, and Letters*. Ithaca, NY: Cornell University Press.

Collins, Patricia Hill. 1990. *Black Feminist Thought*. New York: Routledge.

Collins, Patricia Hill. 1994. "Shifting the Center: Race, Class, and Feminist Theorizing about Motherhood." In *Representations of Motherhood*, edited by Donna Bassin, 371–89. New Haven, CT: Yale University Press.

Collins, Patricia Hill. 2006. "Black Women and Motherhood." In *Motherhood and Space: Configurations of the Maternal through Politics, Home, and the Body*, edited by Sarah Hardy and Caroline Wiedmer, 149–59. New York: Palgrave Macmillan.

Constable, Liz. 2004. "Unbecoming Sexual Desires for Women Becoming Sexual Subjects: Simone de Beauvoir (1949) and Catherine Breillat (1999)." MLN 119, no. 4: 672–95.

Cvetkovich, Ann. 2003. *An Archive of Feelings: Trauma, Sexuality, and Lesbian Public Cultures*. Durham, NC: Duke University Press.

Daniel, Drew. 2016. "News from Home: Remembering Chantal Akerman." *Feedback*, January 25. http://openhumanitiespress.org/feedback/film/remembering akerman/.

Dargis, Manohla. 2019. "The Many Ways of Seeing Agnès Varda." *New York Times*,

December 18. https://www.nytimes.com/2019/12/18/movies/agnes-varda -retrospective.html.

Dargis, Manohla. 2022a. "*Happening* Review: An Abortion Story, an Existential Thriller." *New York Times,* May 5. https://www.nytimes.com/2022/05/05/movies /happening-review-abortion.html.

Dargis, Manohla. 2022b. "Rewriting Women Back into Screen History." *New York Times,* August 22. https://www.nytimes.com/2022/08/19/movies/nasty -women-cinema.html.

Davis, Angela. 1985. "Art on the Frontline: Mandate for a People's Culture." *Political Affairs,* March. http://www.politicalaffairs.net/art-on-the-frontline -mandate-for-a-people-s-culture/.

Dienstag, Joshua Foa. 2019. *Cinema Pessimism: A Political Theory of Representation and Reciprocity.* New York: Oxford University Press.

Dillon, Sarah. 2018. *Deconstruction, Feminism, Film.* Edinburgh: Edinburgh University Press.

Diop, Mati. 2019. "Mati Diop on *Atlantics* and Her Filmmaking Process." New York Film Festival 57. https://www.youtube.com/watch?v=X2lRPUstAOk.

Doucouré, Maïmouna. 2020. "I Directed *Cuties*: This Is What You Need to Know about Modern Girlhood." *Washington Post,* September 15. https:// www.washingtonpost.com/opinions/cuties-director-maimouna-doucoure -why-i-made-the-film/2020/09/15/7e0ee406-f78b-11ea-a275-1a2c2d36e1f1 _story.html.

Du Bois, W. E. B. [1903] 2014. *The Souls of Black Folk.* New York: Vintage.

Du Graf, Lauren. 2018. "Cinema in the Eyes of Simone de Beauvoir." *Screen* 59, no. 3: 381–90.

Ebert, Roger. 1999. Review of *Romance.* RogerEbert.com, November 12. https:// www.rogerebert.com/reviews/romance-1999.

Elkin, Lauren. 2022. "'It Plunged Me Back to Waiting for a Period': Annie Ernaux and Audrey Diwan on Abortion Film *Happening*." *Guardian,* April 3. https://www .theguardian.com/film/2022/apr/03/audrey-diwan-annie-ernaux-happening -interview.

English, Darby. 2010. *How to See a Work of Art in Total Darkness.* Cambridge, MA: MIT Press.

Ernaux, Annie. 2001. *Happening.* New York: Seven Stories Press.

Farrow, Ronan, and Jia Tolentino. 2021. "Britney Spears's Conservatorship Nightmare." *New Yorker,* July 3. https://www.newyorker.com/news/american -chronicles/britney-spears-conservatorship-nightmare.

Felski, Rita. 2008. *Uses of Literature.* New York: Wiley Blackwell.

Ferguson, Kathy. 2023. *Letterpress Revolution: The Politics of Anarchist Print Culture.* Durham, NC: Duke University Press.

Firestone, Shulamith [1970] 2015. *The Dialectic of Sex: The Case for Feminist Revolution.* London: Verso.

Flitterman-Lewis, Sandy. 1990. *To Desire Differently: Feminism and the French Cinema*. Urbana: University of Illinois Press.

Flitterman-Lewis, Sandy. 2003. "What's Behind Her Smile? Subjectivity and Desire in Germaine Dulac's *The Smiling Madame Beudet* and Chantal Akerman's *Jeanne Dielman, 23 quai du Commerce, 1080 Bruxelles*." In *Identity and Memory: The Films of Chantal Akerman*, edited by Gwendolyn Audrey, 27–40. Carbondale: Southern Illinois University Press.

Foster, Gwendolyn Audrey, ed. 2003. *Identity and Memory: The Films of Chantal Akerman*. Carbondale: Southern Illinois University Press.

Fowler, Catherine. 2021. *Jeanne Dielman, 23, quai du Commerce, 1080 Bruxelles*. BFI Film Classics. London: British Film Institute.

Frank, Jason. 2021. *The Democratic Sublime: On Aesthetics and Popular Assembly*. New York: Oxford University Press.

Frank, Priscilla. 2017. "Your Guide to the Feminist Films and Video Art Featured in 'I Love Dick': The Art History Lesson Begins Here." *Huffington Post*, May 12. http://www.huffingtonpost.com/entry/i-love-dick-feminist-art_us_590232c9e4b0af6d718cc8b4.

Fuery, Kelli. 2020. "Empty Time as Cinematic Duration: Towards a Cinematic *Aevum*." *Film-Philosophy* 24, no. 2: 204–21.

Fuery, Kelli. 2022. *Ambiguous Cinema: From Simone de Beauvoir to Feminist Film-Phenomenology*. Edinburgh: Edinburgh University Press.

Galt, Rosalind. 2021. *Alluring Monsters: The Pontianak and Cinemas of Decolonization*. New York: Columbia University Press.

Galt, Rosalind. 2022. "The Spirits of African Cinema: Redemptive Aesthetics in Mati Diop's *Atlantics*." *Movie: A Journal of Film Criticism*, no. 10: 97–106.

Galt, Rosalind, and Annette-Carina van der Zaag. 2022. "'C'est grave': *Raw*, Cannibalism and the Racializing Logic of White Feminism." *Journal of Visual Culture* 21, no. 2: 1–20.

Garcia, Manon. 2021. *We Are Not Born Submissive: How Patriarchy Shapes Women's Lives*. Princeton, NJ: Princeton University Press.

Gillespie, Michael Boyce. 2016. *Film Blackness: American Cinema and the Idea of Black Film*. Durham, NC: Duke University Press.

Girish, Devika. 2022. "Interview: Alice Diop on *Saint Omer*." *Film Comment*, October 10. https://www.filmcomment.com/blog/interview-alice-diop-on-saint-omer/.

Gorfinkel, Elena. 2019. "Against Lists." *Another Gaze*, November 29. https://www.anothergaze.com/elena-gorfinkel-manifesto-against-lists/?fbclid=IwAR3xbionPTpsmXA2G5QL68yBybGO7xcoMlgoPQh6u5odx3Z35bqSUyIEOuE.

Gorfinkel, Elena. 2021. "*Wanda*, Loden, Lodestone." Program essay for screening of *Wanda* at the Institute for Contemporary Art, London. London: Institute for Contemporary Art.

Gorton, Kristyn. 2007. "The Point of View of Shame: Re-viewing Female Desire in Catherine Breillat's *Romance* (1999) and *Anatomy of Hell* (2004)." *Studies in European Cinema* 4, no. 2: 111–24.

Gornick, Vivian. 2020. "The Obligation of Self-Discovery." *Boston Review*, October 22. https://www.bostonreview.net/articles/vivian-gornick-sex-love -and-letters-review/.

Guyot, Jules. [1859] 1931. *A Ritual for Married Lovers (Breviaire de l'Amour Experimental): Meditations on Marriage from the Point of View of the Physiology of Man.* Translated by Gertrude Minturn Pinchote. Baltimore, MD: Waverly Press.

Gyarkye, Lovia. 2022. "'Saint Omer' Review: Alice Diop Crafts a Spellbinding Courtroom Drama." *Hollywood Reporter*, September 7. https://www.hollywood reporter.com/movies/movie-reviews/saint-omer-alice-diop-1235212533/.

Hall, Stuart. 1980. "Encoding/Decoding." In *Culture, Media, and Language*, 51–61. New York: Routledge.

Hansen, Miriam Bratu. 1986. "Pleasure, Ambivalence, Identification: Valentino and Female Spectatorship." *Cinema Journal* 25, no. 4: 6–32.

Hansen, Miriam Bratu. 2012. *Cinema and Experience: Siegfried Kracauer, Walter Benjamin, and Theodor Adorno.* Berkeley: University of California Press.

Haraway, Donna. [1984] 1990. "Cyborg Manifesto." In *Simians, Cyborgs, and Women: The Reinvention of Nature*, 149–82. New York: Routledge.

Hargraves, Hunter. 2023. *Uncomfortable Television.* Durham, NC: Duke University Press.

Harper, Phillip Brian. 2015. *Abstractionist Aesthetics: Artistic Form and Social Critique in African American Culture.* New York: New York University Press.

Hartman, Saidiya. 2008a. *Lose Your Mother: A Journey along the Atlantic Slave Route.* New York: Farrar, Straus and Giroux.

Hartman, Saidiya. 2008b. "Venus in Two Acts." *Small Axe* 12, no. 2: 1–14.

Hartman, Saidiya. 2016. "The Belly of the World: A Note on Black Women's Labors." *Souls* 18, no. 1: 166–73.

Hartman, Saidiya. 2019. *Wayward Lives, Beautiful Experiments.* New York: W. W. Norton.

Hawkins, Joan. 2000. *Cutting Edge: Art-Horror and the Horrific Avant-garde.* Minneapolis: University of Minnesota Press.

Hegarty, Paul. 2017. "Grid Intensities: Hearing Structures in Chantal Akerman's Films of the 1970s." In *The Music and Sound of Experimental Film*, edited by Holly Rogers and Jeremy Barham, 149–65. Oxford: Oxford University Press.

Hennefeld, Maggie. 2016. "Death from Laughter: Female Hysteria, and Early Cinema." *differences: A Journal of Feminist Cultural Studies* 27, no. 3: 45–92.

Hennefeld, Maggie. 2021. "Affect Theory in the Throat of Laughter: Feminist Killjoys, Humorless Capitalists, and Contagious Hysterics." *Feminist Media Histories* 7, no. 2: 110–44.

Hesford, Victoria. 2013. *Feeling Women's Liberation.* Durham, NC: Duke University Press.

Heyes, Cressida J. 2020. *Anaesthetics of Existence: Essays on Experience at the Edge*. Durham, NC: Duke University Press.

Hogg, Joanna, and Adam Roberts. 2009. *Chantal Akerman Retrospective Handbook*. London: A Nos Amours.

Honig, Bonnie. 2021a. "Bonnie Honig on *Promising Young Woman*." Fordham University Press, April 22. https://www.fordhampress.com/2021/04/24/bonnie -honig-on-promising-young-woman-warning-spoilers/.

Honig, Bonnie. 2021b. *A Feminist Theory of Refusal*. Cambridge, MA: Harvard University Press.

Honig, Bonnie. 2021c. "Promising Young Country." *Politics/Letters Live*, April 22. http://politicsslashletters.org/commentary/promising-young-country -warning-spoilers/.

Honig, Bonnie. 2021d. *Shell-Shocked: Feminist Criticism after Trump*. New York: Fordham University Press.

hooks, bell. 1992. "The Oppositional Gaze: Black Female Spectators." In *Black Looks: Race and Representation*, 115–31. Boston: South End.

Ince, Katherine. 2006. "Is Sex Comedy or Tragedy? Directing Desire and Female Auteurship in the Cinema of Catherine Breillat." In *Thinking Through Cinema: Film as Philosophy*, edited by Murray Smith and Thomas E. Wartenberg, 157–64. London: Blackwell.

Ince, Katherine. 2017. *The Body and the Screen: Female Subjectivities in Contemporary Women's Cinema*. New York: Bloomsbury.

Irigaray, Luce. [1974] 1985. *Speculum of the Other Woman*. Translated by Gillian C. Gill. Ithaca, NY: Cornell University Press.

Irigaray, Luce. [1977] 1985. *This Sex Which Is Not One*. Translated by Catherine Porter. Ithaca, NY: Cornell University Press.

Jacobs, Steven. 2012. "Semiotics of the Living Room: Domestic Interiors in Chantal Akerman's Cinema." In *Chantal Akerman: Too Far, Too Close*, 73–87. Exhibition catalog. Antwerp: Ludion.

Karlyn, Kathleen Rowe. 1995. *The Unruly Woman: Gender and the Genres of Laughter*. Austin: University of Texas Press.

Keeling, Kara. 2007. *The Witch's Flight: The Cinematic, the Black Femme, and the Image of Common Sense*. Durham, NC: Duke University Press.

Kourlas, Gia. 2023. "The Dance Delight in 'Barbie' Belongs to the Kens." *New York Times*, July 28. https://www.nytimes.com/2023/07/28/arts/dance/ken-dance -barbie-movie.html.

Kraus, Chris. 1997. *I Love Dick*. New York: Semiotext(e).

Kruger, Barbara. 1983. "'The Golden Eighties' Directed by Chantal Akerman; 'Heart Like a Wheel' Directed by Jonathan Kaplan." *Artforum* 22, no. 4. https:// www.artforum.com/print/reviews/198310/the-golden-eighties-directed -by-chantal-akerman-heart-like-a-wheel-directed-by-jonathan-kaplan -64944.

Landry, Olivia, and Christinia Landry. 2019. "Torlasco's 'Philosophy in the

Kitchen': Image, Domestic Labor, and the Gendered Embodiment of Time." *New Review of Film and Television Studies* 17, no. 4: 456–80.

Lane, Anthony. 2008. "Carrie." *New Yorker*, June 9 and 16. http://www.newyorker.com/magazine/2008/06/09/carrie.

Lane, Anthony. 2023. "How 'Oppenheimer' and 'Barbie' Bring Monumental Figures to Life." *New Yorker*, July 20. https://www.newyorker.com/magazine/2023/07/31/oppenheimer-movie-review-barbie.

Liss, Andrea. 2009. *Feminist Art and the Maternal*. Minneapolis: University of Minnesota Press.

Lorde, Audre. [1984] 2007. *Sister Outsider*. Berkeley, CA: Crossing Press.

Lowenstein, Adam. 2022. *Horror Film and Otherness*. New York: Columbia University Press.

MacKinnon, Catherine A. 1989. "Sexuality, Pornography, and Method: Pleasure under Patriarchy." *Ethics* 99, no. 2: 314–46.

Margulies, Ivone. 1996. *Nothing Happens: Chantal Akerman's Hyperrealist Everyday*. Durham, NC: Duke University Press.

Margulies, Ivone. 2009. "A Matter of Time: *Jeanne Dielman, 23 quai du Commerce, 1080 Bruxelles*." *Current*, August 17. https://www.criterion.com/current/posts/1215-a-matter-of-time-jeanne-dielman-23-quai-du-commerce-1080-bruxelles.

Margulies, Ivone. 2016. "Elemental Akerman: Inside and Outside *No Home Movie*." *Film Quarterly* 70, no. 1: 61–69.

Margulies, Ivone. 2019. "Our Way of Working: A Conversation with Claire Atherton about Chantal Akerman." *Camera Obscura: Feminism, Culture, and Media Studies* 34, no. 1: 13–29.

Marso, Lori J. 2006. *Feminist Thinkers and the Demands of Femininity: The Lives and Work of Intellectual Women*. New York: Routledge.

Marso, Lori J. 2010. "Feminism's Quest for Common Desires." *Perspectives on Politics* 8, no. 1: 263–69.

Marso, Lori J. 2015. "Feminism." In *Encyclopedia of Political Thought*, edited by Michael Gibbons. New York: John Wiley and Sons. https://www.academia.edu/6156496/_Feminism_In_Encyclopedia_of_Political_Thought_Ed_Mike_Gibbons.

Marso, Lori J. 2016a. "Perverse Protests: Simone de Beauvoir on Pleasure and Danger, Resistance, and Female Violence in Film." *Signs: A Journal of Women in Culture and Society* 41, no. 4: 869–94.

Marso, Lori J. 2016b. "The Second Sex." In *Oxford Handbook of Classics in Contemporary Political Theory*, edited by Jacob Levy. Oxford: Oxford University Press. https://academic.oup.com/edited-volume/34715/chapter-abstract/296447474?redirectedFrom=fulltext.

Marso, Lori J. 2017. *Politics with Beauvoir: Freedom in the Encounter*. Durham, NC: Duke University Press.

Marso, Lori J. 2018. "Birthing Feminist Freedom." *HA: The Journal of the Hannah Arendt Center for Politics and Humanities at Bard College*, no. 6: 98–106.

Marso, Lori J. 2019. Review of *Mothers: An Essay on Love and Cruelty* by Jacqueline Rose and *Full Surrogacy Now: Feminism against Family* by Sophie Lewis. *Los Angeles Review of Books*, July 18. https://lareviewofbooks.org/article/find-our-mothers/.

Marso, Lori J. 2021. Review of *Deconstruction, Feminism, Film* by Sarah Dillon. *Hypatia* 36, no. 4: e8, 1–4. https://www.cambridge.org/core/services/aop-cambridge-core/content/view/FC02A31E53D145AC386FC23AC07554ED/S0887536721000052a.pdf/deconstruction_feminism_film_sarah_dillon_edinburgh_edinburgh_university_press_2018_isbn_9781474434225_paperback.pdf.

Marso, Lori J. 2022a. Review of *Why We Lost the Sex Wars* by Lorna Bracewell. *Perspectives on Politics* 20, no. 1 (March): 312–13.

Marso, Lori J. 2022b. "Winning the Sex Wars in Feminist Cinema and Media." *Contemporary Political Theory*. https://link.springer.com/article/10.1057/s41296-022-00589-y#article-info.

Marso, Lori J. 2022c. "Simone de Beauvoir et la rencontre cinématographique." *Cités* 90: 131–44.

Marso, Lori J. 2022d. Review of *Beauvoir in Time* by Meryl Altman. *Simone de Beauvoir Studies* 33, no. 1: 177–83.

Marso, Lori J. 2024a. "Burn Book: On *Priscilla* and Sofia Coppola's White Girls." *Los Angeles Review of Books*. January 20. https://lareviewofbooks.org/article/burn-book-on-priscilla-and-sofia-coppolas-white-girls/.

Marso, Lori J. 2024b. "Frame Tale: On Christine Smallwood's 'La Captive,' and Chantal Akerman." *Los Angeles Review of Books*, April 4. https://lareviewofbooks.org/article/frame-tale-on-christine-smallwoods-la-captive-and-chantal-akerman.

Marso, Lori J. 2024c. "Phenomenology in the Kitchen: Feeling Time Like a Feminist." In *Film Phenomenologies: Temporality, Embodiment, Transformation*, edited by Kelli Fuery, 41–60. Edinburgh: Edinburgh University Press.

Marso, Lori J. 2024d. "What Women Want, per Catherine Breillat." *Los Angeles Review of Books*, July 19. https://lareviewofbooks.org/article/catherine-breillat-shows-us-what-women-want/.

Maslin, Janet. 1999. "With Her Libido as Navigator, One Woman's Adventures." *New York Times*, September 17. https://www.nytimes.com/1999/09/17/movies/film-review-with-her-libido-as-navigator-one-woman-s-adventures.html.

Mathon, Claire. 2019. "Claire Mathon, AFC, Discusses Her Work on Mati Diop's Film 'Atlantics.'" AFC, May 21. https://www.afcinema.com/Claire-Mathon-AFC-discusses-her-work-on-Mati-Diop-s-film-Atlantique.html?lang=fr.

Mavor, Carol. 2007. *Reading Boyishly: Roland Barthes, J. M. Barrie, Jacques Henri Lartigue, Marcel Proust, and D. W. Winnicott*. Durham, NC: Duke University Press.

Maxwell, Lida. 2017. "Queer/Love/Bird Extinction: Rachel Carson's *Silent Spring* as a Work of Love." *Political Theory* 45, no. 5: 682–704.

McBane, Barbara. 2016. "Walking, Talking, Singing, Exploding, and Silence: Chantal Akerman's Soundtracks." *Film Quarterly* 70, no. 1: 39–47. https://filmquarterly.org/2016/09/16/walking-talking-singing-exploding/#r2.

McFadden, Cybelle H. 2014. *Gendered Frames, Embodied Cameras: Varda, Akerman, Cabrera, Calle, and Maïwenn.* Madison, NJ: Fairleigh Dickinson University Press.

McGill, Hannah. 2023. "Hello, Dolly!" *Sight and Sound* 33, no. 7: 30–33.

McGillvray, Maddi. 2020. "The Feminist Art Horror of the New French Extremity." In *Women Make Horror*, edited by Alison Pierce, 122–32. New Brunswick, NJ: Rutgers University Press.

McHenry, Jackson. 2021. "Paris Hilton, Musical Theatre, and Wagner: How *Promising Young Woman*'s Soundtrack Came Together." *Vulture*, February 2. https://www.vulture.com/2021/02/how-promising-young-womans-soundtrack-came-together.html.

Mehra, Nishta J. 2017. "Sara Ahmed: Notes from a Feminist Killjoy." *Guernica*, July 17. https://www.guernicamag.com/sara-ahmed-the-personal-is-institutional/.

Miller, J. Hillis. 2006. "Derrida's *Destinerrance*." MLN 121: 893–910.

Mizejewski, Linda. 2014. *Pretty/Funny: Women Comedians and Body Politics.* Austin: University of Texas Press.

Morgan, Daniel. 2016. "Where Are We? Camera Movements and the Problem of Point of View." *New Review of Film and Television Studies* 14, no. 2: 222–48.

Moten, Fred. 2003. "Black Mo'nin'." In *Loss: The Politics of Mourning*, edited by David Kazanjian and David L. Eng, 59–76. Berkeley: University of California Press.

Moten, Fred, and Stefano Harney. 2013. *The Undercommons: Fugitive Planning and Black Study.* New York: Minor Compositions.

Murray, Ros. 2022. "The Practice of Disobedience." *Another Screen.* https://www.another-screen.com/the-practice-of-disobedience.

Mulvey, Laura. 1975. "Visual Pleasure and Narrative Cinema." *Screen* 16, no. 3: 6–18.

Mulvey, Laura. 2006. *Death 24x a Second: Stillness and the Moving Image.* London: Reaktion.

Mulvey, Laura. 2022. "The Greatest Film of All Time: *Jeanne Dielman, 23 quai du Commerce, 1080 Bruxelles*." *Sight and Sound Weekly Bulletin*, December 1. https://www.bfi.org.uk/sight-and-sound/features/greatest-film-all-time-jeanne-dielman-23-quai-du-commerce-1080-bruxelles.

Nash, Jennifer. 2009. "Black Maternal Aesthetics." *Theory and Event* 22, no. 3: 551–75.

Nelson, Laura. 2023. "Fracture and Assembly: On Lizzie Borden's *Regrouping*." *Los Angeles Review of Books*, January 26. https://lareviewofbooks.org/article/fracture-and-assembly-on-lizzie-bordens-regrouping/?mc_cid=4f64eeab19&mc_eid=9d87ef5a55.

Nelson, Max. 2018. "A Hard Road Home: The Films of Chantal Akerman." *New York Review of Books*, May 24.

Ngai, Sianne. 2007. *Ugly Feelings*. Cambridge, MA: Harvard University Press.

Nicholas, Lucy. 2023. "Ken's Rights? Our Research Shows That *Barbie* Is Surprisingly Accurate on How Men's Rights Activists Are Radicalized." *Conversation*, July 25. https://theconversation.com/kens-rights-our-research-shows-barbie-is-surprisingly-accurate-on-how-mens-rights-activists-are-radicalised-210273.

Nussbaum, Emily. 2017. "What Women Want on '*I Love Dick.*'" *New Yorker*, June 26. http://www.newyorker.com/magazine/2017/06/26/what-women-want-on-i-love-dick.

Orange, Tommy. 2018. *There, There*. New York: Knopf.

Osterweil, Ara. 2014. *Flesh Cinema: The Corporeal Turn in American Avant-Garde Film*. Manchester: Manchester University Press.

Panagia, Davide. 2024. *Sentimental Education*. New York: Fordham University Press.

Paskin, Willa. 2023. "Greta Gerwig's *Barbie* Dream Job." *New York Times Magazine*, July 11. https://www.nytimes.com/2023/07/11/magazine/greta-gerwig-barbie.html.

Peirse, Alison, ed. 2020. *Women Make Horror: Filmmaking, Feminism, Genre*. New Brunswick, NJ: Rutgers University Press.

Popova, Maria. 2015. "The Artist's Reality: Mark Rothko's Little-Known Writings on Art, Artists, and What the Notion of Plasticity Reveals about Storytelling." *The Marginalian*, February 17. https://www.themarginalian.org/2015/02/17/the-artists-reality-mark-rothko/.

Price, Yasmina. 2023. "An Interview with Alice Diop: Language, Law, and Living Histories." *Screen Slate*, January 16. https://www.screenslate.com/articles/interview-alice-diop-language-law-and-living-histories?fbclid=IwAR0xTLwGxZvz6sfkMI_7fACOhUyngVhgKfE4vV9fxd14CA6PGcDWcJTbo9g&mibextid=Zxz2cZ.

Rapold, Nicolas. 2015. "Chantal Akerman Takes Emotional Path in Film About 'Maman.'" *New York Times*, August 5. https://www.nytimes.com/2015/08/06/arts/international/chantal-akerman-takes-emotional-path-in-film-about-maman.html.

Reinhardt, Mark. 2017. "Visions Unseen: On Sovereignty, Race, and the Optical Unconscious." In *Photography and the Optical Unconscious*, edited by Shawn Michelle Smith and Sharon Sliwinski, 174–222. Durham, NC: Duke University Press.

Rennebohm, Kate. 2021. "Chantal Akerman and Stanley Cavell: Viewing in *La Captive* and Reviewing in Moral Perfectionism." In *Movies with Stanley Cavell in Mind*, edited by David LaRocca, 253–73. New York: Bloomsbury Academic.

Rennebohm, Kate, and Simon Howell. 2021–23. *The Akerman Year: A Monthly Podcast Miniseries on the Work of Chantal Akerman, Hosted by Kate Rennebohm and Simon Howell*. https://akermanyear.fireside.fm/.

Richardson Viti, Elizabeth. 1999. "Simone de Beauvoir and the Reproduction of Mothering." *Simone de Beauvoir Studies* 16: 114–22.

Roberts, Adam. 2014. "Unfettered Expression: Adam Roberts on Chantal Akerman's *Golden Eighties*." ICA. https://archive.ica.art/bulletin/unfettered -expression-adam-roberts-chantal-akermans-golden-eighties/.

Rose, Jacqueline. 2018. *Mothers: An Essay on Love and Cruelty*. New York: Farrar, Straus and Giroux.

Rosen, Christopher. 2020. "*Promising Young Woman* Understands the Power of the Perfect Pop Song." *Vanity Fair*, December 24. https://www .vanityfair.com/hollywood/2020/12/promising-young-woman-soundtrack -score.

Rothko, Mark. 2006. *The Artist's Reality: Philosophies of Art*. Edited by Christopher Rothko. New Haven, CT: Yale University Press.

Saito, Stephen. 2022. "A Common Secret: Audrey Diwan and Anamaria Vartolomei on the Making of *Happening*." *Moveable Fest*, May 2. https://moveablefest .com/audrey-diwan-anamaria-vartolomei-happening-film/.

Sandberg, Sheryl. 2013. *Lean In: Women, Work, and the Will to Lead*. New York: Knopf.

Scherffig, Clara Miranda. 2022. "Interview: Audrey Diwan's *Happening*." *Screen Slate*, May. https://www.screenslate.com/articles/ndnf-interview-audrey -diwans-happening.

Schmid, Marion. 2010. *Chantal Akerman*. Manchester: Manchester University Press.

Schmid, Marion. 2016. "Self-Portrait as Visual Artist: Chantal Akerman's *Ma mère rit*." *MLN* 131, no. 4: 1130–47.

Schoolman, Morton. 2020. *A Democratic Enlightenment: The Reconciliation Image, Aesthetic Education, Possible Politics*. Durham, NC: Duke University Press.

Schwartz, Selby Wynn. 2022. *After Sappho: A Novel*. New York: Liveright.

Scott, Joan. 2011. *The Fantasy of Feminist History*. Durham, NC: Duke University Press.

Sedgwick, Eve Kosofsky. 2003. *Touching Feeling: Affect, Pedagogy, Performativity*. Durham, NC: Duke University Press.

Serpell, Namwali. 2015. "Uses of Criticism." *Los Angeles Review of Books Quarterly Journal*, Fall: 18–27.

Shapiro, Michael. 2021. *The Phenomenology of Religious Belief: Media, Philosophy, and the Arts*. New York: Bloomsbury.

Sharpe, Christina. 2016. *In the Wake: On Blackness and Being*. Durham, NC: Duke University Press.

Sharpe, Christina. 2023. *Ordinary Notes*. New York: Farrar, Straus and Giroux.

Shaviro, Steven. 2007. "Clichés of Identity: Chantal Akerman's Musicals." *Quarterly Review of Film and Video* 24: 11–17.

Shreir, Daniella. 2019. "Another Gaze: Feminist Filmmaking and the Work

of Chantal Akerman." *Suite 212* podcast, April 29, 2019. https://podcasts
.apple.com/bs/podcast/another-gaze-feminist-filmmaking-and-the-work
/id1366889715?i=1000436833971.

Shulevitz, Judith. 2011. *The Sabbath World: Glimpses of a Different Order of Time.*
New York: Random House.

Shulman, George. 2020. "Fred Moten's Refusals and Consents: The Politics of
Fugitivity." *Political Theory* 49 (April): 272–313.

Smith, Dinitia. 1998. "Film: Chantal Akerman and the Point of Point of View."
New York Times, April 26. https://www.nytimes.com/1998/04/26/movie
s/film-chantal-akerman-and-the-point-of-point-of-view.html.

Smith, Shawn Michelle. 2013. *At the Edge of Sight: Photography and the Unseen.*
Durham, NC: Duke University Press.

Sobchack, Vivian. 1992. *The Address of the Eye: A Phenomenology of Film Experience.* Princeton, NJ: Princeton University Press.

Sobchack, Vivian. 2004. *Carnal Thoughts: Embodiment and Moving Image Culture.* Berkeley: University of California Press.

Spielberg, Theo. 2024. "Ocean of Sound." *Los Angeles Review of Books*, April 11.
https://lareviewofbooks.org/article/ocean-of-sound/.

Srinivasan, Amia. 2021. *The Right to Sex: Feminism in the Twenty-First Century.*
New York: Farrar, Straus and Giroux.

Steinbock, Eliza. 2019. *Shimmering Images: Trans Cinema, Embodiment, and the
Aesthetics of Change.* Durham, NC: Duke University Press.

Syedullah, Jasmine. 2022. "Becoming More Ourselves: Four Emergent Strategies
of Black Feminist Congregational Abolition." *Palimpsest* 11, no. 1: 108–40.

Taylor, Liza. 2022. *Feminism in Coalition: Thinking with US Women of Color
Feminism.* Durham, NC: Duke University Press.

Tronto, Joan. 2015. *Who Cares?* Ithaca, NY: Cornell University Press.

Ugwu, Reggie. 2020. "How *I May Destroy You* Got Its Stunning Soundtrack." *New
York Times*, July 15. https://www.nytimes.com/2020/07/15/arts/television/i
-may-destroy-you-soundtrack.html.

Vicino, Mia Lee. 2023. "Interview: The Official Barbie Watchlist: Greta Gerwig on the Classic Film Influences behind Her Fantasy-Comedy-Kind of
Musical." *Letterboxd*, July 13. https://letterboxd.com/journal/the-official
-barbie-watchlist-greta-gerwig/.

Warner, Kristen. 2017. "In the Time of Plastic Representation." *Film Quarterly* 71, no. 2. https://filmquarterly.org/2017/12/04/in-the-time-of-plastic
-representation/.

Wheatley, Catherine. 2010. "Contested Interactions: Watching Catherine Breillat's Scenes of Sexual Violence." *Journal for Cultural Research* 14, no. 1: 27–41.

Willet, Cynthia, and Julia Willet. 2013. "The Seriously Erotic Politics of Laughter: Bitches, Whores and Other Fumerists." In *Philosophical Feminism and
Popular Culture*, edited by Sharon Crasnow and Joanne Waugh, 15–36. Lanham, MD: Lexington.

Williams, Linda. 1991. "Film Bodies: Gender, Genre, and Excess." *Film Quarterly* 44, no. 4: 2–13.

Wilson, Emma. 2002. "Deforming Femininity: Catherine Breillat's *Romance*." In *France on Film: Reflections on Popular French Cinema*, edited by Lucy Mazdon, 145–57. London: Wallflower.

Young, Damon R. 2018. *Making Sex Public and Other Cinematic Fantasies*. Durham, NC: Duke University Press.

Zuckerman, Esther. 2023. "For the Documentarian Alice Diop, Only Fiction Could Do Justice to a Tragedy." *New York Times*, January 16. https://www.nytimes.com/2023/01/16/movies/alice-diop-saint-omer.html.

Index

187–188n6; on pregnancy and maternity, 93; promise as key term for, 58, 75; race not addressed by, 58, 129–131, 201nn28, 29; reader/text relationship, view of, 18; "second sex" concept, 2, 137; on "waiting," 91–92; "Woman" debunked by, 15; *Writings: All Said and Done*, 13–14, 76, 194n20; *America Day by Day*, 13; autobiography, 12; "Brigitte Bardot and the Lolita Syndrome," 14–15, 21, 128; *Force of Circumstance*, 17, 171n26; *Inseparable*, 190n18; *Les belles images*, 12–13; preface to Lanzmann's *Shoah* text, 14, 15. *See also The Second Sex* (Beauvoir)

Bechdel, Alison, 99

Bechdel rule, 99, 115, 146, 155, 159–160, 205n7

"becoming a Woman," process of, 16, 18, 93, 107

Béghin, Cyril, 179n18

Les belles images (Beauvoir), 12–13

Bennett, Jane, 172n9, 199n14, 201n27

Bergson, Henri, 76, 172n31, 190n22

Berlant, Lauren, 2–3, 106, 111, 153, 195n4

biology, "data" of, 107–108

birth: and feelings about mothers, 27, 29; in *Romance*, 82–83, 109, 114–115, 136–137; in *Titane*, 82, 101–102

Black female viewers, 19

Black feminist theory, 10, 21, 26, 55, 166n13

Black film, 203–204n2

Blackhurst, Alice, 8

Black mothers, 26–27, 49–54

black noise, 76–77

Black Utopias (Brown), 76

Blow Up My Town (Akerman), 6, 10–11, 22, 59, 62–67, 63, 115; dancing scene, 131, 132; "harmonics" in, 188–189n12

body: denial of, 136–137; and laughter, 106; materiality of flesh, 110, 114; responses to feminist cringe comedies, 23, 106; strange in the everyday, 100; waiting, 92; writing from, 136

body horror, 22, 81, 82, 98; invasion of female body, 86; men's horror of women's bodies, 123–124, 136–137; responses elicited by horror's gaze, 102–103; unwanted pregnancy, 89–96; as women's everyday experience, 106. *See also* horror

body politic, 106, 111, 195n1

Borden, Lizzie, 159

borders, 39–40

Born in Flames (Borden), 159

"Boys" (Charli XCX), 67, 76

Bracewell, Lorna, 198n8

Bradley, Rizvana, 166n13

Bradshaw, Peter, 113

Breillat, Catherine, 22–23, 100, 101, 107; feminism, relationship to, 198–199n12; incompatibility of films with liberal view of individual, 115; materiality of flesh in work of, 110, 114; men's responses to, 110, 198n10; rules about filming sex violated by, 108–109. *See also Romance* (Breillat)

"Brigitte Bardot and the Lolita Syndrome" (Beauvoir), 14–15, 21, 128

Brinkema, Eugenie, 103, 110, 114, 166n12, 194nn22, 23

Brown, Jayna, 76–77

Butler, Octavia, 76

Byrd, James, 185n39

camera: Latin meaning of, 28; mothers compared to, 21, 28, 30, 44, 46; as orifice, 28. *See also* technology

Camera Lucida (Barthes), 21, 28, 30, 31, 44–45; Winter Garden photograph, 45, 183n34

camerawork: disorienting, 4; motherwork linked to, 27; point-of-view perspective, 9; "realist" shots, 40–41. *See also* motherwork camerawork

camerawork motherwork, 10, 54–56, 176n3. *See also* motherwork camerawork

Campion, Jane, 118
Campt, Tina, 177n7
Cannes Film Festival, 81
cannibalism, 97–98
capitalism, 12–14, 165n11; challenges to in feminist horror films, 84, 88; and women's waiting, 91–92
capture, 36, 39–41, 45
Cardamenis, Forrest, 167n15
Carroll, Noël, 103
Charli XCX, 67, 76
Cinema and Experience (Hansen), 5
cinema of experience, 5, 15–19, 155–157; *Barbie* as, 23, 155; and cringe, 137–138; discovery/recovery by, 15; experiencing women's experiences, 18–19; movement images in, 130–131. *See also* experience
"Cinema's First Nasty Women," 203n1
Cixous, Hélène, 136, 137
"Closer to Fine" (Indigo Girls), 148
Clover, Carol, 102
Coel, Michaela, 22, 59, 71–75
Coffin, Judith, 16
collective: and *Barbie,* 23; and cringe, 106, 126; film as collective praxis, 10; individual versus, 2, 26, 172nn33, 34; and reproduction of expectations, 19–20; and resistance, 78, 86, 88, 160; shared experiences, 2–3, 23, 39–40, 76, 79–80, 83, 95, 157
Collins, Patricia Hill, 26, 27
color, 23
Coltrane, Alice, 76
comedy, 195–196n4; feminists said to be humorless, 105–106. *See also* cringe comedy
common sense, "male," 5, 91, 107; feminist alternatives to, 16, 65, 104
complaint, female, 153, 155
consumerism, 12–13
control, 23, 48, 60
Coppola, Sofia, 82, 191n3
Couple, A (Wiseman), 185n41
Creative Mind, The (Bergson), 76
cringe comedy, 22–23, 105–138, 160,

195–196n4; collectivized, 120–121; desire in, 106, 112, 117–118, 123, 127, 138; feminist possibilities within, 106, 138; linked with feminist realism, 107; and motherwork camerawork, 122; and shared feelings, 106, 123, 138. *See also I Love Dick* (Soloway's television adaptation); love letters; *Romance* (Breillat)
cruel optimism, 2–3, 111
Cukor, George, 159
cultural objects, 139–140, 148
Cuties (Doucouré), 191–192n6
Cutting Edge: Art-Horror and the Horrific Avant-garde (Hawkins), 81
Cvetkovich, Ann, 164n7
cyborg, 31, 56, 102, 106

"Daguerréotypes" (Varda), 30
Dakar (Senegal), 87
dancing, images of, 129–138, *130–135*
Daniel, Drew, 181n29
Dargis, Manohla, 92, 203n1
Dash, Julie, 204n3
Daughters of the Dust (Dash), 204n3
Davis, Angela, 183n39
Demy, Jacques, 144
Denis, Claire, 83, 98, 193–194n19
Derrida, Jacques, 169–170n22, 200n22
desire, 13, 23; as active, 123–125; embarrassment/shame as part of, 114–115; in feminist cringe comedies, 106, 112, 117–118, 123, 127, 138; fluidity of, 110, 119, 123–124, 131, 200n21; Freudian view of, 119–120; of girls, interrupted by patriarchy, 58, 60–61; male, 118, 119, 121, 123; as monstrous, 98; new language of, 127; patriarchal contamination of, 106–107, 111, 123, 125, 137; public displays of, 128–129, 195n2; racialized, of viewer, 129–131, *130*; in relationship to others, 130–131; space of possibility for, 94–95; in writing and reading of letters, 107, 127
Dialectic of Sex, The (Firestone), 159, 163n2

feminist filmmaking, 6–8, 49–51, 165n11; acts of repair in, 51; Akerman's influence on, 49; European arthouse films, 22; feelings as political act in, 50; "feminist arrogance" of, 8; love letters to, 22, 107, 118, 127, 152, 155; male gaze countered by, 7, 144; "rules" for, 115, 146, 155, 159–160, 205n7, 99100; strategies of, 19. *See also* camerawork motherwork; cringe comedy; horror genre; motherwork camerawork; specific filmmakers and films

feminist realism, 22, 82–83, 99, 106–107, 120. *See also* realism rule

feminized subjects, 20, 23

Fennell, Emerald, 22, 58, 59, 67–71, 143

Ferrell, Will, 147, 148, 203n4

Firestone, Shulamith, 16, 111, 159, 163n2, 178n10

Flitterman-Lewis, Sandy, 193–194n16

Force of Circumstance (Beauvoir), 17, 171n26

formal strategies, 9, 19; in Akerman's work, 62–63; close reading of, 103, 194n23; formalism, "radical," 103

Fowler, Catherine, 8, 167–168n17

France, abortion policy, 93

Frank, Jason, 190n21

Frankenstein (Shelley), 30, 31

freedom: blocked by patriarchy, 16, 172–173n34; cameras as technology in service of, 27; director's appeal to, 17; holding spaces for, 28; home linked with, 42; as relational, 2, 5, 47; sensed through film, 5; soft side of patriarchy offered in place of, 61; staging, 47; through feminist realism, 106

Freud, Sigmund, 108–109, 119, 122

From the Other Side (Akerman), 11, 21, 26, 35–41, 45, 54, 55, 181n28, 184n39; border and desert in, 39–44, *41, 43, 44*, 54, 55, 182n32; documentary characteristics of, 27, 35–36; fabulation in, 36–38, *38,* 192n9; infrared footage from US helicopters, 40–41; motherwork in, 27; presented in Kassel, Germany, 35; "realist" shots, 40–41; voiceovers, 36–38

Fuery, Kelli, 17, 167n16, 170n25

Galt, Rosalind, 81, 86, 192n7

Gaslight (Cukor), 159

gaze: assaultive and reactive, 102; of Black viewer, 19; of camera, 30; and gender, 102–103; male, camera as, 30; male, challenges to, 19, 23, 25–26, 106, 144; and mothers, 29, 45

gender: difficulty in following rules of, 112; and gaze of viewer, 102–103; as genre in French, 80; in modern horror film, 102; and narrative arc, 7; viewer and identification with, 102, 108

"generic" sense, 104

genre, 79; genre trouble *as* gender trouble, 98. *See also* horror genre

Gerwig, Greta, 13, 23, 165n10, 191n4; on "authentic artificiality," 144; and creative control, 148; response to feelings about movie, 141

Gillespie, Michael Boyce, 203–204n2

Girlhood (Sciamma), 191–192n6

girls: Akerman on staying a girl, 29; bodies of encroached on, 60–61; desires of interrupted, 58; requirements for posture and clothing imposed on, 75; in *The Second Sex,* 11

Gorfinkel, Elena, 8, 166–167n14

Gornick, Vivian, 157

Grand-mères (Grandmothers) (documentary television series), 31–32, 178n11

grandmothers, 31–32, 49, 83–84, 178n11, 182n30, 200n24

Gray, Francine du Plessix, 171n26

grief, 30, 31, 43–44

Guyot, Jules, 60

Gyarkye, Lovia, 184n38

Medea, 27–28, 52, 53, 177n5
Medea (Pasolini), 174n43
Medusa myth, 99
#MeToo era, 67
memory, 15, 51, 53, 59; in Barthes, 31, 45, 183n34
Men, Women, and Chainsaws (Clover), 102
men's rights activists, 142
menstrual blood, 124–125
Merleau-Ponty, Maurice, 5
metonymic reading, 169n22
Midge (doll), 143–144, 152
Miller, J. Hillis, 200n22
Millet, Kate, 174n42
Mirren, Helen, 142
Mizejewski, Linda, 195n4
Morrison, Toni, 159
Moten, Fred, 173n38, 177n7, 183n34
mothers: ambivalence inspired by, 54; Black, 28, 49–54; borders complicated by, 29; broadening of category of, 27; compared to cameras, 21, 28, 30, 44, 46; conventional perspectives of, 31; cyborg, 31, 56; disappearance/erasure of, 27, 31, 35, 44–46, 48, 49, 51; as fantasies, 29, 44–45; filming of as political act, 50; as home, 29; lost, 31, 36–38; myths of as disciplining norms, 26; myths of challenged, 47; nonnormative, 26–27, 55; as objects, 44–45; patriarchal views of, 29, 49; proximity to both death and life, 29; and *studium*, 49
Mothers: An Essay on Love and Cruelty (Rose), 29
motherwork, 21; defined, 26; and technology, 27, 48; and violence, 10, 26–27
motherwork camerawork, 10, 25–56, 160, 176n3; as aesthetic form of motherwork labor, 26; and cringe comedy, 122; defined, 25; joining of filmmaker and camera, 31; multiple encounters, 46. *See also* camerawork motherwork; *From the Other Side* (Akerman); *Jeanne*

Dielman, 23, quai du Commerce, 1080 Bruxelles (Akerman); *No Home Movie* (Akerman); *Saint Omer* (Diop)
movement: images of, 129–138, *130–135*; within moments, 16; and plasticity, 141
Mulvey, Laura, 6, 18, 30, 127, 144, 173n40, 175n44; *Riddles of the Sphinx* (film), 178n9; "Visual Pleasure and Narrative Cinema," 7
Murray, Ros, 168n17
music, 62, 87, 94, 190n22
My Mother Laughs (Akerman), 180n23

Nash, Jennifer, 177n4
Native American people, 41–42
"neck aesthetics," 103
Nelson, Laura, 159
Nelson, Max, 181–182n30
neoliberalism, 12, 85, 165n11; fantasy of progress in *Barbie*, 142, 143, 152. *See also* capitalism
Never Rarely Sometimes Always (Hittman), 3–4
Newton, Juice, 70
Ngai, Sianne, 106, 195n4
No Home Movie (Akerman), 11, 21, 26–28, 41–48, 181n29, 183n33; audience silence at New York Film Festival, 183–184n35; desert in, 39–44, *41, 43, 44,* 54, 182n32; domestic objects in, 184n37; fabulation in, 45–46; motherwork in, 27; *In My Room* compared to, 83–84; origin story of, 182n32; *punctum* and *studium* in, 43; Skype conversations in, 47–48
Nous (We) (Diop), 51
Nowhere (Papaioannou), *150*
Nussbaum, Emily, 105, 128

object: mother as, 44–45; and twoness of sex, 137
Oedipus complex in women, 109
opaque characters, 7, 34–35, 80–81, 84, 131, 168–169n19
"Oppositional Gaze, The" (hooks), 19

Orange, Tommy, 41–42
Ordinary Notes (Sharpe), 49
orifice, camera as, 28
other: embodied position of, 166n13; mother as, 29; outside/outsider/alien as, 39; as transformational figure in horror films, 81; (*m*)*others*, 27; as unfamiliar and dangerous, 29

Palme d'Or (Cannes Film Festival), 81
Panagia, Davide, 171n27, 183n34, 187–188n6
Papaioannou, Dimitris, *150*
Pasolini, Pier Paolo, 174n43
patriarchy: Barbie/*Barbie* as threat to, 142, 148; brought to Barbie Land, 147–148; cognitive dissonance created by, 151; contamination of female desire by, 106–107, 111, 123, 125, 137; credibility and authority of women questioned, 106, 108; as "dispositional power of domination," 171n27, 187–188n6; encroachment of on girls, 60–61; enhanced by women's feelings, 202n3, 203n1; film as ideological apparatus for, 165n11; freedom blocked by, 16, 172–173n34; mothers, views of, 29, 49; racialized, 17, 39, 57–59, 184n39, 192n9, 203n1; romance, script of, 111–112; senses ordered by, 16, 61; whore/virgin binary, 60, 113. *See also* sensorium, male; white noise of patriarchy; white supremacy
Peirse, Alison, 103
philosophy, genre and gender of, 80
"Philosophy in the Kitchen" (Torlasco), 200n25
photography, 30, 31, 177n7, 180n24; capture by, 36, 39–41; and Hartman's fabulation, 36; optical unconscious of, 201n29. *See also* Barthes, Roland
pink: in *Barbie*, 3, 141, 143, 149, 152–153, 165n10; defined, 139; plasticity intensified by, 141. *See also Barbie* (Gerwig)
placenames, 55

plasticity, 23, 139, 202n1; double evocation of in *Barbie*, 141; "plastic representation," 143, 155; queering of, 143. *See also Barbie* (Gerwig)
poetry, 156
Politics with Beauvoir (Marso), 172n31
Polley, Sarah, 173n36
"pontianak" figure, 81, 192n7
Popova, Maria, 202n1
pornography, 81, 100, 108–110; anti-pornography feminism of 1970s, 109, 110
Potter, Sally, 118
pregnancy, 89–96, 101–102; birth scene in *Romance*, 82–83, 109, 114–115, 136–137; Midge doll, 143–144
Pretty/Funny (Mizejewski), 195n4
"pretty picture," disruption of, 14–15
promise, 92; feminist alternatives to patriarchal, 61–62, 75; patriarchal as false, 58, 75
Promising Young Woman (Fennell), 22, 58, 59, *69*, 76, 187n2; soundtrack, 67–71, 76
punctum, 30, 39, 43, 49, 53, 169n22

Quadiri, Fatima Al, 87

race, appropriation of, 130, *130*
racialized desire of viewer, 129–131, *131*
racialized patriarchy, 17, 39, 57–59, 184n39, 192n9, 203n1
"radical" formalism, 103, 194n22
Raw (Ducournau), 97–98
reader: Beauvoir's archive of experience as appeal to, 17–18; discovery/recovery by, 15; passivity attributed to, 18–19. *See also* viewer
reader/text relationship, 18
"real," 192n9, 200n21
realism: anticolonial, 86; visual realisms, 22. *See also* feminist realism
"realism" rule, 99, 159–160
"reality": as construction, 10
A Real Young Girl (Breillat), 110

refusal, politics of, 21, 38, 180n26, 192n7; collective, 78

Reinhardt, Mark, 201n29

Removed (Uman), 121, *121*

Rennebohm, Kate, 168–169n19

representation, 175n45, 204n3; as construction, 13; "plastic," 143, 155

resemblance, 44

Resnais, Alain, 51

revenge films, 97–98

Riddles of the Sphinx (Mulvey), 178n9

Right to Sex: Feminism in the Twenty-First Century, The (Srinivasan), 109

Ritual for Married Lovers, A (Guyot), 60

Robbie, Margot, 142

Rogers, Anna Backman, 42, 82

Romance (Breillat), 22–23, 100–101, 107, 109–115, *114*, 124, 195n1; birth scene in, 82–83, 109, 114–115, 136–137; as early version of cringe comedy, 110–111; voice-overs in, 111–113, 118

romance, patriarchal script of, 111–112

Rose, Jacqueline, 26, 29, 183n33

Rothko, Mark, 139, 141, 202n1

Saint Omer (Diop), 10, 21, 26, 27–28, 49–54, *52*, 54–55, 174n43; fabulation in, 49; feelings of actresses during filming, 50, 53; home video of Diop's mother in, 51, 53; *Jeanne Dielman* compared with, 50; opening shots, 51–52; origin story of, 27, 49, 184n38; triangulated space in, 49–50

Sappho, 161

Saute ma ville. See Blow Up My Town (Akerman)

Schmid, Marion, 180n23

Schoolman, Morton, 188–189n12

Schwartz, Selby Wynn, 161

Sciamma, Céline, 50, 191n6

Scott, Joan, 29

Second Sex, The (Beauvoir), 6; author-reader intimacy in, 16; "Biology" chapter, 12; as cinematic, 16, 18; destiny, history, and myth in, 59–60; "eternal feminine" in, 11, 99, 159; negative power of images, 171n28; reception of, 170–171n26; volume 1, *Facts and Myths,* 59–60; volume 2, *Lived Experience,* 60, 172n33; "What is a woman?," 11–12, 153, 157

Sedgwick, Eve Kosofsky, 200–201n25

Senegalese viewers, 87–88

sense experience, 17, 173n38

sensorium, in horror films, 104

sensorium, male, 5–6, 22, 58, 171n27; feminist challenges to, 6, 59, 65; soft side of, 61; touted as common sense, 108. *See also* patriarchy

Serpell, Namwali, 205n6

sex, public, 129, 131, 201n26

Sex and the City TV series, 197n7

Seyrig, Delphine, 8, 13, *34*, 145, 167–168n17, 179n16

Shapiro, Michael, 172n31

Sharpe, Christina, 49, 178n8

Shaviro, Steven, 144

Shelley, Mary, 30

Shell-Shocked (Honig), 159

"She's Not There" (Zombies), 100

Shoah (Lanzmann), 14, 15

shock, language of, 61

Shreir, Daniella, 8

Shulman, George, 173n38

Sight and Sound (McGill), 149–151

Sight and Sound magazine, 6

Singin' in the Rain (1952), 149

slasher films, 102

slavery, 27, 173n38, 175–176n1, 176, 177n3

Smith, Shawn Michelle, 177n8

Snow, Michael, 9

Sobchack, Vivian, 5

Soloway, Joey, 194n21; *I Love Dick,* 22–23, 107, 111–128

sound, 187n2; in *Blow Up My Town,* 62–65; feminist countering of patriarchal white noise, 61–62; *Happening,* 93–94; patriarchal, 58–59; of trauma, 72. *See also* images; soundtracks; white noise of patriarchy

to, 22, 118, 122, 152, 161, 200n25; passivity attributed to female, 7, 18–19, 173n40; racialized desire of, 129–131, *130*; Senegalese, 87–88; as subject, 20; "to be looked at" status of female, 7; woman-identified, 2, 4, 11, 16, 20, 108, 111, 137, 164n5. *See also* reader

Virgin Suicides, The (Coppola), 82

"Visual Pleasure and Narrative Cinema" (Mulvey), 7

voice-overs, 23, 36–38, 64–65, 89, 178n11; in *Barbie*, 142; in *Romance*, 111–113, 118

"waiting," 91–92

Walker, Alice, 177n4

Warner, Kristen, 143

"Wayfaring Stranger" (16 Horsepower), 96

Wayward Lives, Beautiful Experiments (Hartman), 36

Weather Girls, 68–69

Welfare (Wiseman), 185n40

wetness, 119, 123–124

White, Jennifer, 149

white noise of patriarchy, 22, 57–78, 108, 160, 187n2; as betrayal, 59; black noise as resistance to, 76–77; Black women's responses to, 71–75; and "harmonics," 188–189n12; "locker-room talk" of men, 67–68; media examples of, 59, 61; nonsynchronous and anti-realist sound effects as counter to, 61–62; pop music mantras about boys, 67–68; *punctum* and *studium* of white supremacy, 49, 56, 178n8; stasis created by, 57, 59;

"Woman" as "man-stringed" instrument, 59–62, 187n4. *See also Blow Up My Town* (Akerman); *I May Destroy You* (Coel); patriarchy; *Promising Young Woman* (Fennell); soundtracks; stasis

Williams, Linda, 191n1

Window Shopping (Golden Eighties) (Akerman), 13, 23, 165n10, 172n30; song-and-dance numbers, 144–145, *145*

Wiseman, Frederick, 50–51, 185nn40, 41

Witherspoon, Reese, 3

Wittgenstein, Ludwig, 53

"Woman": debunked by Beauvoir, 15; as horror for man, 123–124, 136; as "man-stringed" instrument, 59–62, 187n4

"woman-child," 129

woman-identified viewers, 2, 4, 11, 16, 20, 108, 111, 137, 164n5

women: credibility and authority of questioned, 106, 108; everyday experiences as horror, 22, 82, 106; feeling projected onto, 151; love letters to creativity of, 22, 107, 118, 127, 152, 155; men's horror of bodies of, 123–124, 136–137; two-ness of, 137; as "waiting," 91–92

"Women in the Movies" series, 3

Women Make Horror (Peirse), 103

Women Talking (Polley), 173n36

Wong, Ali, 196n4, 199–200n20

Young, Damon R., 115, 129, 201n30

Zombies, 100–101

www.ingramcontent.com/pod-product-compliance
Lightning Source LLC
Chambersburg PA
CBHW020507020225
21237CB00004B/21

9 7 8 1 4 7 8 0 3 1 2 2 2